My Troubles Are Going to Have Trouble with Me

THE DOUGLASS SERIES
ON WOMEN'S LIVES
AND THE MEANING OF GENDER

MY TROUBLES ARE GOING TO HAVE TROUBLE WITH ME

Everyday Trials and Triumphs of Women Workers

KAREN BRODKIN SACKS and
DOROTHY REMY, editors

Rutgers
University
Press
New Brunswick,
New Jersey

Library of Congress Cataloging in Publication Data
Main entry under title:
My troubles are going to have trouble with me.

Based on papers from a symposium organized at the 1979 meetings of the American Anthropological Association and from a 1982 conference on "Research to Make a Better Living for Working Women."

1. Women—Employment—United States—Addresses, essays, lectures. 2. Sex discrimination in employment—United States—Addresses, essays, lectures. I. Sacks, Karen, 1941– . II. Remy, Dorothy, 1943– .
HD6095.M9 1984 331.4 83–23079

ISBN 0–8135–1038–4
ISBN 0–8135–1039–2 (pbk.)

Manufactured in the United States of America

Contents

Acknowledgments

The articles in this book come from two sources. The first was a symposium organized by Dorothy Remy and Helen Safa at the 1979 meetings of the American Anthropological Association. The second was a conference, Research to Make a Better Living for Working Women, in 1982, funded by the Business and Professional Women's Foundation; organized by Lyn Goldfarb, Phyllis Palmer, and Karen Sacks; and cosponsored by their respective institutions, the Service Employees International Union, the George Washington University Women's Studies Program, and the Business and Professional Women's Foundation. This meeting joined researchers and working women activists in pursuing a practical goal: to determine and promote the research most likely to help women workers improve their jobs and work lives in the coming decades. Some thirty participants formed the Working Women Research, Education and Action Project (WWREAP) and drew up an agenda of priority research topics. With a grant from the Sperry-Hutchinson Foundation, the Business and Professional Women's Foundation was able to help fund four research projects as a step toward implementing this research agenda.

This book represents a commitment by the Business and Professional Women's Foundation to encourage and publicize research that can help working women improve their work lives and gain economic independence. The foundation has been a sustaining force in a wide range of activities—from funding some of the research that appears here, to bringing researchers together with each other, to building ongoing ties between feminist scholarship and working women's needs. Mary Rubin and Patricia McDonough of the foundation shared in the organization and conceptualization of the WWREAP conference, as did Winnie Bayard, who also orchestrated most of the preconference communication and travel arrangements for the participants and who did prodigious typing and publication coordination for the book manuscript. Jenrose Felmley, the foundation's executive director, offered a wide range of support and assistance throughout the entire endeavor. Lyn Goldfarb and Phyllis Palmer co-organized and co-conceptualized in the morning and co-chauffered and co-cooked in the afternoon so that the conference could happen.

Both the conference and the anthropology symposium grew out of a much wider informal and cooperative network of researcher-activists committed to doing research of use to women workers in their struggles for equity and equality. In a more fundamental sense, then, this book is the collective product of an almost decade-long dialogue, a sort of ragged, rolling conversation among perhaps fifty feminist scholars and many, many more women workers. It began in early 1977, when most feminist research about and with women workers was scattered and not quite legitimate and when most researchers were not known to each other. Dorothy Remy and Heidi Hartmann used letters and word of mouth to find those who had done, were doing, or were hoping to do research about and for the use of working women in clerical, sales, service, and manufacturing jobs—where some 80 percent of all working women were. As a result of their efforts, some twenty people, ranging from graduate students to tenured faculty from a variety of fields, turned up for a weekend in the Connecticut woods. They brought sleeping bags, groceries, and a good deal of intellectual energy. The agenda was to share ideas, problems, and questions, rather than to read papers, and to focus discussion around three topics: What are the forces against women in both the workplace and the community? What strategies for coping have working-class women workers developed? How do women go beyond coping to resistance, both organized and unorganized? These have been enduring themes for shaping our research, and they form the structure of this book.

Six months later, Lynn Bolles, Patricia Fernández Kelly, and Charity Goodman, with the assistance of Helen Safa and the late Vera Greene, hosted a second conference at Rutgers University's International Center. Discussion focused on comparing problems of women workers in the Third World with those in the United States, since many of those who attended this meeting had worked in Latin America, the Caribbean, Africa, or Asia. That spring, Helen Safa hosted still another group in Massachusetts. Each of these confabulations brought some new people together with the old, in a mushrooming and overlapping network.

It did not occur to anyone to ask for funding for these meetings, and in retrospect, it is probably a good thing. Collective cooking, eating, and cleaning made it much easier to think about the daily-life interconnections between women's paid and unpaid labor and to keep the practical goals of feminist theorizing in fairly clear view.

During this period, too, a whole variety of formal and informal study and research groups sprang up among those doing research on women and work. Projects began to take shape; some that were in process were completed; and the widening ripples of informal networks have become an established and legitimate—though not stuffy—field of learning. This book is one of a happily growing number of works on women and work. Its birth was collective, just as was its conception and gestation. The title is a line from *I Had Trouble Getting to Solla Sollew* (Random House) and is used by permission of its author Dr. Seuss.

While there were many more papers from both symposia than could be fitted into one volume, this book grew from and with the direct written and verbal insights and nurturance of all the participants in both meetings, from five unfortunately anonymous but marvellously insightful reviewers, from sisterly critiques and assistance from Eileen Boris, Phyllis Palmer, Roberta Spalter-Roth, and Ronnie Steinberg, from Amiel Franke's help in restoring Dorothy Remy's vision, and from Sylvia Brodkin's help in sharing her visions of work and family with her daughter Karen Brodkin Sacks. Last but not least, it has been pure pleasure to work with Marlie Wasserman, our editor at Rutgers.

My Troubles Are Going to Have Trouble with Me

THE DOUGLASS SERIES
ON WOMEN'S LIVES
AND THE MEANING OF GENDER

Introduction

KAREN BRODKIN SACKS

This book is about the realities of the kinds of underpaid jobs the overwhelming majority of women hold today and are likely to hold in the future unless some radical changes are made. We hope the book will be a contribution to working women's ongoing efforts to fight back and change their life chances. The book has twin themes. One theme is the ways in which capitalism's introduction of new technologies and workplace reorganization has affected and is likely to affect the kinds of jobs for which women are recruited and the working conditions they can expect to face. These are the constraints and circumstances within which, in spite of which, and against which women workers create their own forms of organization and values at work and in their family lives. The second theme is the fund of experience developed to cope with, limit, and end a variety of exploitative working conditions. The essays capture something of the give and take of daily workplace life—between what capitalism does to women workers and what women workers do in response—or to quote Dr. Seuss, how "my troubles are going to have trouble with me." The essays do not deal with headline-making events. We have deliberately chosen to focus on women's *daily* experiences, in part to highlight their active, ongoing resistance and dispel the debilitating myth that women workers are somehow docile or passive; in part to share the lessons of their experiences; and in part to indicate the major significance of what may appear to be local or small-scale work reorganizations and technological innovations.

In developing these themes—what capitalism has done to women's work, and how women resist and do *for* each other—it became increasingly clear that some discussion of women's unpaid labor in their families was needed for an understanding of women's paid labor experiences. Love and sex have been mixed up with work and money for a long time, and in complex ways that we have only just begun to explore. Today's feminism is challenging sexist ways of thinking as well as acting. It has deromanticized the home, insisted on the legitimacy of the unpaid work women do there, shown the existence of emotions in the so-called rational public sphere, and asked for new views and visions of women's work lives that look for continuities and interrelationships.

While working women may shape their own lives and create their own collective history, they necessarily do so under circumstances they do not control. Women may demand equal access to jobs, but they do not control the regional and international movements of factories and offices, nor do they control the kinds of jobs that exist. Especially since World War II, American corporations have become international, employing workers throughout the world. In one sense, this has resulted in a certain amount of job flight from the United States (there is an enormous literature on this subject; see Frobel, Henrichs, and Kreye, 1980 and NACLA, 1975, 1977 for overviews; for bibliographies on the impacts on women, see Elson, n.d. and Scerbak, 1982). In another sense, the internationalization of monopolies has also set in motion the internationalization of a working class with shared experiences, shared problems, and shared interests in opposition to capital. Within the United States there have been sectoral as well as geographical shifts, from manufacturing jobs to service-sector jobs, and from the Northeast and Midwest to the Southeast and Southwest.

At one level, this whole process is motivated by business's never-ending search for cheaper labor. This search is part of a larger engine of exploitation that no capitalist can control for long. In the early days firms competed with one another. Today, much larger units such as international monopolies compete, regardless of how large they are. Failure to meet or beat the competition threatens business disaster. This engine has been the simultaneous generator, on the one hand, of a certain kind of technological progress, especially in the development of labor-saving machinery, and, on the other hand, of human misery in the form of speedups, unemployment, and reductions in real wages and their ramifying consequences (Braverman, 1974; Gordon, Edwards, and Reich, 1982; Marx, 1965; Zimbalist, 1979). Capitalists find themselves linked in lockstep: as one finds a way to decrease his cost of production, whether through speedup and layoffs, lower wages, or mechanization, he is able to drop his prices, capture a competitor's market, and put him out of business. Without competition, he may raise prices again. While the actual ways that capitalists today do and do not compete are enormously more complex than can be detailed here, the search for ever-cheaper human labor power is a constant amidst all the variety, a constant that forces business to subject women around the world to a variety of similar life circumstances and to link their fates to those they may never see. It is considerably easier for women of different races, languages, and ethnic groups on the same shop floor in New England to forge a unity against divisive competition, as Lamphere describes (this volume), than it is for, say, Levi-Strauss workers in Mexico, the Philippines, and Texas to do the same (see Fernández, this volume; Enloe, 1980). Yet, as the reader compares the issues raised by apparel workers in New England in Lamphere's essay with those of Ciudad Juarez workers' in Fernández's essay, it becomes apparent that the same corporations divide and exploit them both and that women workers' unity in the twentieth century needs to be international as well as interracial and interethnic if it is to be at all effective.

There is a second set of consequences that have emerged from inter-capitalist competition in the last two decades. We experience it as "the economic crisis," as stagflation. Observers have long pointed out that there has been a relative decline in the number of jobs available in primary production, especially in heavy industry such as steel and automobiles. In part, this is the result of almost a century-long effort to speed up workers through automation and scientific management. In part, it is the result of a postwar extension and expansion of an earlier textile industry strategy to run from unions and higher wages in the Northeast and Midwest to the lower waged South. These largely unionized jobs, which have been the mainstay of much of the working class, have been disappearing, perhaps since the mid-1960s, as American companies moved operations to such varied places as South Africa, Mexico, and England—or more recently, as they have lost some of their markets to competitors. As a consequence, American corporations have sought other sectors of investment where they can compete more effectively and where they do not have to face international competition. Until recently, microelectronics and electronic data processing were virtual American monopolies internationally. Domestically, American business sought to create new and profitable industries where none existed before. Fast foods, cleaning services, health care, and care of the aged, the so-called service sector, mushroomed. In addition, and as a result of the social movements of the 1960s, there has also been an expansion of social services provided by the federal, state, and local governments. These shifts have been described as a shift in the American economy from production to service (Braverman, 1974; Rothchild, 1981). While this description is not entirely accurate, it does highlight the relative decline in basic (and unionized) manufacturing and the relative increase in a whole variety of old and new clerical and information-processing jobs as well as an absolute increase in the kinds and numbers of health, food, and cleaning service jobs.

There is a relationship between the creation of a service *industry* by large corporations and the decline of heavy manufacturing. To a certain extent American industry is running away to cheaper labor areas of the world, but more significantly, the market for its goods has shrunk relatively, now that European and Japanese products are successfully competing. This has led American industrialists to speed up some workers in the United States and to replace others with machines, so that fewer workers are producing goods. In the long run, too, fewer heavy industrial goods are being produced. Many large corporations are actually conglomerations of companies producing everything from missiles to milkshakes. They are finding, given the state of the economy and international competition, that there is profit to be made in fast foods, nursing homes, cleaning services, and possibly even child care—what some have labeled "Kentucky Fried Children" (Petchesky and Ellis, 1972). Much of this profitability comes from the low wages and low benefits paid to the largely female and minority work forces in these jobs.

To a large extent, the areas of decline are areas where relatively highly paid men predominated, whereas growth areas are in low-paying jobs that have been sex-typed as women's and race-typed as minorities'. More and more women are, of course, working in the wage labor force for more of their lives. Most women workers are concentrated in a very few occupations and industries: manufacturing (garments, textiles, jewelry, food processing, and canning), clerical work, cleaning, and health and food services. The "lucky" fifth in professional and technical jobs are crowded into librarianship, public school teaching, nursing, and social work, among the lowest paid of all professions. Many women have found both professional and clerical jobs in local, state, and federal governmental offices. As the economic crisis has deepened, however, there have been massive layoffs in the public sector. These have affected women and minorities disproportionately (Saperstein, 1982).

Women's increase and men's relative decrease in work-force participation, combined with the rise in female-headed households, only highlight the obvious: that the fates of women and men outside the plant gates, office buildings, and shopping malls are very directly linked and that family and household life are shaped by the availability, types, and conditions of wage work. In two-parent families, inflation combined with sectoral shifts in the work force mean that women's wages are carrying more of the cost of raising a family; and more families are being raised on women's wages alone, either because of male unemployment or because the women are single parents. Given the low wages most women earn, this has resulted in more women and children living somewhere between poverty and desperation. As relatively secure, unionized, and well-paid men's jobs become scarcer, more women—and increasingly, children—are forced to look for work in their particular sex, race, and age job ghettos.

The first part in this volume explores some of the continuities between family and workplace life. Sacks presents a theoretical overview for analyzing the linkages between working-class family and kinship on the one hand and the particular historical and sectoral demands of capital on the other. The essay attempts to repoliticize kinship, to reveal its nature as historically changing relations of production. It focuses both on generational patterns of structural conflict that wages and the ideologies attached to them introduce into families and on the family and community relations sustained by working-class women's wageless work that counters such fission. It also queries possible connections between family organization and workplace resistance.

Frankel's historical study of textile unionization in a southern mill town demonstrates these connections. It shows the unity of family and work organization as workers relied on the ties of kinship and community support centered around women to sustain themselves in a battle with the company that spanned several generations.

Ferree looks at the persistence of a sexual double standard in contemporary relations of family to work and how it affects the kinds of tacit bargains women make with their families as conditions of taking paid work. For men, home and work are assumed to be mutually supportive, but for women, conflict is presumed because the unpaid domestic job is still assigned only to women. At one level, women may have won the "right" to a double day. Ferree deals with the different ways women define their paid work to themselves and to their families and with the different class-based logics and consequences these definitions can have on the allocation of household authority responsibilities on the one hand and women's behavior on the job and in the labor market on the other. She points up how the notion that women work *either* from necessity *or* for fulfillment hinders the efforts of both working-class and middle-class women to negotiate less exploited paid and unpaid work lives.

Palmer's analysis of the history of domestic work, until very recently one of the very few occupations open to black women, reminds us that the relationships and nature of household labor are closely linked to technological changes and to the wider economy. The 1920s saw the beginnings of mass-produced domestic goods whose initial impact was probably on the structure of private households long before its impact elsewhere. With the introduction, albeit on a limited scale, of washing machines, stoves, refrigerators, vacuum cleaners, canned food, and commercial bread, many domestic chores became less strenuous and time consuming. Those affluent enough to purchase these new goods were also those who had formerly hired young immigrant or black women as live-in cooks, maids, child carers, and laundresses. As Palmer shows, domestic service was transformed at this time from a live-in job performed by several specialists, to day work handled by a single maid-of-all-work who was generally black. As alternatives to domestic work opened to white, but not to black, women, the former left these low-paid jobs. Palmer shows the conflict between black maids and their white employers over the nature of the job. Employers saw the new technology as labor saving and the real work as that of managing and directing; they added all manner of tasks and expanded the labor that household workers had to perform. Household workers, for their part, organized themselves and struggled to have their work defined as real work requiring skill as well as stamina. In some ways this laudable goal is now being appropriated by corporations who seek to make profits by collecting fair pay for wage workers—and paying them less than fair wages.

The essays in Part II deal with the impacts of computer technologies and industrial reorganization on sectors of the work force where the numbers of jobs for women have been growing. A major issue is whether or not women are being robbed of their skills and subjected to assembly-line conditions in clerical, service, and even some professional jobs, despite corporate assertions that they are upgrading these jobs.

Protective labor legislation limiting the hours, industries, and conditions under which women were allowed to work was gradually introduced in every state by the 1920s. Its proponents had a variety of contradictory intents that ranged from ending the hazardous factory conditions women faced, to driving women from the work force and preventing employers from using them to drive down men's wages (Hill, 1979). The latter approach, taken by some trade unions, attacked the victim rather than the culprit. That any positive effects on men's wages resulted has yet to be demonstrated. What is clear is that women were driven out of jobs in the better regulated, more unionized, and better paid sectors of manufacturing. These became "men's jobs." Kessler-Harris (1981: 99–100) implicates protective laws in strengthening and hardening occupational segregation by race as well as by sex. Women's need to work continued, drawing women into the embryonic clerical and sales sectors. These were billed as clean and high-prestige work for women, but they were for native-born, English-speaking, and white women. When these areas boomed after World War II, they were already sex and race typed.

Protective labor laws did not totally exclude women from the unionized manufacturing sector. Remy and Sawers deal with the impact of new technology on women in the meat-packing industry, where certain skilled jobs have long been women's. They describe the rise of centralized operations in meat-packing—from feedlot to boxed beef production and shipping—as well as the growth of vertical control by large grocery chains who capture a larger share of the market. This has undercut the jobs of better paid and unionized male and female meatpackers. The work force now being recruited to work the new and highly automated plants, which are far from urban influence, is largely minority, female, and miserably paid. As women's and men's skilled labor became incorporated into new machinery, workers in the plant studied by Remy and Sawers were driven to ever greater feats of strength and speed as plant owners sought to meet the competition. In this context the owners used the equal rights legislation of the 1960s and 1970s to implement sexually discriminatory patterns of automation and speedup and to deprive women of their jobs when they were unable to do the heaviest work.

Seeds for changing the shape of America's work force from industrial toward more sales, service, and clerical workers were planted in World War I, but they did not really blossom until after World War II. The flowering of a consumer economy was postponed by the Depression of the 1930s and World War II. The postwar years saw the shape of stores and selling radically transformed, as Benson describes in her essay. She traces the homogenization and deskilling of retail sales work to the rise of monopoly discount chains that relied on standardized buying and on a part-time, short-term, and poorly paid labor force of women. While computers, scanners, and inventorying cash registers have become more common in large chains, the major transformation of the work force in retail sales preceded them. It was also a period in which clerical and office work mushroomed enormously. While clerical and retail sales work are not the same, they underwent parallel transformations in recent times and perhaps even became sex typed as women's jobs in the same way.

Still more recently the silicon chip and microelectronic circuitry have revolutionized virtually all areas of work in which information storage and communication are important. Clerical, sales, and library work seem to be changing almost hourly, if one follows new advances in computer technology. Machung's discussion of word processors (the same word is used for the machine and the worker) points to similar restrictions in the scope of work, its deskilling, high turnover, and decreasing pay. Here, however, the impetus comes directly from managerial introduction of a kind of computerized typewriter to enormously increase typing output. Machung characterizes word processing as representing "the intersection of repetitious typing with repetitious computer work." It removes a time-consuming part of a secretary's all-around job and turns it into something akin to industrial labor complete with productivity criteria. Though word processing skills are advertised as a key to women's advancement in clerical work, the reverse is becoming more the case.

Murphree deals with this technology's impact on Wall Street legal secretaries, traditionally an elite among clerical workers. Word processing and microcomputers are stripping legal secretaries of their more routine work; at the same time, an increasing division of lawyering labor among lawyers and paralegals has decreased legal secretaries' ability to develop and exercise their traditional lawyering and administrative skills. The more routine work tends in large law firms to be performed under factorylike conditions by working class and minority women, while white seven sisters college graduates tend to become the paraprofessionals. Legal secretaries are by default left to become specialists in the nonroutine and unpredictable, but undervalued, tasks.

Estabrook shows how the rise of private data banks is creating a private-sector information industry in competition with the public-service philosophy and organization of libraries. As libraries are forced to compete, librarians are subjected to business principles of efficiency and find their work deskilled and their job opportunities curtailed in educational and public libraries. Their counterparts in private industry are "information specialists," primarily men with business or computer backgrounds.

Sacks deals with how one group of ward secretaries in a hospital responded to the introduction of video data terminals at their workplace. They believed that their new skills, together with their previously unrecognized skills, mandated a raise and more autonomy in their working conditions. Mainly black women, they were ranked two pay levels below mainly white secretaries. Computerization legitimated and crystallized their determination and helped them sustain an effective walkout.

The theme of business use of technology and reorganization of work to manipulate sex and race differences and divisions so as to lower pay and speed up the work emerges from many of the essays and cuts across the parts. Palmer's essay in the first part shows that as housework went from being a mixed to a black occupation, at the same time that new machines changed household technology, the division between employer and servant was transformed from an (unequal) sharing in a joint enterprise to one where the employer became more manager and the maid did increasing amounts of heavy labor unaided. Black women have not been able to make headway in retail sales jobs until fairly recently, as the work became transformed by discount chains, mass buying, and self-service into high-turnover, part-time, low-paying cashiering and stock tending at self-service stores. To meet competition from newer meat-packing operations, management at the plant studied by Remy and Sawers used equal rights laws *against* women workers by merging seniority lists to get rid of women because they could not perform at the rapid pace that management was able to coerce from men. Nevertheless, offstage, the machines against which these modern-day John Henries competed were tended by women for near-minimum wages. Estabrook's, Murphree's, and Machung's essays raise questions about new sources of racial and sexual dividing and conquering. Will female librarians be able to preserve their jobs and raise their pay to match that of mainly male information specialists, or will corporations ultimately replace these men with women and lower the pay? Will black women be tracked into word processing and away from secretarial work? Will word processors replace much of the secretarial work force at lower wages, or will word processors and secretaries organize against this sort of destructive division of labor? The success of the ward secretary walkout indicates that management does not always have to win and that conscious collective action can prevent gender and race from being manipulated to divide and defeat.

Part III deals with women in manufacturing work, because clerical and service work are not so internationally organized. Two essays focus on textiles and apparel work mainly because these industries and the struggles of their workers loom so large in the history of women workers. In less than thirty years these industries have become international in scope, placing women workers in Asia, Latin America, and the Caribbean in situations similar to those faced by North American and Western European women much earlier. Plants ran away from New England to spring up in the Carolinas and Tennessee in the 1920s and in industrial parks set up jointly by multinational corporations and Third World governments of Asia and Latin America in the 1960s and 1970s. Despite their global organization, textiles and garments share a number of characteristics with other industries that depend heavily on women's labor. The jewelry industry described by Shapiro-Perl, microelectronics discussed by Katz and Kemnitzer as well as clothing manufacture as treated by Lamphere and Fernández are all labor intensive. They depend on what is really a highly skilled work force; relatively little skill is embodied in the machines, and much is in the heads and hands of experienced workers. Even in the most technologically sophisticated microelectronics plants, the worker's skill is still key, so much so that women have set up subcontracting operations in their own kitchens. These four firsthand participant studies of the labor process underscore the exploitative contradiction between demands for real skill and corporate assertions that the work is entry level and unskilled. They show, too, that management policies are to seek a female work force in part because they believe women are more skilled (especially at sewing) and in part because they believe them less likely to rebel.

The central thread linking the essays in this part is that women workers do have a sense of their skill, are anything but passive, and do resist oppressive conditions. The essays detail the variety of conscious strategies workers have developed. They range from the individual to the collective, from strategies designed to change unsatisfactory conditions to those that help women create meaning and joy in spite of and within their oppression.

Carothers and Crull, and Fernández each address sexual harassment to remind us that women workers face additional forms of workplace coercion and oppression. Carothers and Crull analyze why the forms harassment takes differ by type of workplace. They contrast the political and economic messages of harassment when women enter male-dominated work forces with those they face in mainly women's workplaces. Both they and Fernández describe the tensions and divisions sexual harassment fosters and stress the importance of public exposé as a necessary part of resistance. Fernández describes *maquiladora* women's "jocular" harassment of an occasional lone man, an oblique but incomplete expression of and resistance to their shared victimization.

Lamphere shows how, in a multiethnic work force, new workers are socialized by others to resist management's manipulation of piece rates to divide and speed them up. She shows how "familizing," or bringing family to, the workplace is a means both to overcome divisions among women and to bring pleasure into the daily grind. Fernández deals with some of the ways *maquiladora* workers make their work hours bearable. Shapiro-Perl's study demonstrates that even what looks from the outside like nonresistance is actually a daily battle. But the strategies employed in this jewelry plant, perhaps because of (but also contributing to) high turnover, are mainly individual ones, of low risk, but also of low gain—like quitting itself. Katz and Kemnitzer's essay also focuses on women's efforts to change their low-paying and dead-end jobs. Here, too, they job-hopped and occasionally became subcontracting entrepreneurs in a higher risk, higher gain strategy. The women co-workers of Katz and Shapiro-Perl were aware of the limited and temporary nature of the gains they made.

Though the process is apparent only with the hindsight of historical perspective, women's daily resistance, like water on a boulder, has had a cumulative effect that has sustained and transmitted the lessons of their more concerted collective and dramatic efforts. Runaway shops are testimonies to workers' success in resisting greater output for less pay. If management always won this battle, they would have considerably less incentive to relocate. The effect is perhaps easiest to see in textiles and apparel, but it is also visible in electronics assembly. In both industries, plants have run away from the unionized parts of the country to nonunion Texas and the Carolinas, to Korea, Taiwan, Thailand, Mexico, Jamaica, and Haiti. Let us remember that early New England millowners gladly replaced feisty farm daughters with what they hoped would be docile families of first Irish and French Canadian, and then southern and eastern European, landless workers. The farm daughters, while they left no lasting organization, left their mark for future workers through their leadership in the fight for a ten-hour day and their role in the antislavery movement (Dublin, 1979; Flexner, 1968). European immigrants proved anything but docile, as mainly women waged sustained and successful struggles—in the New York garment workers' strike of 1909, the Uprising of Twenty Thousand, which led to a functioning International Ladies Garment Workers' Union—and in the partly successful International Workers of the World–led Lawrence textile strike in 1912, the Bread and Roses strike (Tax, 1980). Corporate hope sprang eternal as it sought new sources of cheaper and more docile labor in the southern piedmont. With the help of millowner policies, an independent, initially antiunion farming population transformed itself into a very militant proletariat that rose up across the South in a decade of costly, bloody, but ultimately unsuccessful strikes (McLaurin, 1971). The last two decades have seen the apparel, textile, and electronics industries relocate much of their productive capacities to the Third World. There is every reason to suspect that the daughters of Asia and Latin America recruited to work in these plants will undergo similar transformations. Indeed, young women textile and electronic workers in Korea strike with some frequency, and on at least one occasion they have taken over their factories and held their American bosses hostage (Hamilton, 1982). In Malaysia, where strikes are dangerously illegal, epidemics of hysteria sweep through whole factories, effectively stopping work (Grossman, 1978; Lim, 1978).

It is not always easy for Third World daughters to go home again. They are often caught between their families' poverty and their own low wages, between control by elders (especially male) as dutiful daughters, and their rights as independent adult wage earners (Yoon, 1976). Unlike their nineteenth-century American foresisters, Third World women find it more difficult to seek their fortune in the West. Increasing numbers of Asian, Caribbean, and Latin American women do, however, emigrate to the United States and Europe with that hope. Once here, they may well find themselves again working in garment and microelectronic factories—or worse, as domestics, sweated workers, or unemployed. Both Lamphere and Katz and Kemnitzer describe work forces made up largely of new-immigrant women. Pitted against each other, first at a distance, and now also face to face, women workers struggle to unite in the face of divisive goading. Lamphere's essay shows the effort women invest in sustaining social networks and a work culture of resistance and in incorporating new workers and new ethnic groups in it. The "old hands" in this unionized factory pass on to new workers, by word of mouth, lessons that were written in major actions a long time ago.

In an important sense, the internationalization of monopolies is also the internationalization of a working class with shared experiences, shared problems, and shared interests in opposition to an international business class. At present, this work force is divided nationally, ethnically, and racially. Unity at a distance is more difficult to achieve than unity face-to-face. Perhaps global factories will assist female workers' efforts in this direction.

References

Braverman, Harry. 1974. *Labor and Monopoly Capital.* New York: Monthly Review Press.

Dublin, Thomas. 1979. *Women at Work: The Transformation of Class and Community in Lowell, Massachusetts 1826–1860.* New York: Columbia University Press.

Elson, Diane, n.d. *Women Workers in Export-oriented Industries in Southeast Asia: A Select Annotated Bibliography.* Institute for Development Studies, University of Sussex. Mimeo.

Enloe, Cynthia. 1980. *Sex and Levi's: The International Sexual Division of La-*

bor. Available from author, Government Department, Clark University, Worcester, Mass.

Flexner, Eleanor. 1968. *Century of Struggle*. New York: Atheneum.

Frobel, F., J. Henrichs, and O. Kreye. 1980. *The New International Division of Labour*. Cambridge: Cambridge University Press.

Gordon, David M., Richard Edwards, and Michael Reich. 1982. *Segmented Work, Divided Workers: The Historical Transformation of Labor in the United States*. Cambridge: Cambridge University Press.

Grossman, Rachel. 1978. "Women's Place in the Integrated Circuit." *Pacific Research* 9: 5–6.

Hamilton, Saralee. 1982. "Korean Women Fight Union-busting Tactics." *Women and Global Corporations* 3, nos. 1, 2. In *American Friends Service Committee Women's Newsletter*.

Hill, Ann Corine. 1979. "Protection of Women Workers and the Courts: A Legal Case History." *Feminist Studies* 5, no. 2: 247–273.

Kessler-Harris, Alice. 1981. *Women Have Always Worked*. Old Westbury, N.Y.: Feminist Press.

Lim, Linda. 1978. *Women Workers in Multinational Corporations in Developing Countries: The Case of the Electronics Industry in Malaysia and Singapore*. Occasional Papers in Women's Studies, University of Michigan.

Marx, Karl. 1965. *Capital*. Vol. 1. Moscow: Progress Publishers.

McLaurin, Melton. 1971. *Paternalism and Protest: Southern Mill Workers and Organized Labor, 1875–1905*. Westport, Conn.: Greenwood.

NACLA (North American Congress on Latin America). 1975. "Hit and Run: U.S. Runaway Shops on the Mexican Border." *Latin America and Empire Report* 9, no. 5.

———. 1977. "Capital's Flight: The Apparel Industry Moves South." *Latin America and Empire Report*, 11, no. 3.

Petchesky, Rosalind, and Katherine Ellis. 1972. "Children of the Corporate Dream." *Socialist Revolution* 2, no. 6: 8–28.

Rothchild, Emma. 1981. "Reagan and the Real America." *New York Review of Books*, February 5.

Saperstein, Saundra. 1982. "Study Shows RIFs Hurt Women and Minorities." *Washington Post*, December 30.

Scerbak, Adrienne. 1982. *Selected Bibliography: Women and Structural Dislocation*. Institute for Research on Women, Rutgers University.

Tax, Meredith. 1980. *The Rising of the Women: Feminist Solidarity and Class Conflict 1880–1917*. New York: Monthly Review Press.

Yoon, Soon Young. 1976. "You Can't Go Home Again: Migration of Korean Single, Young Female Workers." Paper presented at annual meeting of the American Anthropological Association.

Zimbalist, Andrew, ed. 1979. *Case Studies in the Labor Process*. New York: Monthly Review Press.

ONE
WORKING FAMILIES AND THE DOMESTIC CODE

1

KAREN BRODKIN SACKS
BUSINESS AND PROFESSIONAL WOMEN'S FOUNDATION

Generations of Working-Class Families

Women's lives, especially those of women workers, are bursting out of the cultural categories that for so long have simultaneously described and constrained them. The conventional dichotomy of society into a home or family sphere of love and emotion as women's place and responsibility, and a public sphere of power and work as men's place is often called the Domestic Code. This code is out of joint with experiences that families require prodigious amounts of unpaid labor as well as increasing amounts of paid labor from women. It is also out of joint with women's recognition that family and kinship relations are very much about economics and power.

In the last decades women entered the labor force in unprecedented and unexpected numbers, and the "typical" woman can now expect to spend most of her years, including those when her children are young, in the paid labor force. This typical woman is also a working-class woman: she works for wages in clerical, service, manufacturing (and even some technical and professional) jobs that pay poorly and give her little possibility for advancement, little control over her work, and little decision-making power in her work. One recent analysis of the U.S.

Eileen Boris, Carol MacLennan, Phyllis Palmer, Nina Shapiro-Perl, Randy Reiter, Dorothy Remy, Mary Rubin, and Joan Skolnick were delightfully helpful and supportive in collectively helping me to wrestle an inside-out set of ideas into coherence. I would also like to thank five anonymous reviewers, one in particular who went far beyond the call of duty. A portion of this research was supported by a grant from the National Science Foundation.

class structure using such criteria concludes that women now make up the majority of the working class and that women—together with minority men—constitute a *large* majority of the U.S. working class (E. Wright et al., 1982).

There is a need for new categories and frameworks to describe more accurately the relationships among family, wage work, class, race, and ethnicity. What is work when viewed through the eyes of a woman performing it? Is class membership still to be understood on the basis of an individual's relationship to a wage? Do families have a single class or multiple classes? Feminist critiques have made conventional approaches to these questions problematic (see Vogel, 1981, for a good summary and analysis of recent efforts to relate family and workplace). This essay builds on the increasingly rich body of feminist theory, social history, and social science in a comparative, anthropological direction. It abstracts trends and themes from the diverse and particular histories by which today's very heterogeneous working class evolved. I will discuss working-class development in generational terms, where each "generation" has its own characteristic relations of production. These are family and kinship relations that organize the unified paid and unpaid labor of class maintenance and reproduction.

It is important to think about kinship, especially under capitalist and industrial conditions, as political and economic relations, as relations of production. For this reason I use "generations" of working-class kinship dynamics rather than, say, stages. Part of breaking down the Domestic Code involves confronting our association of kinship with sentiment and its opposition to power and wealth (Medick and Sabean, 1983). To liberate ourselves from these constraints, it is important to begin seeing family and kin relations as about love, money, and power simultaneously.

This essay is in three sections. The first analyzes the material and ideological aspects of wages as they affect gender and age dynamics within working-class families. Capitalists have consistently tried to recruit specific groups of workers by age, gender, and ethnicity. These efforts have set up ethnically segregated communities within the working class, and patterns of age and gender conflict and cooperation within these communities. This section deals with three generations of age and gender dynamics as working-class responses to capitalists' demands for and against particular kinds of workers. The brief second section focuses on the development of the contemporary generation and the economic forces that are leading women to challenge the wage ideology and the Domestic Code directly. The third section looks at the other side of the process—how each generation of working-class family relations acted on capitalism. It deals with efforts to resist and curtail capitalism's divisiveness and with efforts to alter the conditions of wage labor. Here, family and kinship are treated as political and economic relations for carrying out working-class women's unwaged work and for struggling against oppression in waged work. It concludes with the hope that the unity of work and family demands on women workers may be providing a basis for a fundamental challenge to the wage system and the ideology that sustains it.

Wages and Family Relations over Three Generations

The development of industrial capitalism meant the growth of a proletariat, a working class dependent on cash wages for its livelihood and for its continuity over the generations. In the United States, among the first industrial wage workers were the young farm daughters who went to work in New England's textile mills. Over the succeeding 150 years, they have been followed by descendants of African slaves and by European, Asian, and Latin American indentured and free immigrants. Despite the extraordinary diversity and division within this class, all share a daily reality that centers around a unified labor of acquiring and transforming cash into life's necessities and pleasures. This labor requires the cooperative work of women and men and also of several generations organized in households and families of various kinds. All these families depend on money wages. Hence, earning money and spending it are central life-maintaining activities.

Generations of workers have lived with a daily reality of a unified labor that persistently contradicts a cultural language attached to their wage packet that denies this unity. Often called the domestic ideology or Domestic Code, it is an interpretation of what work is and what it is not, about who works and who does not, about what a man is and does, what a woman is and does. These ideas have become part of our way of talking and thinking about our lives to each other and ourselves. They have also been the basis of structural conflicts that have divided the genders and generations in both the family and factory (Ryan, 1981).

The Domestic Code presents society as composed of a public sphere and a private sphere, each operating according to different, though complementary, natural laws. Work is in the public sphere, which is governed by cutthroat competition and survival of the fittest; whereas the home, in the subordinate but necessary private sphere, is the place for love and morality, though not for work. Men and women have different fundamental natures that suit them to different spheres of activity: men, to the public world of work; women, to the private world of domesticity. Women's nature is to raise families with and for husbands, a nature that is incompatible with public-sphere activity in general and working for wages in particular. A century and a half of social science and medical expertise has articulated this hostility to women workers on the one hand and has romanticized women's unpaid family labor on the other (Barker-Benfield, 1977; Cott, 1977; Ehrenreich and English, 1979; Ryan, 1979; Welter, 1966).

The Domestic Code has been a ruling set of concepts in that it did not have to do consistent battle with counterconcepts (Gramsci, 1971). It has also been a ruling concept in the sense that it "explained" an unbroken agreement among capitalists, public policymakers, and later, much of organized labor, that adequate pay for women was roughly 60 percent of what was adequate for men and need be nowhere adequate to allow a woman to support a family or herself (Kessler-Harris, 1975).

Until very recently, this ideology was part of the social milieu within which women have, however unwillingly, had to act. Most nineteenth- and early twentieth-century feminists manipulated it more than they challenged it. When they sought to enlarge women's places in education, jobs, the professions, or politics, they felt themselves constrained to argue that these were proper places for women's particular nature to have an influence because they called for extensions of household skills and family morality into the public sphere. Many nineteenth- and early twentieth-century feminists argued that women's natural piety and purity made them valuable contributors to the "helping professions," as they came to be called when women entered them, and to politics alike (Bordin, 1981; Epstein, 1980; Flexner, 1968; Kraditor, 1971; Rothman, 1979).

It is important to indicate that, even though the Domestic Code has been something of a ruling ideology, it has not ruled the thoughts of all women all the time. There were certainly varied challenges from a variety of places. Socialists like Charlotte Perkins Gilman questioned assigning housekeeping and child care to women; the "new women" of the early twentieth century rejected the sacrificial Victorian ideal of motherhood and sought their own identities in the professions (Cooke, 1979; Gilman, 1913). Unfortunately, we do not know enough about the working-class women whom the Domestic Code stigmatized as inadequate and immoral members of their gender because they could not meet the criteria of proper homemakers. We are only just beginning to ask whether these women had their own visions of the relationship of work and family, and of men and women.

Wages and Working-Class Generations

Along with wages comes an ideology that wages are paid an individual in fair exchange for labor performed by that individual alone. Marx (1935, 1965) long ago pointed out the inequality of the exchange, for workers create commodities of much more value than their wage equivalents. Subsequent feminist analysis has stressed the extent to which a wage must be used to cover the cost of labor done for no wages, generally by women—labor necessary for the maintenance of the wage earner and for the reproduction of the whole family and class of wage earners. At the workplace, conflicts have tended to center on the unfairness of the wage-for-work exchange.

In families, tension takes a different form, centering on conflicts between individualist ideology and the collective or familistic nature of working-class survival. The conflict centers on how much of the wage belongs to whom and for what (Spalter-Roth, 1983). Historically, conflict over ownership rights of the wage has remained the same, but the lines of conflict have shifted by gender and generation along with shifts in who earned wages and how much they earned (see Sen, 1980; Tilly and Scott, 1978; for discussions of generation and kin relations as analytical concepts linking family and work relations).

From the perspective of women's work and family relations, there seem to be three generations of a white working class, each with its own pattern of conflict and resolution. These generations, I should stress, are analytical concepts rather than real historical periods, but they are a sort of "abstract history" that is helpful for thinking about the integration of family and work lives in real history. In the *first generation*, a farming population with some family or corporate ownership of or access to land as its basic means to livelihood becomes involved with wages. Characteristically, it is either daughters or sons who become the wage earners. Wages are not yet a family's major source of livelihood, and children are only supplementary workers for their natal families. Wage levels are far too low to maintain a family, so it is not surprising that the first wage workers are unmarried children. Indeed, capitalists here target "dependents" for their work force precisely because their precapitalist social roles sanction both work and low pay. This generation is succeeded by a *second generation* of working-class families, the first proletariat dependent on wages for survival and reproduction. Husbands, daughters, and sons are typically earners, but families also require involvement by mothers and other non-wage-earning adults in the informal economy for significant amounts of their cash needs. A *third generation* has grown up since World War II. Increasingly, mothers, and once again children, are entering the labor force and taking up new forms of wage work as capital penetrates and breaks down many areas of community-based informal economic activity. This generation is characterized by multiple wage earners and the dominance of wage employment over informal and entrepreneurial activities of married women.[1]

In the first generation, wages are at once both sources of conflict dividing daughters and sons from parents, and levers by which sons and daughters can gain independence from parental, often paternal, authority. The analysis is sharpest if we contrast farming families with first-generation proletarian families under circumstances where the former resist loss of their land and heightened dependence on wages.

1. Gutman (1977) discusses similar sequences experienced by different European ethnic groups in American cities over the nineteenth and early twentieth centuries. These similarities need to be viewed in relation to variations stemming from the changing nature of capital over this period and to variations stemming from the industrial and geographical particulars faced by different groups. Safa (1981) confronts a similar interplay of similarities and differences internationally in her discussion of stages in the development of the U.S. garment industry's labor force. She describes an initial phase of native-born, single women who leave the work force on marriage, followed by a stage of immigrant workers where motherhood is combined with home sewing, followed by the present stage of runaway shops in the Third World. Where the object of Gutman's periodization is ethnic communities and Safa's is the garment industry, mine is patterns of family and kin relations.

Landowning farmers pass on farmland and other productive property through inheritance; but a proletarian family has no such inheritable means of subsistence. The characteristic intergenerational tensions and balance of power between parents and sons and daughters are radically different as a result. When farm sons and daughters become the first generation in their families to work for wages, they find themselves pulled in contradictory directions. The farming system dictates that wages belong to the household, usually represented by the father; the capitalist system dictates that wages are the individual property of whoever earns them. Agrarian fathers in nineteenth-century Europe or the United States, or in twentieth-century Asia, might hold their sons to them in reluctant obedience by the power of inheritance. In many parts of the world, daughters were even more constrained because parents controlled their dowry and their marriage, both of which were necessary for their survival. In contrast, proletarian parents often find themselves dependent on their children's wages to keep the household afloat and expect their children to contribute to the collective endeavor; but the individualist pull of the wage tends to undermine this perspective. The stress increases when sons and daughters migrate away from home in search of work and have to support themselves in addition to their natal households. This conflict has been managed (but not resolved) in different ways by different peoples and families over time. Thus, young women factory workers in Hong Kong are dutiful daughters contributing their earnings to the family fund and remaining under patriarchal authority (Salaff, 1981). In South Korea today, however, many wage-earning daughters of peasant families are especially reluctant to give up their new-found, though ambiguous, liberation to return home and face subordination to parents, spouses, and in-laws (Yoon, 1976, 1979).

Yesterday's American daughters may have come from Eastern Europe, Ireland, and Japan. Today's come from the Philippines, Vietnam, Malaysia, Thailand, Korea, Mexico, El Salvador, Haiti, the Dominican Republic, and Jamaica. As several essays in this book show, they now find themselves in California's Silicon Valley and in the deunionized garment plants of the Southwest and Northeast. The growing literature on women's migration shows that many of these daughters work to support parents and siblings, but many are also parents and wives as well and thus have two families—often both overseas—to support in addition to themselves, as the generational transformations pile up and overlap one another like waves on a beach (Mortimer and Bryce-Laporte, 1981).

There is also a gender dimension to the conflicts over wages, between husbands and wives over whether the husband has the use of "his" wages or whether the wife has first claim because of her responsibility for buying food and children's clothing and for paying the rent. Among the second-generation proletariat of nineteenth-century

United States and England, this conflict gave the temperance movement much of its vitality (Bordin, 1981; Paulson, 1973). For women especially, liquor embodied the philosophy that wage earners owned their wages as private property. In contrast, a family-ownership philosophy underlay the practice of "tipping," where all earners of the household put their wages in a family pot to be allocated, usually by the mother or whoever played the role of household administrator (Humphries, 1977; Tilly and Scott, 1978).

In today's third generation, with wives and mothers of small children heavily involved in the wage labor force, the gender dimensions of the wage conflict have changed somewhat. Now these women, too, see wages as their private property and use them to assert their rights to autonomy and to resist subordination to husbands in much the same way that wage-earning daughters did in the first generation. Yet mothers and wives lack the mobility of fathers and daughters because it is still mothers who bear responsibility for dependent children. In this context two contradictory aspects of wages-as-private-property become apparent. On the one hand, wages represent a basis for resisting gender and generational *subordination*; on the other, they represent resistance to *interdependence*. Today's wage-earning women seem to be resisting subordination more than interdependence: Men are less able to enforce unequal obedience from wives; more working mothers are leaving oppressive marriages even though the consequences may well be having to carry both the wage and unpaid labor burdens of raising children on poverty-level wages, a situation that has come to be termed the feminization of poverty (Ehrenreich and Stallard, 1982; Pearce and McAdoo, 1981; Rubin, 1982).

The Birth of the Third Generation

The material realities of women's lives have changed in the last forty years. Today's "average woman" now has two jobs, one unpaid, the other underpaid by some 40 percent relative to men in comparable work. After a generation's experience with a double workday, women, whether or not they identify themselves as feminist, have come to believe that their jobs should be compensated well enough to support themselves and their children. It is the women of this generation of the working class who are becoming increasingly impatient with manipulating or acting within the confines of conventional ideology in order to achieve any kind of gender equity. Increasingly, they are coming to see the gender and generational conflicts and the notions of sexual nature of the Domestic Code as obstacles that need to be swept away.

This generation has seen the rise of suburbs, shopping malls, and a "service economy" that has broken up many older working-class community networks and replaced women's informal economic activities with mass-produced commodities and services. Women workers now make up almost half the American labor force and are the large majority of workers in some of the fastest growing and lowest paying industries, such as electronics manufacturing, hospitals and nursing homes, fast foods, and data and word processing. More women head families and are sole supporters of children than ever before. A deteriorating economy has made women's earnings central even in families where a man is also working.

The dramatic rise in the numbers of wage-earning mothers and in the importance of their wages for their own lives and those of their families have battered away at the illusion that family and work worlds are separate. When women make paid maternity leaves and child care into workplace issues, they are beginning to challenge the Domestic Code of separate spheres and separate sexual natures. When they demand equal pay with men in comparable jobs, they are doing so as part of a changed consciousness of their rights to living wages and an end to economic and social subordination.

This consciousness was fostered in the social and economic aftermath of World War II. During the war, women worked not so much in unprecedented numbers, as in unprecedented kinds of jobs, notably in the well-paid, heavy industrial ones, and with unprecedented social legitimacy. Rosie the Riveter became a stock heroine of wartime popular culture. It was acceptable for women, even mothers, to work (Anderson, 1981; Chafe, 1972; Milkman, 1982; Trey, 1972).

But this was to be a temporary situation justified by the war. During the 1940s politicians, economic analysts, and industrialists were all haunted by the fear that the Great Depression was not over, that it had only been held in temporary abeyance, to return when the boom from the war economy ended (Milkman, 1976, discusses women in the Depression). After the war they made peace with a labor union establishment purged of its communists and radicals and that was becoming more and more conservative (Caute, 1978). They were joined by a combination of Madison Avenue and popular social science promotion of a new lifestyle based on mass consumption of mass-produced goods. The entire coalition shared in a consensus that the health of the American economy depended heavily on women returning to the home and leaving their relatively well-paid wartime jobs to men. In return, these men were supposed to support their wives and children in a higher, middle-class lifestyle in the new suburbs that pop psychologists and financiers alike were promoting as integral to a solid peacetime economy. Politicians and public policy analysts in the coalition successfully urged massive federal support for the roads and low-interest mortgages that allowed white—but not black—working-class suburbs to proliferate. They also helped create policies that allowed workers to furnish their homes in what Madison Avenue had begun to call a "middle-class" style (G. Wright, 1981). A new version of the domestic ideology emerged in this milieu: There were no more women workers; indeed, there was no more working class. Those who lived in the suburbs were middle class in income, attitudes, and aspirations. Those who did not conform and make this transition tended to be viewed as deviants to be cured of their ills lest they cause problems to others (Ehrenreich and English, 1979; Ryan, 1979; Weisstein, 1970). For the most part, working women were invisible during the 1950s. Those caught by a spotlight appeared as social problems, the cause of almost everything ranging from homosexuality and juvenile delinquency to the Great Depression.

It is now clear that the reality was very different from what the ruling consensus claimed. Most of the Rosie the Riveters of World War II did not leave the work force when they were forced out of their wartime jobs (Anderson, 1981; Gabin, 1982; Trey, 1972). Instead, they found other jobs in offices, hospitals, and banks; in nonunionized small factories; and in a variety of personal services; and these jobs did not pay as well as those they lost. Behind the image of working-class prosperity lay the reality that working-class families needed more than one paycheck to make it in the postwar inflation and to participate in the more expensive suburban life. Part-time work, "mothers' shifts," seasonal jobs that allowed "vacations" when the kids were out of school (as Benson's essay in this volume discusses), all helped these "deviant" women disguise themselves as proper homemakers. During the 1950s and 1960s the number of such white women grew steadily. Black women, both married and single, had long been working in higher proportion than white women, but at jobs that paid abysmally little—notably, domestic work and laundry work. Even in wartime, black Rosies were last hired and lowest paid (Anderson, 1981; Lerner, 1973). In the mass culture of the media and in the paradigms of social science, to be a working woman or to be black—regardless of one's sex—was to be deviant, something to be alternately cured, brought into the mainstream, or wished away. These contradictions matured throughout the 1950s and 1960s. Overt challenges began with the struggle to desegregate the schools and rapidly expanded into a broadly based movement against racist discrimination and subordination.

The 1960s were a decade when those who had been defined as marginal or deviant and those who were invisible asserted their identities and rights to equity. They reanalyzed and reclaimed their histories as part of this effort. Black women were an early and continuing—but often forgotten—force in this movement. Leaders in many of the most significant national civil rights struggles were women. So too was the less visible but sustaining core of leadership in both the North and South (Evans, 1980; Hansberry, 1964; Moody, 1970; Rywell, 1974). Sustained by the force of the civil rights movement, workers, minorities, women, and students joined in uneasy and uneven alliance to become visible and to reassert their existence in class, race, and gender terms. For a time they destroyed the media image of American society as a democratic collection of middle-class individuals and generated an awareness that race, class, and gender were sources of social and economic oppression as well as of cultural identity and strength.

In this process, black and white working women came to see, and to spread an awareness, that they too were social beings rather than an idiosyncratic collection of deviant individuals. They showed that they were groups that *had* economic, legal, and institutional problems with low wages, sexist and racist laws and customs, and domestic organization, rather than *being* problems themselves. Under the slogan "The personal is political," the women's movement clarified the political and economic roots of personal life (Cade, 1970; Freeman, 1975; Morgan, 1970).

These new feminist consciousnesses were born from the contradictions of women's increasing need to work a double day in the face of social denial and disparagement of their efforts. As more women work a double shift for more years of their lives, and as more women find themselves raising their children on their own, as they also have in the last two decades, the cultural ideal of a dependent homemaker looks more clearly like a cruel and crippling "catch-22." The new consciousness has also stimulated and informed a scholarly reexamination of women's work lives. No longer ideologically constrained to deal with work *or* family, there is a growing recognition that part of family *is* work—in the double sense of unpaid labor and of creating and maintaining social, economic, and affective relations—and that analyses of work need to incorporate an understanding of family and kin relations. Analysts are also exploring how women's wage work and family lives have both been shaped by the needs of corporate capital and how this directly affects the kinds of work and work lives women can expect to face in the immediate future. This indeed is the center of the new feminist scholarship.

Kinship as Working-Class Relations of Production

As women's contemporary life experiences and the new scholarship it has stimulated reveal more about the ways that gender and generational specificity of wage work have shaped women's family lives, there is increasing curiosity about the other side of the process. What effects might family relationships have on the organization of the labor force and on its ability to resist oppressive conditions? While such research is still in its infancy, there is a growing sense that the answers are important for a full understanding of women's wage work and that there are very likely to be connections between waged and unwaged relations of production. In other words, kin relations, as relations of production governing women's unpaid family labor, may affect the structure of the work force and perhaps the successes and failures of workplace struggles.

This section highlights four areas where we are beginning to see—even if dimly—the shapes of some of those connections: How prewage family organizations may have shaped capital's first-generation work forces in various parts of the world; how the informal economic activities of second-generation mothers may have affected the organization of working-class families and communities; how second- and third-generation working-class families may act as bases for resistance to workplace-generated oppression; and how third-generation women workers may be forced to develop new forms of workplace resistance to maintain and reshape family and community life as capital increasingly penetrates working-class communities.

First-Generation Family and Work-Force Interplay

Family relations seem to have been variously involved in shaping the kinds of paid labor women have engaged in. Nineteenth-century U.S. mill girls did not enter the labor force as generation-free or gender-free beings. They came from families whose main subsistence was farming, families who were not about to allow their men to leave farming to become wage workers (Dublin, 1979; A. Hamilton, 1957). Prospective employers had a role in determining who would be acceptable to them, but this was often shaped by family labor needs and by the cultural division of labor. Thus, the women workers of New England were farm daughters, single women who expected to spend a relatively short time in the mills before they married and returned to take their mothers' places on the nineteenth-century farm. Employers advertised for and recruited daughters rather than mothers, fathers, or sons, but they did so because daughters were the only family members, on the one hand, whose labor the farm population regarded as "expendable" and, on the other, whose wages they regarded as a proper contribution to the household economy and to a young woman's self-subsistence and preparation for marriage. American farming practices and family values justified and supported the low wages millowners paid to women workers. Neither daughters nor their families expected wages adequate to sustain a family, since they did not expect to be in the mills that long nor to depend on wages as their major source of subsistence.

In the United States, a wage labor force of agrarian daughters was short lived. But more recently, textile, apparel, and microelectronics firms in Asia and parts of Latin America have drawn much of their first work forces from a similar population of young women from rural families, most likely for similar reasons (Grossman, 1978; Heyzer, 1982; Kung, 1976; Lim, 1978; Salaff, 1981; Wong, 1981; Yoon, 1976, 1979).

By way of contrast, in many parts of Africa it was sons rather than daughters who were recruited—often forcibly—as the first wage labor forces in the mines, plantations, and factories. When they were paid at all, it was not a living wage, for it was expected that farming would continue to support their families and that young men would work before their marriage in order to accumulate needed marriage payments (see Goody, 1976, for a contrast between European dowry and African bridewealth systems). Here, too, the sexual division of labor and family values helped colonial rulers and corporations justify low wages, but for sons rather than daughters (Rodney, 1972).

Clearly this is not an explanation of *how* a proletariat was created; that explanation needs to deal with the whole gamut of circumstances by which capitalists and landlords force peasants and farmers to seek wages. The interplay between *who* these families sent to earn the needed wages and who the employers sought or accepted becomes significant in this context. One can consider these sons and daughters a first-generation proletariat, a work force defined by their kinship relations as a group of people who are not held socially responsible for reproducing themselves. Their meager wages are supported by the unwaged agricultural labor of their families, and all their labor power contributed mightily to the primitive accumulation of capital.

In the United States the heavy industrialization between 1870 and 1920 involved large numbers of European and Asian immigrants. Most came initially as single women and men, daughters as well as sons. While many intended to be temporary migrants and were able to return, many more stayed and brought over siblings, parents, and spouses to form working-class communities of wage-working families, a second-generation proletariat. A similar process is being repeated today as the sons and daughters of Asia, the Caribbean, and Latin America, the dubious beneficiaries of corporate capital's expansion, either stay and fight the multinationals (S. Hamilton, 1982) or emigrate to the United States in search of less poverty-stricken lives for themselves and their kin. We know less about the lives of the new immigrants and about the structures of their communities than we do about the immigrants of the turn of the century. Many women work at home, sewing or assembling microelectronics in a revival of cottage industry; still others may be taking in boarders or boarding themselves. Many hope to return home, but many others are working to bring over family (Bolles, 1981; Garcia Castro, 1982; Pessar, 1982; and papers in Mortimer and Bryce-Laporte, 1981; see also Katz's essay in this volume). It is again the case that new working-class ethnic communities are organizing a second-generation (and in many cases simultaneously a third-generation) proletariat in U.S. cities.

Second-Generation Mothers and the Informal Economy

The second generation came of age in the United States in the late nineteenth century and the first decades of the twentieth. This period was marked by intense and extensive labor conflict, what historian Brecher (1972) has characterized as virtual class warfare, as a largely immigrant work force of mine, railroad, steel, meat-packing, textile, and garment workers fought the Carnegies, Rockefellers, and other rising robber barons for living wages, secure jobs, and safe working conditions. Daughters of these families—as well as fathers, sons, and an occasional married mother—were an important part of the work force and its majority in textile and apparel manufacture. Throughout this period, as in earlier times, the pay for women assumed that they were dependent for their main support on either a father or a husband. Women forced to support themselves, with or without children, often faced the most desperate poverty. Single women could not begin to live on their own voluntarily before the 1920s (Kessler-Harris, 1981).

Even though the labor struggles of this period won very real improvements, "one of the basic facts of family economics during the early decades of the twentieth century was that most working-class males, and many of those in the middle class, were not paid enough to support their families according to the American standard of living" (Wandersee, 1981: 1). Before World War I, the white female labor force was made up of young, single women as well as some widows and divorced women with children. Daughters often worked outside the home and contributed their wages to the family. If they were forced to move away from home to find work, as was particularly the case for black women, they sent money home. Sons sent home less than daughters, as sons were often encouraged to try to make it on their own. While mothers tended to cluster in the informal economy, they tended to be working for wages in textile mill communities in New England, and later in the South. Single mothers also tended to migrate to mill towns, where they pooled wages with their children in order to subsist and assigned one of their number (often, but not always, the mother) the task of managing the household and its labor (Kessler-Harris, 1981).

Black women, like black men, were excluded from most well-paid industrial jobs, and faced the greatest poverty (Kessler-Harris, 1981). Black mothers worked for wages at a much higher proportion than white mothers; their choices were usually fieldwork, domestic work, or laundry work. As white immigrant daughters found jobs in industry, black daughters and mothers increased their proportion of the domestic work force in the urban North, as Palmer's essay in this volume shows. Because so many black mothers have always worked, it is more accurate to see their life experiences as combining simultaneously those of the second and third generation of the working class. White women of the third generation are only now beginning to experience the intensity of wage labor and its consequences that black women have long faced (Palmer, 1983).

Second-generation mothers' earning efforts were often hidden—and unrecognized—in what has now come to be called the informal economy: a mixture of petty entrepreneurial sales and service activities. Married women whose husbands lived with them were much less likely to appear in the labor force, but they often earned significant amounts of money by taking in piecework or boarders; by doing sewing, laundry, or baking; or by running a small store or pushcart. My mother recalled her mother's workday as a grocery storekeeper:

> In those days you didn't close the store until you were practically dead on your feet, which would have been twelve o'clock, twelve-thirty; you opened six in the morning and worked straight through . . . there were no store hours, and if another little store kept open later, then you kept open later; if they opened earlier, you opened earlier. So they were never free. In between my mother would run back and forth to make the beds or to change the linen or to do what was necessary. (Brodkin, 1978)

Taking in lodgers has been one of the most prevalent income-earning activities of working-class wives and mothers. These women provided to the unmarried of the working-class community some of the domestic services they performed directly for their own families and thereby also made a cash contribution to the household budget (Jensen, 1980; Pleck, 1979; Smith, 1979).

In the steel and coal regions of the Midwest, as in the mushrooming cities of the East, boarders could contribute a significant share of a family's income. For example, some 40 percent of all families of immigrant steel workers in Homestead, Pennsylvania in the early twentieth century took in boarders. With one to four lodgers in a four-room house, a family could add about 25 percent to their income (Kessler-Harris, 1981: 48–49). In the New England communities of Polish silk and cotton millworkers, four out of five people lived in houses with boarders (Lamphere et al., 1980). Taking in boarders involved considerable labor on a woman's part. In these communities she got up at 3 A.M. and cooked breakfast, often before going to work in the mills herself from 7 A.M. to 6 P.M. When she returned home she then had to cook supper and wash everyone's dishes. Saturdays were for washing sheets. Sundays were for building working-class community social relations: one of the Polish women whose life Lamphere et al. describe (1980) had over one hundred godchildren.

Even with the success of unions in heavy industry, it is debatable whether a single wage ever covered the costs of rearing a family in more than a minority of jobs (May, 1982). Many necessary goods and services were obtained outside the capitalist market economy. Most working-class families survived on a combination of wage work, boarders, and miscellaneous entrepreneurial activities held together by reliance on kin.

All these loomed large in my mother's New York City childhood of the 1920s:

> My father worked in a factory as a knitter; his work was seasonal and for probably half a year he was unemployed so that Grandma had to save during the fat months for the lean ones. Grandpa turned over his wages out of which

> Grandma gave him carfare and cigarette money. I suppose we were fortunate in that Grandma came of a large family and in the beginning many of them lived nearby.
>
> I remember our being one of a number of partners in a grocery and delicatessen store, the other partners being Grandma's brothers (two I think). . . . During this time the families lived fairly close, and of course the cousins played together, the families socialized and got together for holidays. . . .
>
> Sometime about here, my grandparents and my parents bought a house in Coney Island which served as both living quarters and income, since they rented the flats and lived in the basement. (Brodkin, 1978)

Many nineteenth- and early-twentieth-century working-class families also made their own clothes, grew a fair amount of vegetables, and occasionally kept pigs or chickens (even in urban areas) and prepared most of their own foods (Byington, 1910). In the course of the twentieth century, working-class families have gradually come to depend on large corporations for many of the things they formerly produced, or did, for themselves. An early-twentieth-century family might buy material from which the mother or older daughter would make the women's clothing and some of the men's. Cooking and washing in working-class neighborhoods without running water were time-consuming and back-breaking domestic chores. Women would buy flour, meat, sugar, coffee, and tea, but would likely can their own vegetables, fruit, and perhaps meat. Those items that were purchased were bought from vendors or from mom-and-pop stores. Until the 1920s affluent families were likely to hire working-class daughters to do their cooking, washing, cleaning, shopping, and child care as full-time, often live-in maids (Katzman, 1978; Strasser, 1982).

Because working-class family circumstances and needs varied over a life cycle, some households were likely to be labor poor while others might be labor rich at any given time. Thus, a family with small children might need more domestic help than a mother could supply—for laundering, sewing, child care, and cash—while a family with older sons and daughters might have less need of outside help and be in a better position to provide it to others. Reciprocity existed to be sure, but it was often mediated by cash, or phrased as buying a service. My parents' description of the working-class neighborhoods in which they grew up is particularly apt: "We lived by taking in each other's washing."

Families as Forces of Resistance

Women shaped new forms of households and played a key role in building working-class communities as part of their efforts to bring cash into their households. Taking in boarders created larger households and sometimes, when the boarders were women, increased the availability of domestic labor. In addition, boarding gave single members of the community a set of social places and links they might not otherwise have. In a similar way, women's entrepreneurial ventures like selling goods and services to neighbors created a web of reciprocity that was endogenous to the community, that heightened intracommunity dependence on the one hand and that gave it a margin of independence from outside (and likely hostile) interests on the other (Humphries, 1977). Day (1982) describes the web of kin ties in South Carolina Sea Island black communities in these terms. She shows the use of these ties in organizing women's urban marketing of fish and vegetables, and in basketmaking. These entrepreneurial activities and the ties that sustained them were important for a degree of *community* independence from a racist wage system. They were also key for maintaining *women's* economic independence and autonomy in marriage relations. Sea Island women are well aware that recent expansion of consumer goods and services has severely undermined both community independence and women's autonomy within it.

Women's family and community links have also provided a significant basis of support for sustained workplace resistance. Kessler-Harris (1981: 91) credits family support networks with helping women garment workers in New York City hold a key strike for three months in 1909. This Uprising of Twenty Thousand was the victory that established a union in a garment industry made up of many scattered, small-scale shops—an amazing feat of organizing and unity. MacLean (1982) has recently analyzed the importance of women's networks both in the strike and in the subsequent building of the International Ladies Garment Workers' Union (ILGWU). To organize such a scattered work force must have taken a very significant, though largely unstudied, family and community organization. Tilly (1981) looks at nineteenth-century French working-class women to analyze conditions under which they have acted collectively. She too stresses the centrality of working-class women's structured associations in the communities and in wage work, and a household organization that gives women a chance to act independently.

Frankel's essay in this part of this volume deals with the struggles of working-class families in a southern mill town. She details the ways in which the kinds of family, neighborhood, and class ties that women formed helped to sustain a long, though ultimately unsuccessful, strike. Tax (1980) has described something of the same kind of infrastructure sustaining the long, bloody, but partly successful, strike of immigrant textile workers in Lawrence, Massachusetts, the famous Bread and Roses Strike. Unfortunately we are only beginning to explore the ways women's informal economic activities may have created networks of class-based community ties and how these may have been mobilized in defense of women's and men's class interests.

We are on somewhat firmer ground when it comes to family and kinship. There is a growing body of work in both anthropology and history that shows working-class family organization as a product of largely women's efforts and creativity in generating new forms of household composition and kin and neighborhood cooperation to cope with and surmount the divisive and disintegrative pressures that come from the intensification of a wage economy (Rapp, 1978, reviews much of this literature; see also Caulfield, 1974; Stack, 1974; Tilly and Scott, 1978). These studies emphasize the variety and importance of extended kinship and friendship networks for coping with poverty and economic insecurity whose source is primarily capitalist wage labor relations. Whether they are European, North American, or Third World families, it seems that working conditions of existence have continually forced women to rely upon each other to perform the unpaid work they have been assigned by an industrial capitalist division of labor. Young and Willmott (1962) refer to the English working-class family as a woman's trade union. Caulfield (1974) characterizes the organization of Third World and U.S. minority and Appalachian families as "cultures of resistance." She argues that capitalist conditions of existence constantly force women to create familistic relations of production that go beyond their households and nuclear families and that form the infrastructure of working-class and poor neighborhoods in many parts of the world. In this sense, then, the pressures of wage labor have stimulated women's family and class solidarity in opposition to its divisiveness.

Conclusion: Third-Generation Transformations

Reciprocity and community self-provision still survive in many working-class neighborhoods, but those neighborhoods have been undermined by suburbanization, urban renewal, and increased penetration by capitalist economic relations. On the face of it, there is a contradiction, for how can a community that depends on wages for its very existence *not* be fully involved in capitalist economic relations? With hindsight, the contradiction is resolved, for it is clear that there was room in, say, 1920 for a great deal more capitalist penetration of household and community economic relations. First, contemporary households buy more of their goods fully processed than did those of the 1920s. This is clearest with regard to clothing and food, where the labor time of cooking (as in frozen dinners and fast food restaurants) and sewing has been incorporated into the goods themselves. In addition, new commodities like washing machines, or visits to laundromats, and cars have become necessary means to carrying out household tasks.

Second, and at least as major a shift, is from whom goods and services are bought. Today, virtually all domestic commodities, including "fresh" fruit and poultry, are bought from large corporations. Many fewer working-class mothers earn cash by boarding, cooking, washing, or sewing for others. There is less possibility for competition with fast-food chains, franchises, and discount store clothes than there was with another little store. The dream of being one's own boss in a mom-and-pop store now incorporates having to compete with the franchised twenty-four-hour minimarts that dot every neighborhood. The more likely option is that mothers and daughters will work at a fast-food restaurant or chain discount store part time or that a husband and wife might aspire to manage a minimart.

From a working-class woman's perspective, her ability to provide cash for household needs by her entrepreneurial activities has been slowly eroded since World War II by competition from chain discount stores and prepared foods, as well as by the breakup and suburbanization of their communities. At the same time, under more dispersed living circumstances, these services and goods are attractive for the unpaid labor time and money they save them. Though the conflict is not apparent at the level of daily life, working-class women have been pressed and encouraged to give up their own entrepreneurial activities and autonomy for wage labor—at minimum wage as often as not—for the very corporations that did them in. Katz's essay in this volume highlights the rise of a new kind of entrepreneurial activity, homework subcontracting in the microelectronics industry, as women chafe under the constraints of dead-end jobs. Yet, this sort of "self-employment" has more in common with the old "putting-out" system than it does with taking in boarders or baby-sitting.

There is an ironic eddy in the tide of monopoly penetration of household labor and the informal cash economy in domestic work. On the one hand, ready-to-eat and ready-to-wear have cut down some types of women's unpaid labor time and paid entrepreneurial opportunities; and the prices of such goods have made it economically more costly to do it oneself. On the other hand, still other mass-produced commodities like furniture and toys are now sold unassembled or unfinished, forcing consumers themselves to do a large part of the labor on mass-produced items (Glazer-Malbin, 1976; Weinbaum and Bridges, 1979). All studies of unpaid domestic labor indicate that, despite "labor-saving" commodities, women still spend as much time (though fewer calories) now as they did in the 1920s on "housework." Only the content has shifted—to less sewing, cooking, and washing and more shopping and chauffering (Hartmann, 1981; Strasser, 1982; Vanek, 1974; see also Palmer in this volume).

As women are forced more intensively into wage labor, they have become much more vocal about wage discrimination. As interpreted by labor unions in the past, the demand for a "living wage" often meant that a *man's* wage be adequate to sustain a whole family. This demand was seldom met, as I have noted. The current feminist movement has pointed out the double-edged nature of the demand, however (Hartmann, 1976; Humphries, 1977; Sen, 1980). On the one hand, such a wage would provide some economic security and limit the number of family members forced into direct subservience to capitalism. On the other, the sexist assumption that men should be wage earners would increase wives' dependency on their husbands and provide a basis for intrafamily oppression of women as well as deprive women without husbands of access to a living wage.

Lack of success in achieving a family wage has been particularly apparent in recent decades as real wages have been seriously eroded, forcing more women into the labor force for more of their lives. The rise of a capitalist "service economy" has meant that less and less of the costs of sustaining family life can be borne outside wage relations with capital and in reciprocal labor and services or the small-scale, informal economy.

While one need not look far for the destructive effects on interhousehold ties that are a basis of working-class communities, I conclude by suggesting the possibility that there may be some positive results of such negative developments. First, women's control over wages, abysmal as they are, seems to have given them some resources for resisting intrafamily oppression, as I have already noted. Second, as Lamphere, Frankel, and Sacks in this volume suggest, women may be bringing some of those organizational skills they formerly used mainly in creating family and community networks into their organizing efforts in the wage labor force. Workplace organizers may find themselves having to pay more serious attention than they have in the past to women's nonwaged work and family relationships (Sacks, 1983). Third, under increased pressures of a double day, working women are trying to force capital to shoulder some of those costs of family life and class continuity that, under the Domestic Code, it has asserted are private and nonwork. Women's everyday struggles over specific issues generated by economic needs—like child care, paid parenting leaves, and comparable worth—may ultimately give birth to a unified working-class and feminist consciousness of both equality and equity.

References

Anderson, Karen. 1981. *Wartime Women.* Westport, Conn.: Greenwood.

Barker-Benfield, C. J. 1977. "Sexual Surgery in Late Nineteenth-Century America." In C. Dreifus, ed., *Seizing Our Bodies.* New York: Random House, Vintage.

Bolles, A. Lynn. 1981. "'Goin' Abroad': Working Class Jamaican Women and Migration." In D. M. Mortimer and R. S. Bryce-Laporte, eds., *Contemporary Studies of the Black Female and the Migratory Experience in the United States.* Washington, D.C.: Smithsonian Institution RIIES.

Bordin, Ruth. 1981. *Woman and Temperance: The Quest for Power and Liberty 1873–1900.* Philadelphia: Temple University Press.

Brecher, Jeremy. 1972. *Strike: The True History of Mass Insurgency from 1877 to the Present.* San Francisco: Straight Arrow.

Brodkin, Sylvia. 1978. Taped interview and letter to Karen Sacks.

Byington, Margaret. 1910. *Homestead: The Households of a Mill Town.* New York: Charities Publications.

Cade, Toni. 1970. *The Black Woman*. New York: New American Library.
Caulfield, Mina D. 1974. "Imperialism, Family and Cultures of Resistance." *Socialist Revolution* 29: 67–85.
Caute, David. 1978. *The Great Fear: The Anti-Communist Purge Under Truman and Eisenhower*. New York: Simon and Schuster.
Chafe, William. 1972. *The American Woman: Her Changing Social, Economic and Political Roles, 1920–1970*. New York: Oxford University Press.
Cooke, Blanche W. 1979. "Female Support Networks and Political Activism: Lillian Wald, Crystal Eastman, Emma Goldman." In N. F. Cott and E. H. Pleck, eds., *A Heritage of Her Own: Toward a New Social History of American Women*. New York: Simon and Schuster, Touchstone.
Cott, Nancy F. 1977. *The Bonds of Womanhood: Woman's Sphere in New England 1780–1835*. New Haven, Conn.: Yale University Press.
Day, Kay. 1982. "Kinship in a Changing Economy: A View from the Sea Islands." In C. Stack and R. Hall, eds., *Holding Onto the Land and the Lord*. Athens: University of Georgia Press.
Dublin, Thomas. 1979. *Women at Work: The Transformation of Class and Community in Lowell, Massachusetts 1826–1860*. New York: Columbia University Press.
Ehrenreich, Barbara, and Dierdre English. 1979. *For Her Own Good: 150 Years of the Experts' Advice to Women*. New York: Doubleday, Anchor.
Ehrenreich, Barbara, and Karen Stallard. 1982. "The Nouveau Poor." *Ms* 10:217–224.
Epstein, Barbara. 1980. *The Politics of Domesticity*. Middletown, Conn.: Wesleyan University Press.
Evans, Sara. 1980. *Personal Politics: The Roots of Women's Liberation in the Civil Rights Movement*. New York: Random House.
Flexner, Eleanor. 1968. *Century of Struggle*. New York: Atheneum.
Freeman, Jo. 1975. *Women: A Feminist Perspective*. Palo Alto, Calif.: Mayfield.
Gabin, Nancy. 1982. "'They Have Placed a Penalty on Womanhood': The Protest Actions of Women Auto Workers in Detroit-Area UAW Locals, 1945–1947." *Feminist Studies* 8, no. 2: 373–398.
Garcia Castro, Mary. 1982. *"Mary" and "Eve's" Social Reproduction in the "Big Apple": Colombian Voices*. Occasional Papers. New York University Center for Latin American and Caribbean Studies.
Gilman, Charlotte Perkins. 1913. *Women and Economics: A Study of Economic Relations between Men and Women as a Factor in Social Evolution*. 6th ed. Boston: Small, Maynard.
Glazer-Malbin, Nona. 1976. "Housework." *Signs* 1, no. 4: 905–922.
Goody, Jack. 1976. *Production and Reproduction: A Comparative Study of the Domestic Domain*. Cambridge: Cambridge University Press.
Gramsci, Antonio. 1971. *Selections from the Prison Notebooks*. New York: International Publishers.
Grossman, Rachel. 1978. "Women's Place in the Integrated Circuit." *Pacific Research* 9: 5–6.
Gutman, Herbert G. 1977. *Work Culture and Society in Industrializing America: Essays in America's Working Class and Social History*. New York: Random House.
Hamilton, Alexander. 1957. "Report on Manufactures." In Samuel McKee, ed., *Papers on Public Credit, Commerce and Finance*. New York: Liberal Arts Press.
Hamilton, Saralee. 1982. "Korean Women Fight Union-busting Tactics." *Women*

and Global Corporations 3, nos. 1, 2. In *American Friends Service Committee Women's Newsletter*.
Hansberry, Lorraine. 1964. *The Movement: Documentary of a Struggle for Equality*. New York: Simon and Schuster.
Hartmann, Heidi. 1976. "Capitalism, Patriarchy and Job Segregation by Sex." *Signs* 1, no. 3 (pt. 2): 137–170.
———. 1981. "The Family as the Locus of Gender, Class and Political Struggle: The Example of Housework." *Signs* 6, no. 3: 366–394.
Heyzer, Noeleen. 1982. "From Rural Subsistence to an Industrial Peripheral Workforce: An Examination of Female Malaysian Migrants and Capital Accumulation in Singapore." In L. Beneria, ed., *Women and Employment*. New York: Praeger.
Humphries, Jane. 1977. "Class Struggle and the Persistence of the Working Class Family." *Cambridge Journal of Economics* 1:241–258.
Jensen, Joan M. 1980. "Cloth, Butter and Boarders: Women's Household Production for the Market." *Review of Radical Political Economics* 12, no. 2: 14–24.
Katzman, David. 1978. *Seven Days a Week: Women and Domestic Service in Industrializing America*. New York: Oxford University Press.
Kessler-Harris, Alice. 1975. "Where Are the Organized Women Workers?" *Feminist Studies* 3, nos. 1–2: 92–110.
———. 1981. *Women Have Always Worked*. Old Westbury, N.Y.: Feminist Press.
Kraditor, Aileen. 1971. *The Ideas of the Woman Suffrage Movement, 1890–1920*. New York: Doubleday Anchor.
Kung, Lydia. 1976. "Factory Work and Women in Taiwan, Changes in Self-image and Status." *Signs* 2, no. 1: 35–58.
Lamphere, Louise, Ewa Hauser, Dee Rubin, Sonya Michel, and Christina Simmons. 1980. "The Economic Struggles of Female Factory Workers: A Comparison between Early and Recent French, Polish and Portuguese Immigrants." In *Proceedings of a Conference on Educational and Occupational Needs of White Ethnic Women*. Washington, D.C.: National Institute of Education.
Lerner, Gerda. 1973. *Black Women in White America: A Documentary History*. New York: Random House, Vintage.
Lim, Linda. 1978. *Women Workers in Multinational Corporations in Developing Countries: The Case of the Electronics Industry in Malaysia and Singapore*. Occasional Papers in Women's Studies, University of Michigan.
MacLean, Nancy. 1982. *The Culture of Resistance: Female Institution-building in the Ladies Garment Workers' Union 1905–1925*. Occasional Papers in Women's Studies, University of Michigan.
Marx, Karl. 1935. *Value, Price and Profit*. New York: International Publishers.
———. 1965. *Capital*. Vol. 1. Moscow: Progress Publishers.
May, Martha. 1982. "The Historical Problem of the Family Wage: The Ford Motor Company and the Five Dollar Day." *Feminist Studies* 8, no. 2: 399–424.
Medick, Hans, and David Sabean, eds. 1983. *Family: Material Interest and Emotion*. Proceedings of the Roundtable on History and Anthropology. Cambridge: Cambridge University Press.
Milkman, Ruth. 1976. "Women's Work and the Economic Crisis: Some Lessons from the Great Depression." *Review of Radical Political Economics* 8, no. 1: 73–97.

———. 1982. "Redefining 'Women's Work'. The Sexual Division of Labor in the Auto Industry during World War II." *Feminist Studies* 8, no. 2: 337–372.
Moody, Anne. 1970. *Coming of Age in Mississippi.* New York: Dell.
Morgan, Robin, ed. 1970. *Sisterhood Is Powerful.* New York: Random House, Vintage.
Mortimer, Delores M., and R. S. Bryce-Laporte, eds. 1981. *Contemporary Studies of the Black Female and the Migratory Experience in the United States.* Washington, D.C.: Smithsonian Institution RIIES.
Palmer, Phyllis M. 1983. "White Women/Black Women: The Dualism of Female Identity in the United States." *Feminist Studies* 9, no. 1: 151–170.
Paulson, Ross Evans. 1973. *Women's Suffrage and Prohibition: A Comparative Study of Equality and Social Control.* Glenview, Ill.: Scott Foresman.
Pearce, Diana, and Harriett P. McAdoo. 1981. *Women and Children: Alone and in Poverty.* Washington, D.C.: National Advisory Council on Equal Opportunity.
Pessar, Patricia. 1982. *Kinship Relations of Production in the Migration Process: The Case of Dominican Emigration to the United States.* Occasional Papers. New York University Center for Latin American and Caribbean Studies.
Pleck, Elizabeth H. 1979. "A Mother's Wages: Income Earning among Married Italian and Black Workers." In N. F. Cott and E. H. Pleck, eds., *A Heritage of Her Own: Toward a New Social History of American Women.* New York: Simon and Schuster, Touchstone.
Rapp, Rayna. 1978. "Family and Class in Contemporary America: Notes toward an Understanding of Ideology." *Science and Society* 42, no. 3: 278–300.
Rodney, Walter. 1972. *How Europe Underdeveloped Africa.* Dar es Salaam: Tanzania Publishing.
Rothman, Sheila. 1979. *Woman's Proper Place.* New York: Basic Books.
Rubin, Mary. 1982. *Women and Poverty.* Research Summary 4. Washington, D.C.: Business and Professional Women's Foundation.
Ryan, Mary. 1979. *Womanhood in America.* New York: Watts.
———. 1981. *Cradle of the Middle Class: The Family in Oneida County, New York 1790–1865.* Cambridge: Cambridge University Press.
Rywell, Martin, comp. 1974. *Afro-American Encyclopedia.* Vol. 1. North Miami, Fla.: Educational Book Publishers.
Sacks, Karen. 1983. "Kinship and Class Consciousness." In H. Medick and D. Sabean, eds. *Family: Material Interest and Emotion.* Proceedings of the Roundtable on History and Anthropology. Cambridge: Cambridge University Press.
Safa, Helen. 1981. "Runaway Shops and Female Employment: The Search for Cheap Labor." *Signs* 7, no. 2: 418–433.
Salaff, Janet. 1981. *Working Daughters of Hong Kong: Female Filial Piety or Intra-Family Power?* ASA Rose Monograph Series. Cambridge: Cambridge University Press.
Sen, Gita. 1980. "The Sexual Division of Labor and the Working-Class Family: Toward a Conceptual Synthesis of Class Relations and the Subordination of Women." *Review of Radical Political Economics* 12, no. 2: 76–86.
Smith, Judith. 1979. "Our Own Kind: Family and Community Networks in Providence." In N. F. Cott and E. H. Pleck, eds., *A Heritage of Her Own: Toward a New Social History of American Women.* New York: Simon and Schuster, Touchstone.
Spalter-Roth, Roberta H. 1983. "Differentiating between the Living Standards of Husbands and Wives in Two-Wage-Earner Families, 1968 and 1979." *Journal of Economic History* 43, no. 1: 231–240.

Stack, Carol. 1974. *All Our Kin: Strategies for Survival in a Black Community.* New York: Harper, Colophon.
Strasser, Susan. 1982. *Never Done: A History of American Housework.* New York: Pantheon.
Tax, Meredith. 1980. *The Rising of the Women: Feminist Solidarity and Class Conflict 1880–1917.* New York: Monthly Review Press.
Tilly, Louise A. 1981. "Paths of Proletarianization: Organization of Production, Sexual Division of Labor, and Women's Collective Action." *Signs* 7, no. 2: 400–417.
Tilly, Louise, and J. Scott. 1978. *Women, Work, and Family.* New York: Holt, Rinehart and Winston.
Trey, J. E. 1972. "Women and the War Economy: World War II." *Review of Radical Political Economics* 4, no. 3: 1–17.
Vanek, Joann. 1974. "Time Spent in Housework." *Scientific American,* November, 116–121.
Vogel, Lise. 1981. "Marxism and Feminism: Unhappy Marriage, Trial Separation or Something Else?" In L. Sargent, ed., *Women and Revolution.* Boston: South End Press.
Wandersee, Winifred. 1981. *Women's Work and Family Values 1920–1940.* Cambridge: Harvard University Press.
Weinbaum, Batya, and Amy Bridges. 1979. "The Other Side of the Paycheck: Monopoly Capital and the Structure of Consumption." In Z. Eisenstein, ed., *Capitalist Patriarchy and the Case for Socialist Feminism.* New York: Monthly Review Press.
Weisstein, Naomi. 1970. "Psychology Constructs the Female." In R. Morgan, ed., *Sisterhood Is Powerful.* New York: Random House, Vintage.
Welter, Barbara. 1966. "The Cult of True Womanhood 1820–1860." *American Quarterly* 18, no. 2 (pt. 1): 151–174.
Wong, Aline. 1981. "Planned Development, Social Stratification and the Sexual Division of Labor in Singapore." *Signs* 7, no. 2: 434–452.
Wright, Erik, Cynthia Costello, David Hachen, and Joey Sprague. 1982. "The American Class Structure." *American Sociological Review* 47, no. 6: 709–726.
Wright, Gwendolyn. 1981. *Building the Dream: A Social History of Housing in America.* New York: Pantheon.
Yoon, Soon Young. 1976. "You Can't Go Home Again: Migration of Korean Single, Young Female Workers." Paper presented at annual meeting of the American Anthropological Association.
———. 1979. "The Halfway House: MNCs, Industries and Asian Factory Girls." Bangkok: UNAPDI.
Young, Michael, and Peter Willmott. 1962. *Family and Kinship in East London.* Baltimore: Penguin.

Bibliography

Cott, Nancy F. 1972. *The Root of Bitterness: Documents of the Social History of American Women.* New York: Dutton.
Groneman, Carol. 1977. "'She Earns as a Child; She Pays as a Man': Women

Workers in a Mid-Nineteenth-Century New York City Community." In M. Cantor and B. Laurie, eds., *Class, Sex and the Woman Worker*. Westport, Conn.: Greenwood.

Hayden, Dolores. 1981. *The Grand Domestic Revolution: A History of Feminist Designs for American Homes, Neighborhoods, and Cities*. Cambridge: MIT Press.

Kessler-Harris, Alice. 1982. *Out to Work: A History of Wage-earning Women in the United States*. New York: Oxford University Press.

Melosh, Barbara. 1983. *The Physician's Hand*. Philadelphia: Temple University Press.

Pleck, Elizabeth H. 1976. "Two Worlds in One." *Journal of Social History* 10, no. 2: 178–195.

Pope, Liston. 1942. *Millhands and Preachers: A Study of Gastonia*. New Haven, Conn.: Yale University Press.

Scharf, Lois. 1980. *To Work and Wed: Female Employment, Feminism and the Great Depression*. Westport, Conn.: Greenwood.

2

LINDA FRANKEL
UNIVERSITY OF MICHIGAN, ANN ARBOR

Southern Textile Women: Generations of Survival and Struggle

Through three generations in many southern piedmont towns between 1900 and 1960, textile work was inherited as the family and community legacy of a poor white working class.[1] The labor of women —paid and domestic—contributed to the growth of the textile industry in the South and to the survival of workers' families in these communities. Low wages, poor working conditions, and limited alternatives placed heavy constraints on women and taxed their energies in the struggle to provide for themselves and their families. Yet in the face of significant obstacles, women—both as workers and as members of mill communities—participated in the daily resistance and collective protests through which southern mill hands pressed their claims for dignity and control over their lives and labor. The history of women textile workers in the South belies a simplistic image of passivity while at the same time it attests to the powerful forces limiting the autonomy of women workers in southern mill villages.

This essay focuses on the experiences of women textile workers in the Harriet-Henderson Cotton Mills in North and South Henderson,

1. Black workers were overtly excluded from production jobs in the mills until the 1960s. They did, however, perform a variety of the hardest, dirtiest tasks such as yard work, lifting and loading, and janitorial services. In Henderson, the community I studied, the work force was virtually exclusively white, although a small number of black men were employed and were also members of the union. For a discussion of black textile workers, see Frederickson (1982) and Newman (1978).

TABLE I PROFILE OF RESPONDENTS

	1895–1904	1905–1914	1915–1924	1925–1934	1935+
Date of birth	7	10	2	2	0
Began work[a]	1	3	5	9	2

[a]Total 20; information on one woman is missing.

North Carolina.[2] The history of struggle in this community is one of relative success but ultimate failure of workers to exert collective control over conditions in the factories and mill villages. After several unsuccessful attempts to organize a union, including a strike in 1927, the workers in Henderson voted for representation, established two locals of the Textile Workers' Union of America (TWUA), and successfully sustained a contract with the company for fourteen years, from 1943 to 1958. In 1958, however, the company launched a campaign to erode the contract and break the union. The outcome of this 2½-year strike-lockout was the demise of the union organization, the loss of jobs in the mills for the one thousand union members who refused to work without a contract, and the break in the link between the multigenerational community of textile workers in the mill villages of North and South Henderson and the plants their labor helped to build. Sixty percent of the unionized workers who participated in this struggle were women. Their experiences as workers and their strong identification with the community fueled their militant defense of the union.

The case of Henderson shows that increasing rationalization of their work and the disruption of accustomed work habits and family life spurred efforts by textile workers to redress their grievances collectively. When management actions violated communal norms and family welfare, the close kinship, work, and neighborhood ties among workers provided a source of oppositional unity among them. The work of women cemented these networks at the same time that the ideology of women's place shaped their participation in public protest and union organization. To understand both the impetus and the constraints on activism, I explore here women's roles in the organization of production and in the family households in this southern textile community, using extensive oral history interviews with twenty-one former Harriet-Henderson millworkers (Table 1). Supplementary material comes from the records of the TWUA in the Wisconsin State Historical Archives, the *Henderson Daily Dispatch*, and other North Carolina and U.S. Government publications.

2. Two mills, owned by the same family, were built at the north and south edges of town in 1895 and 1898 respectively. During the six decades surveyed here, the Henderson Cotton Mill in North Henderson produced yarns and woven class B sheeting while the Harriet Mill in South Henderson was strictly a cotton-spinning operation. Today, the same family continues to control the two mill complexes, which now produce cotton and synthetic blends of yarn.

Paternalism and Women's Work in the First Generation

From the beginning the mills depended heavily on the labor of women and children. Textile work served as the main conduit into industrial waged labor for families unable to make a living in tenant farming. Overseers from the mills traveled the countryside seeking out large families with numerous female children to work in the spinning mills. During the burst of development that took place in the southern textile industry between 1880 and 1905, two-thirds of the work force was comprised of young women and children (McLaurin, 1971: 18–23). Families with insufficient manpower to engage in labor-intensive tobacco farming were attracted to the mills by the promise of wages, the accessibility of schooling for their children, and the desire to escape the extreme poverty they faced on the land. Female-headed households, young girls, and widows predominated in the stream of impoverished tenant farmers and small landowners, swollen by the depression in agriculture after World War I, who sought work in southern mill villages (Janiewski, 1979; Newman, 1979).

Women consistently comprised a significant portion of the work force in southern textile mills, but the proportion, ages, and marital status of women workers changed as economic and political factors affected the labor demands of the mill and as decreasing fertility changed the shape of mill families. Reflecting the general pattern in the industry, the female percentage of the labor force declined in Henderson from a high of 60 percent in 1900 to a fluctuating level of between 30 percent and 40 percent through the first two decades of this century as child labor diminished and adult employment increased. As rationalization of production and modernization of equipment intensified in the late 1920s and 1930s, however, employment of women steadily rose to almost half of the textile labor force (Table 2). Significant in these trends was the shift from young, single girls to mature, married women as the dominant type of female worker.

In the first generation of mill families, children and young women were the primary female wage earners. Work organization in the mills was modeled on preexisting patterns of sex and age divisions in the family. As on the farm, children continued to make important contributions to the family economy. Little children learned their jobs early as unpaid "helpers" to older siblings (a system sometimes used to evade child labor laws). Children turned their wages over to their parents to be used for family needs. Yet the mill hierarchy partially supplanted the authority of "mill daddies," unemployed men whose main task was to carry lunches to their working children. A millowner quoted in the *Fourteenth Annual Report* (1900) of the North Carolina Bureau of Labor and Printing claimed that "the mill discipline is better for them than many of them get at their homes" (H. F. Schenck, p. 196). In the

TABLE 2 NUMBER OF EMPLOYEES AND PERCENTAGE OF WOMEN WORKERS IN THE HARRIET-HENDERSON MILLS

	North Henderson		*South Henderson*		*(North Carolina)*
	Number	*Percentage*	*Number*	*Percentage*	*(Percentage)*
1900	275	61% women and children	*a*	*a*	
1910	516	42% women	456	33% women	
1920	633	43% women and children			
1923–1924	550	27% women and children	650	38% women	
1925–1926	700	*a*	850	*a*	(36% women in total North Carolina textile work force)
1929					(44.6% women)
1940–1960	400–500	*a*	400–500	*a*	(41–47% women)

Sources: Henderson [N.C.] City Directory (1902); Lahne, (1944); North Carolina Bureau of Labor and Printing (1900–1907); North Carolina Department of Labor and Printing (1910–1926); U.S. Bureau of the Census (1940–1960). See Lahne for data about women and children in the textile industry in both New England and the South.

[a]No figures available.

mills, jobs were segregated by sex as well as age. Young girls worked in spinning, winding, and spooling as machine tenders and assistants, while their brothers hauled yarn, "doffed" bobbins, and ran the machines in the card room. In North Carolina in 1907, for example, 68.8 percent of the ring spinners were young women under the age of 16, while women over 16 accounted for another 25.2 percent. The majority of doffers, 71.8 percent, were boys under 16 (U.S. Bureau of Labor Statistics, 1909–1910).

While women experienced greater opportunities for sociability and employment in mill villages than they had on the farm, their lives were more constricted than their brothers'. Education was limited, and advancement in the mills was closed to women. Skilled, higher paid jobs such as loom fixer and mechanic were held by adult men, as were all supervisory positions ranging from second hands to overseers to department supervisors to mill superintendent. Often these male authorities were the fathers, uncles, or brothers of young women in their own or other sections of the mill. Although kinship relations influenced access to work, they did not alter the priorities or rules applicable to the jobs. A spinner who began working at the age of fourteen recalled:

> My mother's only brother was an assistant superintendent in the mill—the overseer of all the spinning. Therefore I think that played a part in all of them [her own and her mother's family] coming to Henderson and going to work in a mill. As they got old enough, all my brothers and sisters went to work in the mill. All my sisters went to work in the spinning room. Some of my aunts were working there too. The rules that applied to everybody else applied to us. Naturally he would give them a job maybe quicker than somebody else, but they had to work and they had to keep up their work or else they wouldn't have been allowed to work.

Those mothers with a sufficient number of children old enough to send to work or husbands who earned better wages as fixers, weavers, or "straw" bosses were able to give up full-time work in the mills.

> My father was an overseer in the mill. My mamma worked a while, but see she had all those children [thirteen] so she couldn't work much. She quit. They put the children to work at twelve years old, took them right out of school. Then they passed a law you couldn't do it; they had to go to school until they were fourteen. I went to work between fifteen and sixteen, I think it was, that I went in the winding room. My sister had to stand on the box in the spinning room; she couldn't reach to work them. All of them worked in the mill, all my sisters, excepting the baby girl and the baby boy.—WINDER TENDER, SOUTH HENDERSON

Mothers in these families focused their energies on domestic production and provided services to the factory hands such as child care for kin and neighbors, taking in boarders, serving as midwives, or sewing to earn extra income. Domestic production—including keeping chickens, hogs, or a cow; raising vegetables; and churning butter—supplemented the low wages and gave an undergirding to the family's standard of living.

> My mother worked harder than I did. Oh Lord, yes. She had worked in the mill when she was young but not in my lifetime. My father worked in the mill but he had a bad heart and couldn't work much. As my brother got old enough he went to work, then as we children got old enough we went to work. She was the one who waited on him. You had to wash your clothes on the board, boil them in a pot outdoors. Yes ma'am, they didn't have any permapress, everything had to be ironed. I've known my mother to iron six hours without stopping. . . . She'd have to do all the washing and everything. We didn't have any carpets or anything. You had to scrub your floors. Mother cleaned the schoolhouse, too.—SPINNER, NORTH HENDERSON

> Mother didn't work in the mill, but she worked. She had ten children. It was so many at home she was working all the time—sewing, cooking, cleaning. . . . We had chickens, cows, and a garden. Mother worked for a short while but it just didn't work out . . . Father got sick and my older sister quit and went to work. She got out very little; church was about it, and a few PTA meetings. Father had more schooling than mother. He was more active in

church because, as she put it, "Who's going to fix supper for all those folks?"
—WEAVER, NORTH HENDERSON

As wages declined and more families became dependent on irregular work after World War I, the family economy of millworkers became more precarious. In impoverished conditions, women, particularly working mothers, bore a disproportionate burden of harder work, lower wages, and access to fewer resources. This legacy was passed on to their daughters. For example, Mrs. R's mother, a widow, moved to town to put her seven children to work as they got old enough. Her mother took in boarders. Mrs. R went to work at fifteen for twenty-five cents a day. Later, in her own family, "someone had to go without—me. I dressed my husband and kids because they had to go out to meet the public. I was the one who did without. I stayed home because I didn't have nothing. Sometimes I wasn't able to go to church because I didn't have shoes. I made sure the others had enough. All my three children finished school."

The fiber of women's work, whether in the mills for wages or at home to sustain family members, was woven by the family and community dependence on the mills. "Public" work for women was part of the tradition in the mill villages necessitated by the low wages and the mills' demands for multiple family members to participate in keeping the spindles and looms running day and night.[3] Women's household labor reproduced the community of workers both daily and generationally to engage in this work. Women's work in both spheres was conditioned by the low wages, paternalistic management practices, and the rhythms and demands of millwork.

In Henderson, as in other mill villages, a particularly pervasive and extensive form of paternalism regulated the working and private lives of mill hands and their families.[4] The millowners created and controlled an institutional infrastructure consisting of housing, schools, a commissary, and churches. Services of a doctor and coal for heating were provided by the mill, and expenses were deducted from weekly wages along with rent and commissary charges. Access to housing was tied to participation of multiple family members in millwork; tenure in

3. Textile wages have always been lower in the South than in New England. While the lower proportion of skilled workers in the South resulted in a smaller sex differential, the range of southern women's wages was more compressed than that of male workers. More than two wage earners per family have consistently been required for families to meet a minimum standard of living. Davis (1929) cites a wage contribution of 44 percent to the family economy by working mothers in 1914. For detailed data on wages, see Davis (1929); Janiewski (1979: 116–119); Lahne (1944); Newman (1978: 210–211, n. 22); and Oates (1975).

4. Paternalism refers to company control of land, buildings, goods, and services in the mill villages as well as to the ideology that overlay the relations between workers and millowners. Pope (1942) defined paternalism as "the height of capitalism's control over culture." For detailed descriptions of paternalism and its effects see Boyte (1972); Herring (1929); Janiewski (1979); McLaurin (1971); Newman (1978); and Pope (1942).

the mill community depended on a family's ability to supply sufficient labor power for the mills on terms dictated by the company. Later, as the need for and profitability of these direct services declined, modified forms of paternalism were retained. The mill donated school books for the use of workers' children, turned unused millowned houses into community centers in the North and South Henderson villages, and hired a welfare officer who organized recreational activities for youths and worked as well with the local magistrate to control domestic and communal problems such as drinking, fights, and family disorder.

Paternalistic management practices initially grew out of the need to attract and keep labor in the mills. The family system of labor required that the company grant some degree of flexibility to workers who coupled long hours in the mill with family responsibilities. A winder tender in South Henderson explained:

> They let them go home at 11:30 to cook dinner and 5:30 to fix supper. We worked eleven hours then. There weren't but so many people here then, and they actually had to put them back [after they had a baby] if they knew how. You see, that would save them money and would be better than having to learn a new one, so they put them back if they could. . . . Mama said they was good to her. If Papa was sick, [the millowner] would send her a load of coal down there. He was as good as I reckon he had to be. He had to have somebody to run the mill.

The mill-dominated infrastructure substituted for wage increases and served to deflect criticism and minimize state interference. Millowners declared a higher moral purpose in providing work for impoverished white rural families and building community prosperity. The other side of this ideological coin, however, was the high degree of control the paternalistic system allowed over workers' labor and private lives. Welfare practices were geared toward molding an efficient work force based on capitalist standards of appropriate work and nonwork activities and behavior. An industry spokesman declared: "Unless the operatives are trained not only to work but also to live efficiently, the local industry cannot hope to succeed in competition with workers bred in a longer tradition of industrial production" (Davis, 1929: 50).

The mill village system of paternalism served to reinforce workers' dependent status and undermine the possibilities for alternatives or choices either within or outside this way of life. Individuals and families were bound into the hierarchical system of relations in the mills and villages through punitive and persuasive measures. Those who protested, broke company rules, or engaged in disruptive, "unrespectable" behavior risked job loss and eviction for their entire families. Employers in a particular area often blacklisted troublemakers. In response to early protests, owners developed an arsenal of weapons and strategies to deal with strikes: injunctions, lockouts, evictions, National Guard troops to protect scabs (McLaurin, 1971). Jobs, survival, and chances for personal advancement depended on ingratiation with the bosses, conformity to company rules, and adherence to the definition of morality supported by the mills and preached in company-supported churches (Newman, 1979: 6). Personalistic recruitment into the mills fostered a sense of obligation. One woman declared, "They gave us jobs when we had little babies."

Paternalism, whether in the form of goods and services or personal favors, did not supplant, but rather, depended on, women's continued responsibility for domestic life. Further, any "flexibility" necessitated by the family system of labor was conditioned by the different roles and opportunities open to men and women. For example, flexibility for adult women took the form of permission to leave the mills during a break to feed their babies or fix supper for their families. While young girls may have had some latitude to mix work with play or socializing, married women were described as "too tired" for such activities. Mothers needed to keep on good terms with the overseer or the "Big Daddy" (superintendent) of the mills in order to request personal favors related to particular family situations or difficulties (e.g., time out to nurse a sick child). For men, "flexibility" took the form of irregular work habits owing to such common practices as taking time off for hunting, fishing, or drinking. As doffers caught up on their work, they were able to leave the mill to enjoy such leisure pastimes as hanging out at the little stores and bars close by the mill, going to the movies uptown, or courting. Furthermore, ingratiation by men might mean promotion to a job with higher status and wages. In the "mill family," where the owner and supervisors served as models of adulthood, hard work and self-discipline by children reaped potentially higher benefits exclusively for males. Only men had access to the roles of greater authority and status in the overlapping hierarchies of work, family, and religion in the community (Boyte, 1972: 27).

The pushes and pulls of patronage and reprisal undoubtedly reduced workers' capacities to recognize and act on collective interests. Irregular work habits and a high degree of mobility among workers in search of a kinder patron or better working conditions indicated, nonetheless, that workers had some expectations of and standards for appropriate treatment and a more balanced definition of rights and duties (Billings, 1979: 112). For example:

> The Southern mill owners complained that the employees did not work regularly, so that spare hands had to be brought into the mill village; and once the spare hands were present, they had to be given work even if the regular employees had to be "sent out to rest" from time to time. Thus a circle was set up—the people worked irregularly because there were too many hands, and there were too many hands because the people worked irregularly. (Lahne, 1944: 151)

Women took advantage of the spare hand system to attend to household and family tasks "without specifically taking time off." Women's double burden accounted for more frequent work absences. According to one reference cited in Boyte (1972), women lost 30 percent more working time than men owing to their own illnesses or to the need to care for sick family members. The Women's Bureau (1926) reported in 1926 that the average woman worker spent almost three hours daily on housework.

In addition to "laying out," dissatisfied workers left the community to seek work elsewhere:

> I come from independent stock. I was independent. In the past I always complained. They would fire me or I would quit. Before my child was born I would quit any time conditions were bad. At that time if you didn't have a job you'd go stay somewheres two or three weeks and go every day and ask for a job. I didn't want to depend on my folks. I saved $100. One time I refused to spin. I had worked there longer and the bossman's wife could spin better. I couldn't have quit if I had not had the money.—WINDER TENDER, SOUTH HENDERSON

Yet this movement tended to be circular, from one mill village to another (Boyte, 1972: 22). For women, millwork was a family inheritance, and when they had their own children, their mobility was further restricted and their dependency increased. The above winder tender continued: "I couldn't drag my daughter all over the place. If you are left with a baby to take care of and you don't have money, you have to have spunk. I had a child to rear; my husband was dead. I had no other income."

Though these forms of resistance—irregular work habits and frequent moves—represented a challenge to the demands of factory work, they did not necessarily confront the private handling of grievances encouraged by the paternalistic system. Also, the reverse side of flexibility and integration of wage and family labor—long hours and low cash wages—imposed hardship on workers and reduced their capacity to take risks.

Yet, the potential for a more collective basis for defense of workers' interests lay in the very basis of loyalty cultivated by the mills and in the networks of mutual aid that developed among families of long-time workers and community residents. On the one hand, this system operated to push "successful" workers toward an alignment with management. Overseers and straw bosses, drawn from the community of workers, represented "that portion of the cotton mill village population which has achieved success" (Boyte, 1972: 26–27). Their jobs depended on their ability to enforce discipline on the job and their visibility as models of community respectability. On the other hand, families of bossmen and skilled workers had access to greater resources. The wives and mothers in these families were able to remain at home or work only part time while using family wages to create a higher standard of living based on more extensive domestic production and management. Around these families coalesced extended kin and friendship networks, channels of support, assistance, information, and contracts that influenced access to housing, jobs, and other necessities.

Ties of kinship, religion, neighborhood, and peer group exerted pulls and obligations in the direction of the larger community of workers, as this comment by the daughter of an overseer in the cardroom shows:

> Mr. Craig [the mill superintendent] told papa to move further uptown, to buy a house up there so he would get more prestige and respect from the help. Mama wouldn't do it. She had ten children. We lived down there in the pines. The children could play out there. We raised chickens, hogs, and a garden and a cow for milk and butter. Mama stayed home and raised the children.

Thus, a key tension in the mill community lay in whether patronage, poverty, and fear would lead individual workers and families to seek their interests through management-sanctioned, personalistic channels, or whether those with greater resources and skills could provide a cushion of stability and support for a broader based pursuit of workers' interests.

The 1927 Strike

The successive efforts of management to reduce flexibility and exert more control over production had a galvanizing impact on the tenuous balance of interests in the mill community. Workers, finding less room for individual solutions, responded collectively; but the conditions that provoked militant reactions also increased economic insecurity and created a pool of workers whose needs were more difficult to address with limited power and resources.[5]

By the mid-1920s an economic slump in the textile industry spurred management to tighten up at the same time that a labor surplus and a depression in local tobacco agriculture further reduced workers' options. In 1924, when overproduction forced cutbacks in mill operations to a three-day week, the Harriet-Henderson Company decided to withdraw a bonus offered to encourage good work attendance and to reinstate a regular workweek with lower pay. The millowner promised workers that the bonus would be returned when business improved. When, three years later, this promise remained unfulfilled, the workers struck. Protest against management's policies originated in South Henderson, where a higher proportion of women were employed than in the North Henderson mill and where a greater number of families were dependent on the declining wages and work opportunities. The

5. Several important textile strikes occurred during the period 1929–1934, in southern towns including Gastonia and Marion, North Carolina and Elizabethton, Tennessee; see Evans (1970); Pope (1942); and Tippett (1931). Jacqueline Hall, Director of the Southern Oral History Program at the University of North Carolina at Chapel Hill, and Sara Evans at the University of Minnesota are currently studying the role of women in the Elizabethton strike through oral history interviews with participants.

workers' petition, declaring that "most of all of the family men were not making enough to decently clothe and feed their families," turned the basic legitimating premise of the paternalistic ideology—the mill as provider of jobs and rewarder of loyalty—into a critique of the existing conditions of low wages and family dependency.

Not only did the mill hands protest against the low wages and the surplus labor that blocked increases,[6] they also reacted strongly to new management policies geared toward greater control over production. Workers complained about the increasing speed of the machinery and the recent practice of locking the mill gates during working hours. This practice caused particular hardship for women, but it also hit at the dignity of the community of workers as a whole: "We are not a class of people to be locked in."

The strike, which took place at the end of the summer, lasted six weeks. The intransigence of the millowner in recognizing the legitimacy of the collective demands and his use of National Guard troops and the threat of evictions eventually broke the strike. Fearing job loss and the breakup of their community, workers returned to the mills without achieving their aims. Nevertheless, the strike was a community affair during which crowds of workers, their families, and local supporters, including small local merchants, farmers, and religious leaders, gathered to hear speakers and pray at frequent support rallies held in the North and South Henderson mill villages. Eight hundred mill hands signed union cards brought by an organizer for the United Textile Workers (UTW), who had come to assist the strikers. After the defeat of the strike, the UTW made no effort, however, to maintain an organization in Henderson. Local union activity remained submerged until the more supportive climate provided by sympathetic New Deal labor legislation and wartime demand for labor facilitated a successful campaign for organization by the TWUA in 1943.

Women's participation in the 1927 strike, to the extent that it can be reconstructed, reflected both their integration into the mill community as mothers of workers and their own work in the mills, primarily as young girls. Although the public spokesmen for the strikers were men of some standing in the mill community, including an overseer in the cardroom and a popular Sunday school teacher who worked in the spinning department, newspaper and oral history accounts indicate women's support and involvement in the protest. Women and children were noted in the crowds that gathered daily to discuss the strike, and at the apotheosis of the strike drama, a woman was among the nine persons slated for eviction by the mills. Two women who had just begun to work in the mills around the time of the strike, while in their midteens, recalled being sent to the countryside to help kin put up tobacco, as was common at this time of year. While this had not

6. During this period of rapidly declining southern wages, 1920–1930, the South surpassed the North in number of textile workers, active spindles, and looms (Boyte, 1972: 11).

prevented them from joining the walkout and attending union meetings—one without telling her father, an overseer—it did reflect the fact that, while millwork conditioned their lives, young women were still under parental aegis.

> The people were not organized, they just came out. . . . I don't know how the news got around that we were going to strike and we weren't going to let the overseers know anything about it. . . . I remember that my father was working in the cardroom. He was an overseer . . . he came in there where I was and he said, "I heard that the mill was going on strike at 10 o'clock," and he thought I would tell him. Well, I didn't tell him a story. I said I heard some say they might. I didn't tell him I was aiming to because I knew I was going to. . . . We went out through the cardroom and I passed him and we was tickled to death because we's striking. . . . I reckon he expected it. He didn't want us to go to the union meetings, but we would slip off and go anyway, but it didn't cause any conflict. We had an uncle that lived in Wake County. . . . Papa took us down there and we stayed two weeks visiting. It was in the summer and we helped them put tobacco in the barn. Then we came back and the strike was over, so we went back to work.

Rationalization

After 1930 adult married women rather than young single girls came to predominate among women workers. The proportion of women in the mills increased, a trend that accelerated during World War II, and a couple-based work unit replaced the parent-child family wage economy.[7] Unlike their mothers, the second generation of women remained in the mills full time on a continuous basis throughout their adult lives.

As these women of the second and third generations matured, they faced a work world that became increasingly rigid and intense while their family responsibilities remained demanding. The regulation of wages and hours that helped the industry recover from the Depression also spurred the adoption of cost-efficiency measures in the mills (Kessler-Harris, 1982: 266–267). In 1936 the Harriet Henderson Company borrowed money to carry out an expansion and modernization program. New machinery intensified the "stretch-out" of workers begun in the previous decade. Production changes in the mills resulted in the introduction of piece rates, ever-increasing work loads, and close monitoring of individual performances. Textile engineers and time-study men began to play a more prominent role on the shop floor.

Millwork retained its importance for women in the villages for a number of reasons. First, this income was critical for family support:

7. In 1930 almost three-fifths (59 percent) of female textile workers were under 25 years old, whereas slightly over one-fourth (27.8 percent) were between the ages of 25 and 44. By 1940 women under 25 accounted for only 35.7 percent of the female work force, whereas almost two-thirds of women workers were in the 25–44 age bracket. The percentage of married female textile workers rose from 48.9 percent in 1930 to 71.8 percent in 1940 (U.S. Bureau of the Census, 1930, 1940).

"Women had to help make a living. It was not any problem about a man not wanting a woman to work." For women whose husbands drank or deserted them, access to paid work was even less of an option and more of a necessity. Second, lack of education and marriage restricted women's opportunities and mobility. "Putting it all together, back then there wasn't a whole lot of things for women. Maybe people in higher brackets of living knew it was more, but we didn't." The company reinforced these limitations by preventing other industry from coming into the town and by selling mill housing to the worker-tenants:

> Since there were no cars, we had to marry the ones we worked with right in the mills. We couldn't go nowhere to meet people. . . . Nobody with any ability or education worked in the mill. But there were no jobs available . . . no other way, no chance. . . .
>
> Most got out as quick as they could but we had children. We bought the company houses. We couldn't walk away and leave them.—SPINNER, SOUTH HENDERSON

Third, compared to other jobs uptown for women, "the mill was the onliest thing here in Henderson that paid anything." Service jobs such as waitressing and sales work, which were beginning to increase in the 1940s, did not pay as well as the mill wages, which had been improved through federal regulation.[8] Further, these jobs often required longer, less regular hours, creating problems for working mothers. The convenience of millwork, which was "five minutes away" and offered a choice of eight-hour shifts, made it easier for mothers to pick up their children from school, arrange child care, shop, and assist elderly parents. As a female weaver and mother of three explained: "You make your eight hours and you come home . . . you can still do housework and be there for the children."

Eight hours in the mill did not limit women's work in the home. Women felt the intensification of work both on the job and in their home responsibilities. As one spinner put it, "When you work, keep house, and have children, it's more than a job." This juggling of demands necessitated that women workers "try to figure all angles at once." Women enlisted each other's aid as well as that of their children, while "some husbands helped and some didn't." The strategy of split shifts was used quite extensively; husbands and wives would work different shifts so that someone would remain at home to care for the children. Mothers, daughters, and sisters would "trade backwards and forwards" to help each other out. Single mothers particularly depended on these networks of assistance.

8. The National Recovery Act Codes of 1933–1934 and the minimum wage legislation of the Fair Labor Standards Act of 1938 upgraded southern wages, but the disparity had again increased by the 1950s. Some gain in southern wages after 1952 was matched by an increase in the gap between men and women. Hourly textile wages today average only two-thirds of the national hourly manufacturing wage.

Finally, familiarity with millwork grew out of women's relationships with kin, neighbors, and peers in the community. It reflected an aspect of "being with the crowd" and a social dimension that made work meaningful: "We worked together like brothers and sisters."

The ability to have some control over choice of shift and a job to return to after pregnancy leaves became critically important for working mothers. Before unionization, under a system that allowed overseers a great deal of power to control access to and conditions of employment, women were particularly vulnerable to discrimination and favoritism. The use of work accessibility to punish or reward workers was exacerbated by the family connections of the overseers and the potential for sexual harassment of young women by male bosses.

> We went to Mr. Bob [the supervisor] and told him we needed a job. He put us to work, but we had to do like Mr. Bob said. It was operated familylike . . . if he wanted to fire you and hire his child he could do it. There was nothing there to protect you.—WINDER, SOUTH HENDERSON

> There was discrimination on every hand. The bossmen would try to date the women. If one got mad they would "send you out to rest." . . . The women that would go with them got the best jobs. They would take you off a job or shift and put you on another. There was no grievance.—WINDER TENDER, SOUTH HENDERSON

> Along then we didn't have no union. . . . If they wanted to hire you back if you quit to have a baby or something, they'd hire you. If they didn't, they didn't. Most of the time the bossmen would try to go with all the girls. . . . If they wouldn't date them, they wouldn't give them a job.—SPINNER, SOUTH HENDERSON

On the one hand, women were exposed to the arbitrary behavior of male bosses. On the other hand, some of these young women were the daughters and kin of lower level supervisors. As the millowners turned to "scientific management" to solve their problems of work control and efficiency, they began to hire college-trained supervisory personnel, who replaced former overseers and fired many older workers. Daughters saw their fathers demoted or retired without pensions. Therefore, in addition to experiencing a diminishing sense of control over their own labor, they also assumed a burden of care for elderly parents whose hard work and loyalty went unrewarded. The grievances that fueled union organization represented both a reaction to changes in the organization of work and a buildup of anger and frustration at the effects of the older style of favoritism and discrimination based on family connections.

Unionization

The organization of two TWUA locals, Number 584 and Number 578 in North and South Henderson, followed on a successful NRLB election in 1943. The locals achieved an impressive 90 percent membership level in a state that passed a right-to-work law that precluded a closed shop.[9] The women I interviewed, who ranged from activists to loyal supporters to mere dues payers, all felt that unionization brought about greater respect, fairer treatment, and more adequate compensation for the "hard, honest work" they performed: "Under the union we had to respect them and they had to respect us. We had rules under the union, job security. If nothing else but for the job security it was worth the dues. You won't find anyone more union than me. The union protected our jobs, our wages, and our characters, but the company finally broke it" (—WINDER, SHOP STEWARD, SOUTH HENDERSON).

These women expressed a sense of pride and competency in their work. They were experienced in a variety of jobs in the mill and saw good supervision as the kind that let them do their work without interference. Unionization provided women who had limited individual options with a collective measure of protection and job security.

> When the union first came in, I was in the spinning department. There's nothing in the cotton mill I don't know how to do unless it's work in a cardroom. I've done everything from spinning on up to reeling, winding, and yarn stamp inspector. I grew up in the mill. . . . We were getting the rough end of the bargain. . . . That's why I became so interested in the union. I said, "When it comes I want to be the first one. I want to do my job and I want to do it right, but I'm so tired of people telling me what I can and can't do when I know I'm right."—WINDER TENDER, YARN INSPECTOR, UNION OFFICER; SOUTH HENDERSON

Despite the protection of "rules," a seniority system, and the grievance procedure that forced the company to "make amends" if they "did us dirty," semiskilled female workers nonetheless faced increasing work loads and daily harassment by male bosses who undermined their efforts to satisfy their own work standards: "Sometimes the work load was so heavy, you worked so hard and got nowhere. Somebody was always wanting you to do more than you could. . . . I wanted to do good. I have a lot of pride but I did not have the time, just like in housecleaning" (—SPINNER, NORTH HENDERSON). Unable fully to confront control issues, the union bargained for higher wages in exchange for concessions relating to work loads and job control. "The union didn't have no control over how much work you had to do. Any time they raised your wages they put double work on you."

Intensification of work also threatened the sociability and mutual assistance that women workers extended to one another on the shop floor as they did at home:

9. Unionization in the southern textile industry has always been low. In the period during which the Henderson mills were unionized, only 15–20 percent of the southern textile work force was organized. Antiunion practices and right-to-work laws have made organization extremely difficult in the South. Some successes are currently being registered, particularly where black workers have taken the lead.

> I've got to tell the good along with it. Some nights my work run real good. I kept it up, worked hard but kept it up, and I helped the girl next to me start her looms. One time the girl filling batteries on my set of looms, I seen her work her can off and she couldn't catch things up. I'd get in front of her buggy and fill two or three of her batteries and be watching my looms all the same time and see one stop, just put my bobbins down and take off about a half a country mile to go start the loom. So I really walked, I mean you worked.—WEAVER, NORTH HENDERSON

> One girl came in with a terrible headache. She wanted me to get a coke for her so she could take a powder and make the night. I had already started. My machine was running. The same bossman came over and said, "I thought I put you to work." . . . I went back to work. The more I thought about it the madder I got. I went into his office and said, "My husband doesn't talk to me like you did and I'm not going to take it off you no more." We made up at it and he tried to be friendly.—WINDER, SHOP STEWARD; SOUTH HENDERSON

Closer supervision of women workers stemmed not only from the nature of their jobs but also from the cultural proscriptions regarding female behavior. When asked if women workers were treated any differently from the men, a woman shop steward and union secretary replied:

> Oh yes, because a man would not take things that a woman would. You know, if a man comes up and says something to a man and he don't like it, he's going to let you know a lot quicker than a woman would, don't you think? . . . But still I don't think it would have the bearing on them coming from a woman as it would from a man. I don't use profanity, but say if a man came up and you were a man, he came up to you and was telling you something, you'd just haul off and let him have it back with all of that profanity. And he same to me and I didn't, naturally he'd think he could get by with it with a man sooner than he could me. I think the woman would feel like the man could get by.—YARN INSPECTOR, UNION OFFICER; SOUTH HENDERSON

The structure of collective bargaining made it necessary to channel worker frustration over increasing work loads and harassment by supervisors into strong, legitimate grievances that took time to resolve and further frustrated some workers. While a few members felt the union "pushed too far" in pressing grievances, "a lot of people thought the union always had a mess going." Others understood that

> it weren't the union, it was the company agitating them to make them do it. . . . They was out to bust the union, you could tell it, the way they acted and the way they'd do things . . . for spite. Like, they'd take one off their job and put them over here and put somebody else on their job; you know, just rotate them, move them around, just looked like to make them fuss and fight with one another. Everything they'd do to us, we'd get against the company for it, because we knew what it was about. They'd have been glad to see us get against each other, because any house divided against itself cannot stand, and they was trying to break it that way, and they couldn't.—WINDER, SHOP STEWARD; SOUTH HENDERSON

The degree of unity and strength the union was able to achieve in an essentially hostile environment was in large measure due to the long-time ties workers had developed to each other and to the community. Significant to the maintenance of these ties was the work of women both in the factory and in the family. The union organization in both villages was sustained by women's work at the same time that the structure of the union reflected the effects of gender inequality. Women served as shop stewards, committee members, and secretary or treasurer of the locals, but men held the top leadership positions of president and vice-president and served on the important general shop committee. The male president of the North Henderson local acknowledged that "my women were at least 50 percent as active as the men in some part. . . . They helped me to do things. I depended on my women 100 percent to get the job done, and they done it." Women were not, however, particularly encouraged or trained to serve in the most visible leadership roles or to participate in contract negotiations. Much of the union's negotiation with the company over work loads and standards was conducted in technical terms—corresponding to the increasing importance of time-study men and engineering controls—a situation that emphasized those skills and knowledge to which men had greater access.

> We had a woman on there [general shop committee] a time or two, but they wouldn't stay. I don't know why unless because they were required to be at meetings, to meet with the company when they had an arbitration case or when they were negotiating a contract. . . . I guess that's why most all jobs were held by men because women just really didn't have the time to put on it, and those that had time didn't feel like they had the knowledge and didn't feel like they were capable of making the decisions because they didn't know enough about the plant in general. Like maybe they just knew their department and that was all. The men would have the opportunity to get around more, find out more, get over the mill more.—SPINNER, UNION OFFICER; NORTH HENDERSON

Inequalities of time, education, and experience originating in prevailing cultural attitudes about women's place were not directly addressed within the union framework. As a woman who served as recording secretary of Local 584 explained:

> Most women had a family, with a small child, some in school. They had to spend more time at home. The men were freer. As they say: Man's work is sun to sun, a woman's work is never done. This is true in the home, in the family where if you care you have duties you want to do them, to keep house. Well, if you don't care how the house is kept you have all the time. When something did come up, it would have to be something urgent. You would have to make a sacrifice.
>
> Sometimes some would come but after you had to pay somebody to keep a baby or small child all day you couldn't afford to hire somebody to keep it. You did not want to come disrupt the meeting with a crying child. Therefore men's attendance was better. They had more and better opportunity to attend.

Activism required that women step out of the mold of the traditional sexual division of labor more than did merely holding a job or becoming a member of the union. Activist women in both locals shared ties as friends and neighbors as well as a number of similar characteristics: long tenure in the mill community and experience in a variety of jobs in the mill; close kin or social relationships with established, respectable families (e.g., fathers who were former overseers or skilled craftsmen); autonomous participation in union activities (e.g., as widows or women whose husbands were not active); and assumption of increased union duties as children grew older. One strong woman leader in the North Henderson local was both appreciated for her abilities and seen as a threat by male union leaders:

> I think they just got tired of her because she was smarter than they. I think Mae was far more capable of being president of our union than any man we had, and I think she would have made a good one. I don't think [the national union representative] or any of those [men] wanted her to be it. I don't think they would really want a woman from either local to be the president. It might be different now since women's liberation.—SPINNER, RECORDING SECRETARY FOR LOCAL 584; NORTH HENDERSON

Despite some barriers, the democratic ideals of the union gave support to women to "exercise their views and ideas just like men." Where unionization was successful, as it was in Henderson between 1943 and 1958, women benefited from the greater security as well as the political education it offered. Yet avenues for individual mobility for women remained limited both within the mills and within the union hierarchy. For this reason, key women leaders, instead of being vulnerable to cooptation into management positions as was the case for men, became some of the most aggressive and adamant defenders of the union when its existence became threatened.

The 1958 Strike

As in 1927, the strike in 1958 was a "conservative" one, that is, one in which the workers demanded the preservation of a previously conceded set of "rights" from the company. In 1958 the demands focused on the contract. The company proposed a substitute contract that wiped out protections workers had enjoyed for fourteen years and challenged the union's limited power to represent workers' collective interests. The central change was an attack on outside mediation as the final step in the grievance process. The company wanted decisions about whether to take a particular case to arbitration to be subject to veto by either the company or the union. This would have forced the union either to strike or to allow managerial prerogatives to go unchecked every time the company refused to arbitrate.

The company clearly knew that their stance would provoke a strong response. Apparently, it felt that it could weather a short strike and break the union, either by forcing the union to accept the weakening changes or by splitting the membership and enticing workers back to the plant on an individual basis. The company president expressed willingness to risk temporary disruption in order to pave the way for greater control over future modernization of the plants:

> Within the past two years, there have been radical changes in the operation of a textile plant. . . . If we are going to operate these plants successfully [efficiently] we must have a contract which will enable us to take advantage of these advances. If I have to pay a [wo]man regardless of skill to tend a machine that does all the work . . . then we cannot take advantage of this progress.—J. D. COOPER, PRESIDENT, HARRIET-HENDERSON MILLS

Aware of the implications, the workers voted to strike when negotiations broke down and the old contract expired; they remained out when the strike turned into a lockout and scabs were recruited from surrounding counties to fill their places. Only a handful of the former workers, wives of foremen and other supervisory personnel, returned to the plants. The rest of the work force, approximately one thousand, remained solidly and militantly on strike for 2½ years.

Women's labor served as the backbone for the strike; women took the major responsibility for the daily agony of managing the extensive support system for the striking workers and their families. As the strike wore on and some of the men were able to get jobs elsewhere, a hard core of women assumed the greatest burdens. The energies of women were harnessed to a much more intense degree during the strike than previously. Some women who had not been especially active in the union were drawn into more active roles. To a certain extent the roles of men and women were equalized during the strike, since solidarity was a crucial issue: both men and women paraded militantly on the picket lines; women were arrested along with men, although not in equal numbers; women speakers were particularly effective in gaining support for their cause at union conventions and local meetings throughout the eastern United States. The strike "brought a lot of harmony with the people that weren't there before." The strike itself was an important educational and politicizing experience for the workers. It brought out the need for workers to stick together and depend on one another (through the union). Loyalty to the union among strikers superseded other alliances and caused cleavages between union and company supporters in town. These feelings remain alive over twenty years later in families and churches torn asunder by the strike.

The strike was defeated by a combination of factors: the availability of an abundant supply of unskilled labor from rural areas experiencing increasing mechanization of agriculture; the use of Highway Patrol and National Guard troops to support the reopening of the mills with scab labor; an injunction against picketing, and numerous arrests of strikers; and finally, the trial and conviction of eight local and national union leaders on charges of conspiracy to dynamite the mill. The costs of this defeat were extremely high both in bitterness and disruption of lives in the community. In trying to come to terms with defeat, many women expressed the feeling that they had saved their health by being forced out of the mills. The national union was able to help some of the women to retrain to enter new areas of employment that they found more satisfying and where they "got out with the public more": nursing, restaurant work, care of retarded children, bookkeeping, hairdressing. The service jobs many women workers entered, while having certain advantages over millwork, were, however, largely low paying and unorganized. Other women found work in a small number of industrial plants that had recently been built nearby or commuted to mills outside the county (when they were not blacklisted). Those who were too old to find other employment but too young to receive social security had to rely on their overburdened families to supplement their reduced income after union assistance was discontinued.

The ultimate loss of the strike by the union dealt a lethal blow to the connection between the mill village communities of unionized workers and the Harriet-Henderson Company. Workers in the long-established mill village were unwilling to sacrifice the self-respect, fellowship, and security gained through the union for what they felt would be the total domination of management. The mills continue to function as a major source of employment for men and women with little training and few opportunities in Henderson; since the 1964 Civil Rights Act paved the way for their integration, the majority of the workers are now black. There is no union.

Conclusion

The experiences of women textile workers in Henderson, through periods of quiescence and conflict, illustrate the changing ways in which traditional claims and communal ties shaped workers' responses to the degradation of their labor and status. Women in the textile villages acted to defend household and communal standards of living and ways of life. As their participation in millwork remained more continuous throughout their mature lives, women came to participate more autonomously—primarily as workers rather than as family members—in collective organization and protest. Yet, the sexual division of labor in the home, factory, and union continued to shape their activities. Women turned to each other for support and assistance in meeting multiple demands on their time and energy. Some of this cooperative labor, which grew out of kin and friendship networks, translated into resistance to supervisors on the shop floor or support work for activities undertaken by the local union groups. The basic premises and structures that underlie the unequal sexual division of labor were not, however, challenged openly or directly in the workers' community. The union movement addressed some of women's needs as workers but did not provide an explicit understanding of the impact of the sexual division of labor on women's lives. Nevertheless, women activists seized the opportunity to participate in building and defending an organization in the community that, within limits, helped workers to gain a measure of control over their lives and labor. This case supports the conclusion that "certain women in positions and situations that promoted their readiness to act, did act" (Tilly, 1981: 417).

References

Billings, Dwight, Jr. 1979. *Planters and the Making of a New South: Class Politics and Development in North Carolina 1865–1900.* Chapel Hill: University of North Carolina Press.

Boyte, Harry. 1972. "The Textile Industry: Keel of the Southern Industrialization." *Radical America* 6, no. 2: 4–49.

Davis, Jean. 1929. "The Economics of Welfare Work in the Cotton Mills in the Southern States." In Southeastern Economic Conference, ed., *The Industrial South*, 49–57. Atlanta: Banner Press, Emory University.

Evans, Sara. 1970. "Women of the New South: Elizabethton, Tennessee, 1929." Typescript, available from the author, University of Minnesota.

Frederickson, Mary. 1982. "Four Decades of Change: Black Workers in Southern Textiles, 1941–1982." *Radical America* 16, no. 6: 27–45.

Henderson [N.C.] City Directory. 1902. Interstate Directory Co.

Herring, Harriet. 1929. *Welfare Work in Mill Villages: The Story of Extra Mill Activities.* Chapel Hill: University of North Carolina Press.

Janiewski, Dolores. 1979. "From Field to Factory: Race, Class, Sex, and the Woman Worker in Durham 1880–1940." Ph.D. diss., Duke University.

Kessler-Harris, Alice. 1982. *Out to Work: A History of Wage-earning Women in the United States.* New York: Oxford University Press.

Lahne, Herbert. 1944. *The Cotton Mill Worker.* New York: Farrer and Rinehart.

McLaurin, Melton. 1971. *Paternalism and Protest: Southern Mill Workers and Organized Labor, 1875–1905.* Westport, Conn.: Greenwood.

Newman, Dale. 1978. "Work and Community Life in a Southern Textile Town." *Labor History* 19, no. 2: 204–225.

———. 1979. "Life in the Mill Village." Remarks presented at the Conference on North Carolina Social History, Duke University, June 9.

North Carolina Bureau of Labor and Printing. 1900–1907. *Annual Reports.* Raleigh.

North Carolina Department of Labor and Printing. 1910–1926. Raleigh.

Oates, M. 1975. *The Role of the Cotton Textile Industry in the Economic Development of the American Southeast 1900–1940.* New York: Arno.

Pope, Liston. 1942. *Millhands and Preachers: A Study of Gastonia.* New Haven, Conn.: Yale University Press.

Tilly, Louise A. 1981. "Paths of Proletarianization: Organization of Production,

Sexual Division of Labor, and Women's Collective Action." *Signs* 7, no. 2: 400–417.

Tippett, Thomas. 1931. *When Southern Labor Stirs*. London: Cape, and New York: Harrison Smith.

U.S. Bureau of the Census. 1930. *Census of Population*, vol. 4, *Occupations*. Washington, D.C.: GPO.

———. 1940. *Census of Population*, vol. 3, *The Labor Force*. Washington, D.C.: GPO.

Women's Bureau. 1926. *Lost Time and Labor Turnover in Cotton Mills*. Bulletin 52. Washington, D.C.

3

MYRA MARX FERREE
UNIVERSITY OF CONNECTICUT

Sacrifice, Satisfaction, and Social Change: Employment and the Family

Most women workers today are married and most have children. In 1982 fully 53 percent of all employed women were married, and 51 percent of married women were employed. Of married mothers, 56 percent were in the labor force, nearly as high a rate of paid employment as that of divorced or single mothers, 61 percent of whom were in the labor force (U.S. Bureau of Labor Statistics, 1982). Young single women, who until World War II comprised the majority of the female work force, are now outnumbered 2.5 to 1 by married women 25–54 years old, and 39 percent of all employed women have children under age 18 (U.S. Bureau of Labor Statistics, 1979). In other words, women who work for pay today are less likely to define themselves as daughters, more likely to see themselves primarily as wives and mothers, than at any previous time in our history.

Important as family status—as wife, mother, or daughter—is in shaping the meaning of paid employment for women, there is really no

---

An earlier and shorter version of this essay was presented at the National Women's Studies Association meetings, Bloomington, Indiana, May 1980, and some of the material was previously included in a paper jointly done with Carole Turbin entitled "On and Off the Job: Work, Family and Community," which was presented at the American Sociological Association meetings, August 1980. The shorter version appears in *Marriage and Family Review*, 1983, under the title "The View from Below: Women's Employment and Gender Equality in Working-Class Families." The essay has greatly benefited from the suggestions offered by Katherine Jones-Loheyde and by members of the Women and Work Study Group funded by a Problems in the Discipline Grant from the American Sociological Association.

reason to assume that it is any less important for men. Most workers, male and female alike, participate in the labor force not only as individuals but also as members of families; and both men and women place higher importance on their families than on their jobs as sources of satisfaction in their lives (Bernard, 1981; Pleck and Lang, 1979). Paid work is a means to satisfy both individual and family needs and to improve both individual and family well-being. While this is true for both men and women, the roles of men and women in the family are culturally differentiated. While men are expected to take pride in the family role of "breadwinner" and "good provider," women's work is supposed to be behind the scenes, supportive, and auxiliary to that of the "head of the household" (Bernard, 1981). Subordinated to male authority in the family, women then find their family status used against them in the labor force. The idea that women are or ought to be dependent on men is used to justify overt discrimination and to give subtle (and not-so-subtle) legitimation to women's subordinate status on the job. Moreover, women whose wages would be barely adequate to support themselves and totally insufficient to maintain their children are scarcely in a position to bite the hand that feeds them at home. Women's status in the family and women's status at work reflect and reinforce each other; so also does the very different family and work status of men (Feldberg and Glenn, 1979).

In attempting to understand and change women's position in the work force, women's position in the family deserves careful scrutiny. This essay offers a brief review of key assumptions in the study of work and family; a critique of some of the misconceptions about working-class women and their families; and then a preliminary, and I hope corrective, look at some particular families. I focus on ways in which working-class women's employment is understood and responded to by their families and how these women actively participate in constructing a relationship between their families and their jobs which they themselves find acceptable.

Work and Family: Women's Double Bind

The classic sociological model portrays the relationship, for women, between family and job as one of conflict and competing demands. Family is assumed to take the higher priority; work performance and satisfaction are viewed as influenced by family circumstances. Work life is seen as interrupted by family demands; work commitment and actual labor-force participation are usually described as contingent on "prior" home responsibilities. In contrast, sociologists tend to see the relationship, for men, between family and job as one of mutual support and complementarity. The family is held responsible for keeping the male worker in the state of highest possible fitness for his job, that is, not only fed and clothed but freed from distractions and given whatever educational and geographical advantages the family can manage.

The male worker's performance of family roles and satisfaction with family life are presented as contingent on his work circumstances. A man who is economically disadvantaged is seen as incapable of filling family roles adequately; a man's involvement in the family is also viewed as limited by the extent and nature of his work (Coser and Rokoff, 1971; Feldberg and Glenn, 1979; Pleck, 1977).

While this description can be true, it is also often exaggerated. Work circumstances themselves can account for many of the differences between male and female workers that have classically been attributed to socialization and family roles (Feldberg and Glenn, 1979; Howe, 1977; Kanter, 1977). In other words, families may reject stereotypes about male and female roles and traits but still be economically constrained to protect or increase the earnings potential of the worker in the family who has the best-paying job or the best chance of getting ahead (Benenson, in press). Low-wage workers, regardless of sex, also typically have very mixed feelings about their jobs (Levitan and Johnson, 1982). Since women are rarely the workers with the best opportunities and often the low-wage workers, they may expect their own families to put higher priority on the men's work, and they may accept this as no great hardship to themselves, without thereby indicating that they subscribe to general principles about women's second-class status or place at home and hearth. Economic subordination can be experienced as limiting aspirations not only on the job but at home.

The present relationship between job and family is so structured that women bear the brunt of the conflict between the two, a conflict that is not in women's roles or in women's heads but reflects the very different needs and demands of the workplace and the home. A family based on principles of "each man for himself and devil take the hindmost" is no family at all; yet for a family to survive, it needs to recognize that this is indeed the ethos of the capitalist economy (Elshtain, 1981; Humphries, 1982). Thinking about change means considering the conditions under which the nature of the interrelationship between job and family could be different from that which has traditionally been prescribed. Can family and job be as mutually supportive for women as they traditionally have been for men?

Socialist states have traditionally operated on the premise that increasing women's economic opportunities and expecting women to enter and remain in the labor force most of their adult lives would resolve the conflict. The state would also support women's employment by providing child care, or maternity leaves, or both. Rather than resolving the problem, this "solution" institutionalized a "double day" for women in which housework hours were simply added on to the hours spent in paid employment (Berch, 1982; Scott, 1974). Family support, the redivision of household responsibilities to reflect real needs and time available, was not forthcoming. The United States' experience is similar: women are more and more likely to be in the paid labor force but experience little change in the division of labor at home. Employed women continue to do 4.8 hours a day of housework compared to the 1.6 hours their husbands do (Walker and Woods, 1976). In the absence of significant domestic participation by men, women's employment may not be to their advantage. For women's employment to benefit women, the relationship between family and job may have to change. While it may be important for women workers to give greater priority to their work lives than they have in the past, it is surely important for families to give greater priority to the needs of women workers.

Work, Family, and Class

When women's employment is portrayed as a positive experience for women, the implicit model used is the dual-career family. This model pervades both sociological research and the mass media, and it distorts our thinking about the meaning of paid employment for women (Benenson, in press). The dual-career model presents women in elite professions as exemplary of the "nontraditional" woman and posits sharing housework and child care between husband and wife as a natural consequence of the marriage partners' shared commitment to egalitarian principles (e.g., Rapoport and Rapoport, 1971, 1976; Pepitone-Rockwell, 1980). Since dual-career wives have husbands who are also "good providers," they are assumed to have purely noneconomic reasons for working. This is then taken, along with the high levels of education characteristic of these elite couples, to be a prerequisite for an "egalitarian relationship" and so for a work experience that is beneficial to women.

The premises of the model itself are questionable. I doubt that most women professionals—or their families—are as indifferent to their earnings as the model assumes, and many studies suggest that commitment to egalitarian principles is a relatively weak predictor of actual household behavior (Ferree, 1979; Hiller, 1980; Huber and Spitze, 1981). But while the model may not even be a fair representation of the work and family relationships of the elite, it imposes far more distortion on our view of the working-class two-job family (e.g., Harding, 1981). In the first place, working-class women are implicitly compared, not to working-class men, but to those women in the professions who most closely conform to male professionals in their career orientation and commitment. The importance of financial reasons for employment for working-class women is directly contrasted to the personal reasons for employment given by dual-career professional women, and these orientations are presented as so totally opposite that financial motivations are often taken to exclude personal ones. Women who "have to" work for the money are assumed not to want to work at all, rather than as merely not liking their present jobs (e.g., Wright, 1978). Social policy is directed at ensuring women a "choice" and protecting them from this presumably evil necessity—which perpetuates the notion that it is the man alone who is responsible for financial support and the woman who is a "natural" dependent. Exploitation is assessed not from the characteristics of women's work itself, which is rarely studied, but from the simple fact of women's employment at all (Feldberg and Glenn, 1979). The complexities of most workers' love–hate relationships with their jobs (Levitan and Johnson, 1982) are transformed into simplistic categorizations of women as either loving or hating their work and, if the latter, needing to be "protected" from working (e.g., Kreps, 1972).

In fact, studies of working-class women conducted from the 1950s to the present consistently show relatively high levels of actual employment as well as considerable interest in working for pay among women who were at home full time (e.g., Berger, 1968; Ferree, 1976; Komarovsky, 1962; Rubin, 1976). Even monotonous or physically taxing jobs may be experienced as a welcome change from social isolation and unrelieved responsibility for young children (Ferree, 1976; Gavron, 1966; Oakley, 1974). This does not mean that working-class women necessarily like their particular jobs, although some do; the idea of "someday" being able to quit may, like the prospect of retirement for blue-collar men, help many of them get through the days and years of labor (Eckart, Kramer, and Jaerisch, 1976). A job is not a career; as Komarovsky (1962) put it, "A good job is a means to a good living, but achievement in a specialized vocation is not the measure of a person's worth, not even for a man" (57). But blue-collar women are proud of their accomplishments on the job, and they are proud of their role as family providers, alone or in conjunction with their husbands (Walshok, 1981); and they are hurt psychologically as well as financially when they lose their jobs (Rosen, 1981). They see their work as something good for them as well as their families (Rubin, 1981). But they clearly do not have the same kind of work commitment that professional women have, and they should not be expected to acquire it, just to measure up to a class-biased standard of nontraditionality. Certainly women who receive psychological rewards from their jobs are more satisfied than those who do not, but there is no reason to assume that family dependence on the income a woman earns decreases the rewards available to her. For working-class women, as for working-class men, the job may be both personally and financially important.

I am not suggesting that economic need in and of itself transforms women's jobs into personally rewarding experiences but that women's work needs to be defined as an essential contribution to the family, as men's work has been, for the family in turn to respect and support women's needs as workers. The definition of women's work as a contribution to the family or, alternately, as a cost the family bears, shapes the context in which family rights and responsibilities are negotiated. Thus, the family's definition of women's paid work as a cost or contribution is reflected in the balance of power and division of labor in the family. While employed women in general report having more decision-making power than full-time housewives (Bahr, 1975; Blood and Wolfe, 1960; Safilios-Rothschild, 1970), I suggest that women who work because of economic necessity may have more power in family decision-making than women whose work is economically optional. The woman whose income is significant for meeting the family's basic needs would seem, in our society at least, to have a legitimate claim upon family resources in support of her paid work. Women who are working for what society disparagingly calls "psychological reasons" would have no such legitimate claim. In this latter situation the family may be most willing to put its demands into conflict with the demands of the job, and women may end up losing out both at work and at home. Lacking a right to demand family support, such women would particularly be susceptible to being cast in the role of supermom and to find themselves feeling grateful for being "allowed" to add a paid job to their other responsibilities. This is scarcely a situation that could be described as optimal for women.

But this is exactly the situation the dual-career model advances as an ideal. In such a context, commitment to egalitarian values by both husband and wife may offer the only lever women can grasp to try to negotiate a more favorable division of labor, so not surprisingly, the dual-career model emphasizes the importance of changing attitudes as a route to equality in the home. Young women and educated women have more egalitarian sex-role attitudes and are thus heralded as the new wave, but age and education actually have relatively little to do with the division of household roles, in comparison with employment status and relative equality of earnings (Ferree, 1979; Heer, 1958; Hiller, 1980). In fact, sharing housework and child care is a result of relative economic equality more than of either sex-role attitudes or social class per se (Hiller, 1980). The mental health benefits of employment are, in turn, associated with shared responsibility at home rather than with age, education, or income level of the job (Kessler and McRae, 1982).

Even when working-class women are not explicitly presented as deficient in the nontraditional attitudes the dual-career model prescribes, the comparison of value systems stressing "equality, individualism and reason" with those stressing "hierarchy, wholism and morality" (Harding, 1981) reveals the author's biases when they are transformed into "egalitarian" versus "hierarchical" strategies rather than, for example, "individualistic" versus "wholistic." The evaluative bias shown in this choice of emphasis conceals the weaknesses of the dual-career ideal. We might agree that equality is good without accepting the equally central assumption of this "strategy" that family relationships ought to be primarily contractual and subordinated to the needs and whims of the market (cf. Harding, 1981: 63).

The focus of the family for the working class may be more on protecting the weaker members by pooling limited financial resources than on achieving the dual-career ideal of maximizing individual opportunities (Humphries, 1982; Rapp, 1978). In practice, the dynamics of shared scarcity and mutual sacrifice are likely to be quite different from the dynamics of relative advantage and individual fulfillment. To take the risks and incur the costs of sharing requires a level of commitment beyond that of simply being good friends; indeed, in the working class, the device of "fictive kinship" brings friends into the network of shared resources, whereas in middle-class families the use of kinship titles is discouraged even among blood relatives (Rapp, 1978). The middle-class ideal marriage "is more like friendship, hopefully the best of one's life" (Harding, 1981: 64), which in practice helps to protect each "partner's" financial resources from claims made by the other as well as by more extended family members (Rapp, 1978). The working class literally cannot afford this level of financial independence; the poorer the family, the more it depends on circulation of resources outside the market system and financial as well as moral support from family members in times of crisis (Humphries, 1982). While middle-class family members, especially women, may experience the family primarily as a restriction on their individuality and independence, working-class family members are more likely to be aware of both the supportive and the oppressive aspects of family life.

In sum, the dual-career model has, by its idealization of middle-class family norms, led to a misunderstanding and denigration of working-class women and their families. It has exaggerated the distinction between working for financial reasons and for psychological reasons and ignored the ways in which this distinction is used to undermine the legitimacy of women's employment for women of both affluent and poor families. It has treated a woman's earnings as less significant than her attitudes, and it has confused lip service to a norm of egalitarianism with real equality in the family. Finally, it has promoted an ideal of family life that subordinates it to the convenience of the employer and the market rather than insuring its integrity as an alternative value system and source of concrete support. In its view of both work and family life, the dual-career model presents working-class women as deficient and backward rather than as subordinated and actively resisting that subordination within the confines of a class system.

Studying Working-Class Women

The following analysis focuses on some of the issues confronting working-class women as they attempt to reconcile the conflicts between personal needs and family demands and between employment and family life. A key issue is the process by which a family defines women's work as essential or inessential to its well-being and the consequences of that definition for women and their families. Since the division of domestic labor is, I believe, of central importance in making paid employment more or less advantageous for women, a major focus of this discussion is the meaning of women's employment for the housework done by both women and men. Finally, I make comparisons between working-class and middle-class families that, though speculative, present a different and I hope less class-biased view of the process of negotiation between women and their families. Central here is the distinction between the rules and norms that shape these negotiations and the actual bargaining position of husband and wife. In the following pages I attempt to strike a balance between describing the dynamics of specific working-class families in my study and venturing some generalizations about the way family negotiations may often be expected to proceed.

Methodology

As part of a larger structured interview about working-class women's employment and attitudes, I included a few questions that attempted to tap norms about women's participation in the labor force and men's participation in domestic work. These open-ended questions asked women to "advise" a woman who is caught in some familiar binds: she wants to work and her husband is opposed; they need the money and he wants to take a second job; he doesn't want her to tell her friends what he does and doesn't do around the house. As they would otherwise be too hypothetical and abstract, the questions presented particular scenarios. The first scenario was as follows: "Anita's husband earns a very good living as a plumber, but now that her children are in school she would like to take a job. She was a bookkeeper before she married and has seen ads in the paper for jobs she might get. Even though she doesn't need the money, do you think she ought to take the job if she wants to? . . . Why? . . . Suppose her husband were against the idea. Should she take the job anyway or give up the idea? . . . Why is that? . . . Suppose there were a financial crisis in the family. She would like to get a job to help out, but her husband is opposed. He plans on looking for a second job. Should he take a second job or should she take a job to solve their money problems? . . . Why is that?" The question about housework was: "Betty often meets with some of the women in the neighborhood for coffee after her children are in school. Recently they have been discussing ways to get their husbands to do more housework, like washing dishes. Is it all right for Betty to tell her friends what work her husband does and doesn't do around the house? . . . Why/Why not?"

In essence, these questions served as simple projective tests and seemed to be effective as such. A number of respondents commented before answering that the questions seemed personally relevant, or as one put it, "That sounds like a page out of my life." But because the questions do not specifically ask about the women themselves, they do not lend themselves to constructing frequency distributions of the number of women who find themselves in similar situations.

The interviews from which these questions were taken were conducted with 135 working-class wives in a Boston-area community. I defined these women as being working class because they resided in a predominantly working-class community and sent their children to the local schools. In this way I sought to avoid a definition based solely on their husband's characteristics or solely on their own education or paid occupations. Nonetheless, these women would be considered working class by these conventional criteria as well. Most of the husbands were manual workers. Only 3 of the 135 women had graduated from college; a little over a third had not graduated from high school; and most were in clerical, service, or factory occupations. Even those who would be exceptions on the basis of one or another or these characteristics conformed in other regards and thus seemed appropriately part of the study.

The sample was drawn from school lists and was designed to include only married women who were citizens, spoke English, and had at least one child in first or second grade and none younger. When talking about women's feelings when the children are all in school, then, these women are speaking from experience. The whole interview took somewhat over an hour, and the response rate was good (75 percent). The resulting sample had a median age of 36, a median marriage length of 15 years, and an average of 3.4 children; slightly over half (55 percent) were themselves employed full or part time in the paid labor force. These, then, are the women whose norms and descriptions of family life have informed the following analysis.

Women's Employment as Contribution or Cost

Because men's work has traditionally been seen as having the family support that women's paid work has so often lacked, it is important to consider how men have obtained that support. Rather than directly employing the "resources" of the job (income, skills, etc.) in the negotiating process as the conventional exchange framework of family studies (e.g., Blood and Wolfe, 1960) suggests they would, the husbands in these working-class families seem to base their claims for family support on the effort they expend and the costs they incur on the job. Because working-class jobs are often exhausting, boring, and alienating, the husband who holds such a job is seen as making a sacrifice for the good of the family. In return, this sacrifice demands consideration for his needs: quiet when he sleeps, time away from the family, leisure in the evening, and so on. "He works hard; he's earned it" is the way these women justify the special consideration shown their husbands.

Women who hold paid jobs can also be seen as making a sacrifice for the family, but this would seem most likely when the family needs the income she earns. When an employed woman demands consideration for her needs—quiet, escape, leisure, and the like—for the family to respond to these demands will mean a shift in responsibilities greater than that introduced by her simply taking a job. Such a shift does not happen automatically but appears to be negotiated more or less successfully among family members. In the process of bargaining, an employed woman can appeal to her husband's sense of justice and equity ("I'm tired when I come home, too"), but such appeals seem most likely to be effective when they carry the implicit warning that she can only continue her job if they are met. When the loss of her income would be a significant loss to the rest of the family, her claims may be more likely to be satisfied. When the family wants her to work but does not create the conditions she finds essential, her quitting may force a change in conditions at home. As one woman put it, "I quit my job in a fit of anger—I was handing over every penny, so why take that? But he [her husband] says no family can survive these days without two people working. . . ."

When, on the other hand, the family would prefer her not to hold a paid job, family members see no reason to accept her definition of the job as a sacrifice for them, and they incur no moral obligation to offer her any return for the effort she expends. In such circumstances these working-class women suggest that a woman might appropriately drop out of the labor force; then, when the family once again found itself in straitened economic circumstances, she might attempt to negotiate the conditions of her reentry on more favorable terms. This cycle might recur repeatedly in economically marginal families, until the value of her contribution is recognized and some appropriate acknowledgment is made.

In contrast to the situation in which a job is defined as a sacrifice for the family, a sacrifice for which there is a legitimate expectation of compensation, a wife's work may be defined by the family as a reward or privilege. While this occurs surprisingly often in working-class families, I think it is still more likely to be characteristic of middle-class families, where the husband's higher income means that women's paid work can more often be defined as unnecessary. In this case, the family—not always or only the husband—does not see its standard of living as materially improved by the woman's employment. Indeed, her job could interfere with some of their pleasures, and the longer she has been a full-time housewife, the more likely it is that these pleasures have solidified into rights. Because women who work for pay generally do less housework, the value of their nonmonetary contribution declines, and their "unnecessary" income does not offset this. Paid employment is then defined not as a *contribution* to the family but a *cost* the family bears, more or less willingly, as a consequence of the woman's desire for a job.

In essence, under these conditions, the job itself becomes a privilege, and if a woman desires it for "personal" reasons, she will have to pay for it. She may pay by becoming the supermother and superwife who can demonstrate that her job "doesn't hurt anything," does not interfere with her meeting family demands. She may promise, explicitly or implicitly, that "dinner will still be on the table." A number of women, in fact, suggested strategies for overcoming opposition that focused on showing how a job does not change "anything" at home, that is, that her level of household production will not drop, nor will she demand additional assistance. Alternatively, the working woman may pay a price in gratitude that her family is so "understanding" of her occasional failure to meet their demands as thoroughly as she might have were she able to devote herself full time to housework. She may so appreciate the fact that no objection is raised to her paid job that she entirely fails to notice how little a shift in the division of labor has occurred at home. One woman was overwhelmingly grateful because her husband made her a cup of tea in the evenings when she came home from work.

Even if her gratitude for lack of opposition or minimal support is not enough to obscure the fact that she is now working twelve- to sixteen-hour days, she is not really in a position to do anything about it. She is allowed to work, and if the job becomes too much for her, she is allowed to quit; but she has no legitimate basis for recriminations about the division of labor or power in the family because she, rather than the family as a whole, is presumed to be the primary beneficiary of the arrangement. If her psychic need for the job is great enough and the job sufficiently rewarding, she will continue to work despite the costs in time and energy the family's lack of support imposes; if not, she will quit and "find other things to do" to make her life more meaningful at less cost.

When a wife's working is viewed as a cost to the family, her lack of power may be reflected in the way the additional income is handled. It may be trivialized and treated as pin money for her to spend. It may be thrown into a common "pot" and used to pay bills, with the surplus it creates being used to buy "extras" for other family members to co-opt their support. Expenditures on the husband's hobbies may be especially likely to mushroom. Only if—and when—the family is sufficiently accustomed to its new luxuries to consider them necessities, and thus to consider her work vital to the continued satisfaction of their "needs," will she find herself in the position of women whose work is based on family necessity—with the leverage to attempt to negotiate family change.

Invisibility of Housework

If the husband's "hard work" earns him respect and consideration from his family, why does housework fail to earn the same rewards for wives? The issue here seems to be the extent to which housework "counts" as a sacrifice on the woman's part and as a contribution to the family's well-being. While being a full-time housewife often appears to be an unattractive alternative for these working-class women, housework itself does not seem to be perceived as particularly arduous. Being a housewife is often described as boring and isolating; having a paid job is often seen as something to "break up the monotony." As another woman said of housework: "You get stagnated if you're in one place. At least if you're out with other people you don't feel like the walls are closing in on you." Full-time housework may even be seen as a source of mental illness. Women advised taking a paid job because a woman "can't be cooped up in four walls; she'd go bats." "There's no point in making yourself crazy by staying home." "A job is healthy." "It's for the emotions." But as much as housework is perceived to cost in personal terms, it is not typically perceived as work. "Once the kids are in school, there's nothing to do," women said; "I can't see sitting home." "She needs to get out to have something to do." "What the heck is there to do?"

While the problem for some women in these working-class families is that housework is simply not demanding enough, the basic issue is that women often do not figure in the time spent doing housework when assessing the family division of labor as fair or unfair. In this, the culture cooperates, socially and linguistically, by defining *work* as that which occurs in the context of paid occupations. This definition of housework as nonwork shows up very clearly in women's reactions to the choice between a husband taking a second job or a wife taking a job to meet economic needs.

These women clearly preferred a woman taking a paid job in addition to housework to a man taking on a second job. For him to take a second job, they felt, would create too extreme a division of labor, that is, he would have no time for the family, and she would not be carrying her fair share of the "work." They argued that, since they were partners, "they should both work"; "if he did all the work and she stayed home all the time, they wouldn't have anything to talk about." As these arguments reveal, wives' paid employment in working-class families is not a matter of absolute economic necessity so much as it is a preferred strategy for dealing with real economic needs. As family historians have repeatedly pointed out, and as these women clearly recognize, there are alternatives: children, especially older children, can work for pay and contribute their earnings to the family; husbands can work overtime or take a second job (Cantor and Laurie, 1977; Tilly and Scott, 1978). These women's values emphasize ideals of sharing and of companionship in marriage that are sometimes discussed as if they were the exclusive property of the middle class. Given the conditions of their jobs, however, actually realizing the ideal of shared labor and shared life may be very demanding of these women's time and energy (Rosen, 1981).

Moreover, there was a widely shared sentiment that "no man can handle two jobs"; "in the long run he ends up sick"; the income is eaten up in hospital bills; and the family is no better off if he "ends up dead or in the hospital." Similar concerns were not expressed about women's ability to handle a "double day." Still, a number of wives indicated that when the husband "insists on killing himself," a wife cannot prevent it. Though she might be willing to take a paid job, if he insists on "carrying the full burden," she has few alternatives. Because her job at home is not seen as demanding, she may be able to convince him to "allow" her to work rather than overextend himself; but then she has no room in which to negotiate a change in the division of labor at home. If he remains committed to her staying at home and willing to bear the costs of that decision, she is forced to see her own sacrifice for the family, not in terms of the time and effort of a paid job, but in giving up her own preferences for the sake of family harmony. Whether or not she likes it, she is "protected" from having to "work."

The good of the family in this instance requires that the wife "try to be happy" at home. Insisting on her personal desire for a job "only starts family troubles, and you end up with a separation," according to one respondent. The moral obligation is strong: "If [a job] was going to disrupt the home, she should not take it"; but there is also a sharp difference of opinion on whether or not husbands can in fact be persuaded to understand their wives' point of view. For some, the criteria for a good marriage include his being able to "see things from her point of view." "A marriage couldn't be good," some argue, "if this would break it up." Others believe that a husband's opposition can be overridden. One woman suggested, "Do what I did; tell him you're bored to death and you have to do something—you'll take a job or have an affair—he can choose." But many women are more resigned to their husbands' ability to define the situation as he chooses. As one woman noted, "With my husband, I don't win an argument." These women accepted that sustained disagreement with or defiance of their husbands would break up their marriages. When the marriage, and thus the welfare of the family itself, is seen to be at stake, these women think the sacrifice of one's desire for a paid job is not too much to ask. In exchange, a wife may receive autonomy and authority within the confines of the home.

Husbands and Housework

Although the sharp demarcation of male and female spheres of activity and authority is not uncommon in this working-class sample, the effects of changing definitions of sex-appropriate behavior are also apparent. Whereas the women generally seem to find male participation in household tasks acceptable, even desirable, their husbands do not necessarily share this opinion. One constraint employed women have to struggle against in negotiating a more favorable division of labor is their husbands' perceptions of housework as demeaning and unmasculine. The individual man who does not share that perception is nonetheless likely to believe that his buddies do, and all-male social gatherings may reflect and reinforce this rejection of housework as unfit for "real men" without fear of contradiction from absent wives. The image of a husband wearing an apron conveys a message about family power and authority as much or more than it depicts the family division of labor, or at least, so many of these husbands and wives believe. For a wife to let other people know what chores her husband does around the house "would make the man seem like he was henpecked," and "it would make the other women think she had him wrapped around her little finger." "Wearing the apron" means displaying subordinate status, just as "wearing the pants" means exercising authority.

While norms are changing to put a positive value on egalitarian family relationships, a wife exercising power or authority in the family is still viewed with some ambivalence. While some women said they would be "proud to tell what my husband does," they underlined that this was because "he does it because he wants to," not because they had the power to demand help. Whenever the inference might be drawn that a husband was doing housework he did not want to do, there was concern that admitting that he did it would "make him a laughing stock." Complaining about how little a husband does at home seems to be a more acceptable topic of conversation among women than "bragging" about how much housework he takes on. The danger of the latter was not only that women friends would "tell their husbands and they'll set on him and tease him" but that they would go home and use his "goodness" to pressure their husbands for change and "start trouble in other families."

My casual observation of middle-class families suggests there is some class difference here. Middle-class women seem to have accepted a norm of household equality that they do not find realized as fully as they think it should be in their own families. Because the norm is that husbands and wives should share housework, "bragging" about the husband's participation is more acceptable than complaining. Thus, by careful selection and omission, middle-class wives present an exaggerated picture of their husbands' actual involvement in housework, not only to burnish his image but also to protect their own self-presentation as equal and "liberated." Like the working-class women, the middle-class women appear to assume that information about the division of labor conveys information about the distribution of power as well and is therefore potentially discrediting. Who does the housework is not just a fact but crucial evidence of whether or not your own family is living up to the ideal of a "good family" and whether or not you yourself are a "good" person. In such a context, it would be expected that such dangerous information would be carefully handled and selectively presented depending on the norms by which credit and discredit are allocated.

These norms differ by class more than the actual division of labor does. In both classes, women still do the bulk of the housework in most families (Berk, 1980; Walker and Woods, 1976). Moreover, there are "exceptions" in working-class families that would rival those found in the middle class. In one family in this sample, for instance, the husband, who was a fire fighter, regularly put in his forty hours of work on the weekend so that he could take full charge of the house and children the rest of the week while his wife worked a regular nine-to-five job. A study of men who worked the night shift reported that a major reason for choosing or staying in a night job for these men was the opportunity it gave them to take on routine child care while their wives worked or to become more involved with their children. As one worker put it:

> I work nights for the money and to be able to babysit during the day while she is working. I am on third shift now primarily because of our youngest child . . . I would like to go on days in a few years when my youngest child is older and can take care of herself after school. Right now . . . everything is going so well. I don't know whether I would want to go on days now. (Robboy, 1983: 514)

As usual, such arrangements reflect more than pure economic necessity.

Because it is generally understood in working-class families that "guys don't want other people to know they help out; it ruins their male image," and wives usually accept a norm of family loyalty that requires protecting that image, the possibility of creating social pressure for changes in family roles is greatly limited. On the one side, the men appear to reinforce resistance to sharing chores by ridiculing other men's accommodation to their wives' demands. On the other, the women do not find pointing to "what other people's husbands are doing" a legitimate way of reinforcing their own claims. As a result, a more egalitarian consensus may be slow to emerge. While some women personally feel there is "no stigma to a man doing housework," the negative connotations of female authority that it carries, even among women, show that such a social stigma does still exist. This stigma appears to limit women's willingness to press their demands for greater male participation in housework even when their financial leverage makes it probable that such demands would be honored: thus the paradox that employment may already give women power in the family that they do not feel legitimately entitled to use. Particularly if the husband's earnings are low and his "male image" shaky, women may refrain from demanding a more egalitarian division of labor because they might obtain it—at a cost they are not willing to incur (cf. Szinovacz, 1977).

Another way of describing this paradox is to emphasize that power and authority in the family are not interchangeable concepts. Authority, or legitimate power, depends more on the ideals and myths that serve to legitimate it, whereas power itself reflects resources that can be used to control the behavior of others. Men have for centuries held authority in the family, but their actual power has sometimes declined to the vanishing point as they have been unemployed or otherwise unable to support their families. Conversely, even when women's household production and earnings have given them power, they have not had this power morally and ideologically legitimated. Illegitimate power is no less real than authority, but it has different consequences. While the middle class has espoused values that put male authority in question, middle-class women have rarely had the resources to exercise equal power. Thus, male power has gone underground (Gillespie, 1971). It may be a point of honor among middle-class men not to "boss their wives around," to "let her have a career," and to "consult" her on major decisions precisely because the power exists to do otherwise, for there is no honor in necessity. Working-class women, who may also possess more power than they are legitimately entitled to use (though still less than men), may similarly take pride in "building their man up," "protecting his ego," and refraining from pressing claims that would "undercut" his authority.

Conclusions and Further Directions

In summary, this account suggests that both the objective circumstances in which families find themselves and the meanings they give to family life and work are important in shaping their response to women's employment. Women themselves see their jobs through the lens of family life as a contribution to the family or as a cost, or perhaps as a bit of both. The invisibility of housework as work makes it hard for women to take it seriously, which both makes a paid job more important psychologically and makes the burden of combined housework and paid work appear less than two paid jobs. While norms have changed to make husbands' sharing in family life more desirable—and the strict division of labor that would leave the husband working more overtime or a second job more undesirable—norms have not really changed enough to remove the stigma from housework or from women's power, limited though it may be. While working-class women and middle-class women may face different problems and possibilities in reconciling a comfortable family life with their involvement in the labor force, neither can be said to have either unqualified support or opposition, nor can either be said to have unalloyed benefit from their paid work.

Without the blinders imposed by contrasting an "egalitarian family" with a "hierarchical" one (for neither middle-class nor working-class women have achieved equality), it is clear that the needs women have for paid work go beyond simply being able to use the income. Although the dual-career model has polarized financial and psychological rewards on a single continuum, the dichotomy misleads and misinforms. Not only do we idealize the employment of the few; we apologize for the employment of the many. We point to the poverty of working women's families as the reason why they "desire" their jobs and their paychecks and shy away from suggesting that they have any inherent right to work. We fail to distinguish between the miserable jobs in which they are trapped on the one hand, and the value of shared labor in all the paid and unpaid tasks that go to constitute social existence, on the other.

Moreover, there are negative political consequences of treating financial need as the only truly legitimate basis for employment for women. There are two dangers inherent in the current emphasis on the economic legitimation of women's work. First, we may overlook the noneconomic reasons working-class women may have for working. Because it is in their interest to stress the financial importance of the job, we need to be particularly sensitive to other meanings that work can have for women in addition to meeting the family's economic needs. Women at all class levels work for a variety of motives, just as men do; and while financial need may bind them to their present jobs or work conditions, there are relatively few who would wish to give up the sense of participation and purpose in society which having a job can provide. There is no evidence that employed working-class women would rather do full-time housework or that freeing them from the necessity of "having to work" would be doing them any favor. The need for additional income may free some women from the necessity of staying home, and the financial leverage of the job may be an advantage to others, even if norms about family authority make them reluctant to exploit this advantage.

Second, stressing the economic importance of *some* women's work may even inadvertently contribute to the delegitimation of middle-class women's desire for a job. Rather than accept a model of employment that describes some women as working only for personal fulfillment, or only because they want to get out of the house, we need to think about ways of defining work as an objective *and* psychological necessity in people's lives. This means broadening our definition of work to include women's unpaid labor in the home without at the same time undercutting the legitimacy of women's need to do paid work. The removal of meaning from much of the work still left in the home makes a paid job necessary in many instances, and this necessity is no less real for being psychic as well as economic. By legitimating rather than trivializing such motives for women of all classes, we may finally stop apologizing for women's work and begin to create the family and community climate which supports it, a climate in which women's employment may benefit women themselves as well as their families.

References

Bahr, S. 1975. "Effects on Power and Division of Labor in the Family." In L. W. Hoffman and F. I. Nye, eds., *Working Mothers.* San Francisco: Jossey-Bass.

Benenson, H. In press. "Women's Occupational and Family Achievement in the U.S. Class System: A Critique of the Dual-Career Family Analysis." *British Journal of Sociology.*

Berch, B. 1982. *The Endless Day: The Political Economy of Women's Work.* New York: Harcourt Brace Jovanovich.

Berger, B. 1968. *Working Class Suburb: A Study of Auto Workers in Suburbia.* Berkeley and Los Angeles: University of California Press.

Berk, S. 1980. *Women and Household Labor*. Beverly Hills, Calif.: Sage.
Bernard, J. 1981. "The Good-Provider Role: Its Rise and Fall." *American Psychologist* 36, no. 1: 1–12.
Blood, R., and D. Wolfe. 1960. *Husbands and Wives*. New York: Free Press.
Cantor, M., and B. Laurie, eds. 1977. *Class, Sex and the Woman Worker*. Westport, Conn.: Greenwood.
Coser, R., and G. Rokoff. 1971. "Women in the Occupational World: Social Disruption and Conflict." *Social Problems* 18: 535–554.
Eckart, C., H. Kramer, and U. Jaerisch. 1976. *Frauenarbeit in Familie und Fabrik* (Women's Work in the Family and Factory). Frankfurt: Campus.
Elshtain, J. B. 1981. *Public Man, Private Woman: Women in Social and Political Thought*. Princeton, N.J.: Princeton University Press.
Feldberg, R., and E. Glenn. 1979. "Male and Female: Job versus Gender Models in the Sociology of Work." *Social Problems* 26, no. 5: 524–538.
Ferree, M. M. 1976. "Working Class Jobs: Paid Work and Housework as Sources of Satisfaction." *Social Problems* 23, no. 4: 431–441.
———. 1979. "Employment without Liberation: Cuban Women in the U.S." *Social Science Quarterly* 60, no. 1: 35–50.
Gavron, H. 1966. *The Captive Wife: Conflicts of Housebound Mothers*. London: Routledge and Kegan Paul.
Gillespie, D. 1971. "Who Has the Power: The Marital Struggle." *Journal of Marriage and the Family* 33, no. 3: 445–458.
Harding, S. 1981. "Family Reform Movements: Recent Feminism and Its Opposition." *Feminist Studies* 7, no. 1: 57–76.
Heer, D. 1958. "Dominance and the Working Wife." *Social Forces* 36, no. 4: 341–347.
Hiller, D. 1980. "Determinants of Household and Childcare Task Sharing." Paper presented at the annual meeting of the American Sociological Association, New York, August 27–31.
Howe, L. K. 1977. *Pink Collar Workers*. New York: Putnam's.
Huber, J., and G. Spitze. 1981. "Wives' Employment, Household Behaviors and Sex Role Attitudes." *Social Forces* 60: 150–169.
Humphries, J. 1982. "The Working Class Family: A Marxist Perspective." In J. B. Elshtain, *The Family in Political Thought*. Amherst: University of Massachusetts Press.
Kanter, R. M. 1977. *Men and Women of the Corporation*. New York: Basic Books.
Kessler, R., and J. A. McRae. 1982. "The Effect of Wives' Employment on the Mental Health of Married Men and Women." *American Sociological Review* 42, no. 2: 216–227.
Komarovsky, M. 1962. *Blue Collar Marriage*. New York: Random House.
Kreps, J. 1972. "Do All Women Want to Work?" In L. K. Howe, *The Future of the Family*. New York: Simon and Schuster.
Levitan, S., and C. M. Johnson. 1982. *Second Thoughts on Work*. Kalamazoo, Mich.: Upjohn Institute for Employment Research.
Oakley, A. 1974. *The Sociology of Housework*. New York: Random House.
Pepitone-Rockwell, F. 1980. *Dual-Career Couples*. Beverly Hills: Sage.
Pleck, J. 1977. "The Work-Family Role System." *Social Problems* 24: 417–427.
Pleck, J., and L. Lang. 1979. "Men's Family Role." Wellesley, Mass.: Wellesley College Center for Research on Women.
Rapoport, R. N., and R. Rapoport. 1971. *Dual-Career Families*. Baltimore: Penguin.

———. 1976. *Dual-Career Families Re-examined.* New York: Harper and Row.

Rapp, R. 1978. "Family and Class in Contemporary America: Notes toward an Understanding of Ideology." *Science and Society* 42, no. 3: 278–300.

Robboy, H. 1983. "At Work with the Night Worker." In H. Robboy and C. Clark, eds., *Social Interaction: Readings in Sociology.* 2d ed. New York: St. Martin's.

Rosen, E. 1981. "Between the Rock and the Hard Place: Employment and Unemployment among Blue-Collar Women." Paper presented at the annual meeting of the American Sociological Association, Toronto, August 24–28.

Rubin, L. 1976. *Worlds of Pain: Life in the Working Class Family.* New York: Basic Books.

———. 1981. "Why Should Women Work?" Working paper, Center for the Study, Education and Advancement of Women. University of California, Berkeley.

Safilios-Rothschild, C. 1970. "The Study of Family Power Structure." *Journal of Marriage and the Family* 32: 539–553.

Scott, H. 1974. *Does Socialism Liberate Women?* Boston: Beacon.

Szinovacz, M. 1977. "Role Allocation, Family Structure and Female Employment." *Journal of Marriage and the Family* 39: 781–791.

Tilly, L., and J. Scott. 1978. *Women, Work and Family.* New York: Holt, Rinehart and Winston.

U.S. Bureau of Labor Statistics. 1979. *Marital and Family Characteristics of Workers, 1970–1978.* Special Labor Force Report No. 219. Washington, D.C.: GPO.

———. 1982. "Earnings of Workers and Their Families." *News.* November.

Walker, K., and M. Woods. 1976. "Time Use: A Mcasure of Household Production." Paper presented at the annual meeting of the Home Economics Association, Washington, D.C.

Walshok, M. L. 1981. *Blue Collar Women: Pioneers on the Male Frontier.* New York: Doubleday, Anchor.

Wright, J. 1978. "Are Working Women Really More Satisfied? Evidence from Several National Surveys." *Journal of Marriage and the Family* 40: 301–313.

4

PHYLLIS PALMER
GEORGE WASHINGTON UNIVERSITY

Housework and Domestic Labor: Racial and Technological Change

Housework might be conceived as the single occupation that unites women's interests, since it is work almost always performed by women. The tasks of housework—cleaning, cooking, caring for children, sick, and elderly—are those tasks common to all women in U.S. society. Paradoxically, domestic work has also been the occupation that most clearly defines women's class, race, and ethnic differences, for it is an occupation in which some women (poor, black, ethnically subordinate) have worked for wages paid by other women (usually middle class, white, or ethnically dominant). Since at least the seventeenth century, these tasks have regularly provided employment, and domestic work has often been the first paid occupation women move into as societies change from subsistence, agricultural economies to commercial or industrial ones (Chaplin, 1978).

The persistence of the occupation and its elements should not be construed as a stasis in housework, however (Smith, 1982; Vanek, 1979). One lack in the scholarship of work has been a thorough history of housework, a description of changes in these basic tasks in relation to changed ideology, technology, and markets, which has only partially been written by Ehrenreich and English (1979), Strasser (1982), Cowan (1974), and Hartmann (1974). Even when these pieces are connected, a history of social relations comparable to those for other kinds of work is just emerging. The relations of mistress to servant, of housewife to help and to domestic have changed over time, as the varying labels indicate. A more striking change, of course, is the removal of services from the home and the transformation of service work from the shared vocation of two or more women in a household into a profit-making commercial activity in which many women work for a contractor who provides services in many settings.

In the twentieth-century United States, domestic service has declined as an occupation, dropping by 1920 from the largest occupation for all women to the predominant one only for black women, and then declining to an insignificant proportion even of black workers by 1970. How this happened and what changes occurred in the performance of housework and the locus of service work is a larger story than can be encompassed in one essay. What I concentrate on here is how differently the occupation of housework was conceived by white mistresses and by black domestics, and how black women ultimately came to think of themselves as workers with occupational needs and demands rather than as women fulfilling women's most praised, though lowest paid, social role. This essay is, first, a study of how black women disentangled social role from occupation, an often difficult distinction for women in female-intensive occupations that have taken on the aura of "womanhood." Corollated with this is a description of the shift of "private" home work into "public" service occupations. Second, the essay speculates about race divisions used to obscure the changing social relations and loci of service work, a field in which the major changes of the twentieth century have not been technological but organizational and social.

To discuss the transformation of domestic work and the categories of women who perform it, it is necessary briefly to review both the changing place the occupation has had within paid employment available to women and the racial composition of the occupation. Although by 1890 the Census Bureau category of "servants" contained almost one-third of black women at work (31 percent as calculated by Katzman, 1981: 292), it was an even more important occupation for foreign-born white women (48 percent of all foreign-born wage earners were in the category) and a substantial one for native-born white women holding jobs (24 percent of all native-born female wage earners). When more opportunities opened to women workers with the proliferation of corporately organized production and the necessity for paper records to link nationally organized firms, native-born and foreign-born white women had an advantage in gaining access to preferred jobs, so that by 1920 only 7 percent of native-born and 19 percent of foreign-born white women working were still servants. In contrast, 27 percent of black women working were servants, and their reliance on domestic service for employment was even more substantial when laundry work is included; 46 percent of wage-earning black women were in these two occupations, compared with 22 percent of employed foreign-born white women and 8 percent of employed native-born white women.

With the development of new "female" occupations, both black and white women apparently sought to reduce their reliance on domestic employment. Black women's rates of domestic employment fell between the 1900 and 1910 censuses but then began to rise to their all-time highs of 63 percent and 60 percent in the 1930 and 1940 censuses before even the black rate began to fall dramatically (U.S. Bureau of the Census, 1979). White rates, on the other hand, were on a steady decline from 1890 onward, accounting for the fact that the number of women employed as domestics fell between 1910 and 1920. From 1920 to 1940 the percentage of women employed as domestics rose almost to the 1910 level of 22.1 percent of female employment, that is, 15.9 percent in 1920, 17.8 percent in 1930, and 20.4 percent in 1940 (Grossman, 1980).

An occupation that had been predominantly white until 1920 became predominantly black for the last two decades of its existence as a significant occupational category. After 1940 the proportion of women working in domestic service for private households plummeted to 8.4 percent in 1950, rising minimally to 8.9 percent in 1960, and then declining steadily to 2.6 percent in 1979 (Grossman, 1980). By 1950 domestic work was not a significant employer of women—a basic result, it would seem, of the vastly expanded job openings created during World War II and by the new office, electronics, and commercial service employment appearing after the war (Chafe, 1972).

The changing racial composition of domestic workers occurred simultaneously with changing notions of what housework was and how it should be performed. White women sought to make housework a fulfilling position for the unpaid wife-manager (Ehrenreich and English, 1979), while black women sought to make it a respectable job for women workers. In some ways, black women's perception won out, even if only as a by-product of the historical transformation of some household jobs from private, unrecognized, and poorly paid labor to socialized and commercial work.

The major revision of white women's attitudes appeared in the context of the home economics and domestic science movement initiated in its modern form by Ellen Swallow Richards at MIT (Hoy, 1980; James et al., 1971), a movement that was built on and that amplified Catharine Beecher's earlier designs for putting housework on a thoroughly professional footing (Beecher and Stowe, [1869] 1975). As Hartmann (1974) and Cowan (1974) demonstrate, professionalization did not necessarily mean that women reduced their work time as they became operators of high-technology machinery; in fact their daily work may have expanded as machinery and appliances useful in homes newly linked to electric and gas systems made possible the performance of more work *in* the house. Work became less arduous, according to Strasser (1978), but more time consuming. In those households where the mistress was able to afford a servant in addition to buying the obligatory washing machine, the most feasible imitation of professions was specialization and division of labor between the housewife and the domestic worker. Training in schools of home economics stressed that women were to become able managers: directors of their own and others' work, wise purchasers, and experts in new fields such as child psychology. As Hartmann's (1974) readings of time studies show, what this could mean in practice was that the housewife spent more time on shopping, light cleaning, and child care while delegating heavier tasks to a domestic servant. The servant ceased being "helper" on projects in which the house mistress also participated and became instead a laborer performing the least skilled tasks in the hierarchy of housework, at least as this hierarchy was defined by home economics textbooks. In this hierarchy, which needs to be better studied, child care and the newly conceived skills of child psychology were preeminent, food purchase and cooking secondary, and cleaning and laundry lowly, relatively mindless tasks. (I hasten to add that this is not an accurate appraisal, but the era's assignment of value.) Indeed, the ideal for white women was to be planners, directing the work of black women in a division of labor more complete than had been possible in the more labor-intensive nineteenth-century household.

At the same time that white women were being taught to conceive of housework as management, even if the only labor they managed was their own, black women were concentrating on developing standards of labor for household tasks. As a first step in investigating black women's conception of housework, I have surveyed records of Nannie Helen Burroughs's school in Washington, D.C.[1] The respect shown for household labor and the houseworker is the most striking characteristic of the school opened by this remarkable organizer in 1909. Burroughs, the corresponding secretary of the Women's Auxiliary Convention to the National Baptist Convention, convinced the convention that it should establish the National Training School for Women and Girls, and the "Training" in the title seems initially not to have indicated vocational training so much as training for a vocation: the Christ-inspired dedication to serve others, and especially to serve in the missions and Sunday schools sponsored by the National Baptist Churches. Burroughs, already a commanding and matronly figure at twenty-eight, set about creating a black-run and black-funded institution that sounded in inspiration and goals much like the religiously motivated white female seminaries of an earlier era (Barnett, 1978).

From its inauguration in 1909, however, Burroughs's school displayed the dual goals found in black self-improvement efforts at the turn of the century, ultimately coming closer to Booker T. Washington's uplift through manual labor than to W. E. B. Dubois's transformation through intellectual achievement. Simultaneously, the school called itself a school of higher education and gave diplomas in Normal and missionary work (including appropriate courses in Latin, English, math,

1. The papers and manuscripts of Nannie Helen Burroughs and of the National Training School are now collected at the Manuscript Division, Library of Congress. All references in this essay are to materials in this Burroughs collection.

and history, including the history of the Negro), and it also had what would now be called a vocational curriculum. Of the seven diplomas granted in 1911, two were in Normal training, and five were in manicuring and hairdressing, a pattern that continued through the 1920s and expanded to include dressmaking and millinery, domestic science, and the commercial or business course, which after 1921 included advanced shorthand and typewriting. The vocational curriculum was designed, moreover, to prepare black women for the best paid women's jobs, the jobs that white women sought (and held).

It is undoubtedly true that the girls whose parents could gather money to send them from all over the United States, Liberia, and Haiti were not the poorest of black society, although in many cases the students do seem to have been daughters of domestic servants who were trying to assure for them better vocational training and wider occupational opportunities than their own. Certainly the range of occupations, especially clerical work, millinery, and dressmaking, reflected ambitions to succeed as well as white women; and graduates in these fields were the most celebrated among the school's successes.

But Burroughs also saw all labor as an aspect of Christian living and very early indicated that domestic science was training for work in one's own home as well as in others' households. No line separated the two, and black women might work equally efficiently and proudly in both settings. The motto of the school was the Three Bs: Bible, Bath, and Broom—subtitled "Clean Lives, Clean Bodies, Clean Homes" (which Burroughs saw as only incidentally those of white employers).

Burroughs believed, apparently, that black women would move back and forth between doing their own and others' housework, as the vicissitudes of racial oppression required. In 1921 she conceived the National Association of Wage-Earners, for which were eligible "INDIVIDUAL wage earners and housekeepers, . . ." and "FEMALES NOT UNDER SIXTEEN YEARS OF AGE who are engaged in any honorable trade, profession or calling as a means of livelihood, and 'household engineers' of servantless homes." Although a membership book lists some ministers, doctors, janitors, and housekeepers, the bulk of the members were apparently homemakers and domestics supporting better training for domestic work, which was essential for the betterment of the Negro home as well as to secure better employment. The association was to support a training house, and annual prizes were to be awarded to members "who offer (1) The most practical and becoming housedresses and aprons, (2) the best plan for simplifying household management, (3) and valuable invention or improvement in household equipment."

With her severe pride in her own race, derived one suspects from her own obvious self-respecting life, Burroughs reprimanded many blacks for their lax approach to work and enjoined them to train and to strive. "Only the workers who have grit and will study and sweat can hold jobs now," she wrote in 1925. Her school was to train young women to have that capacity. But this was as part of a general conception of the necessity and importance of female work, which was essential both to the race and to the individual wage earner. As Burroughs wrote in the early 1930s, "Every Negro girl should learn the fine art of home making, along with general education or as a profession. The negro home is in dire need of women who know what to do with a home. . . . Just now the race is in greater need of home makers than it is of school teachers."

While much of the National Training School's rhetoric—and certainly its mixture of history, English, music, and vocational homemaking courses—was a customary mix for much female education during the 1910s and 1920s, it becomes remarkable because of the recognition that, for black women, housework is likely to be a paid occupation as well as a source of personal pride. Indeed, this expectation of doing housework for wages becomes more evident with the name change during the 1930s to the National Trade and Professional School. It indicates that black women were always aware that the training given for white women to manage their own homes more efficiently was, when taken by black women, occupational training to labor in someone else's home. Or, as the Burroughs catalog said by 1952,

> This is not simply a course in what is commonly known as Domestic Science or home economics. It is a course designed to prepare women for a *wider, more profitable and dignified* service in the field of homemaking and household management.
>
> Those who show aptitude are trained to become managers of large housing projects, apartment houses, general household directors, field demonstrators, caterers. They are technically trained to "service the home," without having to be "supervised." They know the home from basement to attic and are professional "household engineers" to meet the demand for trained household managers. (My emphasis)

Burroughs's graduates, in other words, did not need the supervision of white mistresses, negating the employers' home management role; the notion of commercial work as more profitable and dignified had been developed in opposition to solitary, suburban housework.

Burroughs's assumption, over five decades of school directorship, that improvements for black women workers would come from better training in those skills useful to her own family and to employers' families, was a curious complement to the argument made by programs for white girls studying domestic science, that their training was intended to prepare white women to run their own homes and to supervise servants. Burroughs, realizing she was responsible for the education of women much more likely to need and to seek paid employment, developed a different goal: recognition, not only for the housewife, but also for paid workers, whose skills merited the reward of good wages and job security.

During the 1960s both black women and white feminists gave serious attention to evaluating the work performed in homes. While some white feminists argued that wages should be paid wives for housework, black women were in the vanguard of efforts to make domestic work a commercial and specialized occupation with central agencies supplying specialized workers to perform specific tasks at a profitable margin. No longer would work be directed by the idiosyncrasies of individual employers but, rather, by performance standards set by a supervisory board, training program, or company.

The National Committee on Household Employment (NCHE) was organized in 1964 under the auspices of a number of national women's organizations, with the National Council on Negro Women taking the lead. This new effort of black women was supported by white women, perhaps partially because white women's employment—and consequent need for household help—was rising as dramatically as the supply of domestic servants was dropping. Supported by Esther Peterson and Mary Keyserling of the Women's Bureau, the NCHE set as its two purposes: to upgrade the status of black workers, many of whom were domestic servants, and to improve the supply of workers available to employed wives. The latter, of course, severely limited the options possible in the former effort, at least without substantial changes in the locus and organization of work done in the home. Most employed wives could not pay wages and benefits comparable to those for blue-collar and pink-collar jobs. Nor could individual homes afford to hire workers for general service when it became possible to buy elements of these services at cheaper rates and with less responsibility for the workers producing the services. Thus, fast food services replaced cooks' duties; and window-, furniture-, and rug-cleaning and floor-polishing services reduced weekly chores.

In 1964, however, these trends were not yet evident, and the NCHE program reflects differing goals of white and black sponsors. The three early goals were: to publicize the work situations of domestics and to educate the public about the importance of their work and the lack of labor protections surrounding it (especially noninclusion under the minimum wage); to establish training programs to standardize, and thereby to improve, domestic labor; and to organize specialized home services for contracting that would justify the raising of wages and entitle black women to new respect.

With its links to the Women's Bureau and to the U.S. Department of Labor, NCHE quickly gained (in February 1966) a contract to establish eight model projects to train, recruit, and place household workers in various specialties. As summarized in the final report (M. K. Trimble Associates, 1971), between January 1967 and March 1971, the eight projects took relatively poorly educated, poorly paid, usually unself-confident women and, not surprisingly, taught or polished home-making skills, improved the women's self-images, and gave them a public recognition and certification of the importance and value of their previously unappreciated skills. Most of the women trained in the eight cities ended up with better jobs and higher incomes, although these were usually in private households where employers had been persuaded to offer better wages and conditions. In addition, the training agents acted like employment services, bargaining with employers to pay the minimum wage and social security contributions, as well as time and a half for overtime work. In no instance, however, were the training agencies, even the three that were attempting to transform themselves into profit or cooperative businesses, able to sustain the cost of training and placement, payment of minimum wages, and benefits on the income earned from the workers' services. The agency that came the closest, SURGE in Alexandria, Virginia, a Washington, D.C. suburb, made a profit only during the period it was contracting with apartment buildings to do large-scale commercial cleaning; when its contracts shifted to a heavier balance of private homes, it began to lose money.

The failure of the NCHE-supervised training projects to translate into profit-making, worker-run enterprises that might supply a large number of certified workers did not, however, result in the collapse of NCHE but instead in its separation from the principles of better training for housework that had motivated many of the white female supporters of the early effort. In 1971 NCHE spun off the Household Technicians of America (HTA), a unionlike collective bargaining group that could organize women workers in particular cities and engage in political activity on behalf of specific legislation, most immediately the inclusion of domestic workers under the minimum wage provisions of the Fair Labor Standards Act. As an organization for organizing women workers rather than for training the unskilled, NCHE has sustained itself, partially with the momentum of winning inclusion for household workers in the Fair Labor Standards Act in 1974. Over time, however, many of the black women domestics who organized and worked for NCHE and HTA came to see their efforts mitigated by a new influx of women workers they have not yet been able to organize: immigrant women from Latin America and Asia, some of whom work at lower wages and without legal protections.

Like all efforts of low-paid workers, black women domestics' attempts to organize have been affected by three interrelated and somewhat unpredictable factors: the influx of new female immigrants, which has always kept domestic work resupplied; the transformation of home work, which now has made child and elderly care almost the only essential, indispensable tasks that cannot be shifted to different hours, to weekends, or managed by the working wife when she gets home from work (or more rarely, her husband), or performed by contracting specialists; and the removal and reorganization of home production into commercial production and services, most notably in food preparation, clothes care, and leisure entertainment.

By the late 1970s those women continuing to do housework were suffering from the general degradation the work had undergone. They were older (clumped for both white and black women in the forty-five to sixty-four age range); they were doing, generally, the least skilled work abandoned by women who were earning considerably more per hour than they were paying the women who came to take care of children or elderly and to do general cleaning; and they were working in an occupation abandoned not only by white women but by the younger generation of better educated black women who could find work in other, more respected, and better paid occupations.

The work performed in the past by housewives and domestic servants had not gone away, however. It had shifted in some cases to social, large-scale settings outside the home—day-care and senior citizen centers, nursing homes, and fast-food restaurants. In other cases it had been taken over by companies that hired workers to offer specific services in the home: health care for the elderly; homemaking services for the disabled; or window- and rug-cleaning, for instance. Much of this labor is still being done by black women, joined now by older and immigrant women. The labor of the household continues to dominate the lives of these women. But the social relations have changed. The women still have problems of low wages and job security. Now, however, the work is socially organized, and the work conditions are being set by company and agency employers rather than by individual mistresses or housewives. The changed categories are only partially captured by the statistics on the movement from private household work to other service work, but Table 1 is revealing.

How to think about household and service work, its organization and the status of workers in it, is complicated by the diverse conceptions developed by black and white women during the 1920s and 1930s. For white women, the way to enhance both the society's esteem and self-esteem for housework has been to professionalize the tasks. This has meant raising the levels of formal education considered essential for housework (e.g., courses in textile chemistry, nutrition, and child psychology) and conceiving of the work as *management*, even if, as Strasser (1982) ironically observes, the only person to be managed was the housewife herself. Even though the housewife combined mental and manual labor in her work, the two were seen as distinct elements, with mental labor the superior of the two.

Black women's conception of labor, as developed through Burroughs's school and the NCHE, is much more an artisanal notion of household labor—of cooking, cleaning, child care, and laundry work as craft skills to be learned through craft training by master workers. In this conception, self-esteem comes from improved job performance to meet shared standards of competence and output. Mental and manual labor are integral aspects of the same person and the same work.

A confirmation that black women experience their work as worthy and perform it with self-assurance comes in Dill's (1980) intensive interviews with twenty-six black domestic workers. Dill indicates that

TABLE I PERCENTAGE OF EMPLOYED PERSONS IN SERVICE WORK

	Black and Other Races			*White*		
	1978	*1975*	*1970*	*1978*	*1975*	*1970*
Women:						
Private house	7.7	10.6	17.5	2.2	2.4	3.4
Other	25.8	26.6	25.6	16.6	17.1	15.3
Total	33.4	37.1	43.1	18.8	19.5	18.7
Men:						
Private house	0.1	0.1	0.3	—	—	0.1
Other	15.8	16.2	12.8	7.8	7.7	6.0
Total	15.9	16.3	13.1	7.8	7.8	6.0

Source: U.S. Bureau of the Census, *A Statistical Portrait of Women in the United States: 1978*, Special Studies P- 23, Number 100 (Table 12-17).

the women feel respect within the black community for performing well the only jobs allowed to black women by white society. These black women often felt enough self-confidence to set standards for child training and child discipline. The additional thoughts from my work are that black women feel self-respect because they recognize the merit of their *work*, and they feel greater certainty about the standards of their work because these come from experience and practice rather than from written instructions in experts' manuals.

Despite their differences, both black and white conceptions of housework assumed its continuation as nonprofit, albeit valuable and compensable, work: for housewives to be managers, but only of their own, unique households, and for workers to be skilled enough to work in many homes and even as forewomen of crews in large institutions. Although aspects of each perception—housework as management and housework as skilled labor—have been incorporated into commercial and contract businesses and services during the decade of the 1970s, neither white nor black women foresaw the most striking change that has occurred: the selling of services by companies that make a profit from women's service work.

The hopes of early generations of feminists to socialize housework (Hayden, 1981) and the hopes of black women workers to perform these socialized services for a living wage have been parodied by historical reality. Many services are now performed on a social scale, but they are performed for profit and by women of color at rates that characterize unskilled labor. Neither the craft conception of black women nor the managerial-professional one of white women has been recognized. Perhaps most important, the assumption that service was given for people's benefit and not for profit has been outmoded.

Women, of course, continue to do the bulk of housework and of social, nonprofit, and for-profit service work. The future of this work can be shaped by women. To do so, they must examine the recent history of service work and the race and ethnic divisions within this history.

References

Barnett, Evelyn Brooks. 1978. "Nannie Burroughs and the Education of Black Women." In Sharon Harley and Rosalyn Terborg-Penn, eds., *The Afro-American Woman Struggles and Images*, 97–108. Port Washington, N.Y.: Kennikat.

Beecher, Catharine, and Harriet Beecher Stowe. [1869] 1975. *American Woman's Home*. Reprint. Hartford, Conn.: Stowe-Day Foundation.

Chafe, William Henry. 1972. *The American Woman: Her Changing Social, Economic and Political Roles, 1920–1970*. New York: Oxford University Press.

Chaplin, David. 1978. "Domestic Service and Industrialization." *Comparative Studies in Sociology* 1: 98–127.

Cowan, Ruth Schwartz. 1974. "A Case Study of Technological and Social Change: The Washing Machine and the Working Wife." In Mary S. Hartman and Lois Banner, eds., *Clio's Consciousness Raised*, 245–253. New York: Harper, Torchbooks.

Dill, Bonnie Thornton. 1980. "'The Means to Put My Children Through': Child-rearing Goals and Strategies among Black Female Domestic Servants." In LaFrances Rodgers-Rose, ed., *The Black Woman*, 107–123. Beverly Hills, Calif.: Sage.

Ehrenreich, Barbara, and Dierdre English. 1979. *For Her Own Good: 150 Years of the Experts' Advice to Women*. New York: Doubleday, Anchor.

Grossman, Allyson Sherman. 1980. "Women in Domestic Work: Yesterday and Today." *Monthly Labor Review* (August): 17–21.

Hartmann, Heidi I. 1974. "Capitalism and Women's Work in the Home." Ph.D. diss., Yale University.

Hayden, Dolores. 1981. *The Grand Domestic Revolution: A History of Feminist Designs for American Homes, Neighborhoods, and Cities*. Cambridge: MIT Press.

Hoy, Suellen M. 1980. "'Municipal Housekeeping': The Role of Women in Improving Urban Sanitation Practices, 1880–1917." In Martin V. Melosi, ed., *Pollution and Reform in American Cities, 1870–1930*, 173–198. Austin: University of Texas Press.

James, Edward T., Janet Wilson James, and Paul S. Boyer, eds. 1971. *Notable American Women 1607–1950: A Biographical Dictionary*. Cambridge: Harvard University Press, Belknap.

Katzman, David M. 1981. *Seven Days a Week: Woman and Domestic Service in Industrializing America*. Urbana: University of Illinois Press.

Smith, Joan. 1982. "The Way We Were: Women and Work." *Feminist Studies* 8, no. 2: 437–456.

Strasser, Susan M. 1978. "Mistress and Maid, Employer and Employee: Domestic Service Reform in the United States, 1897–1920." *Marxist Perspectives* (Winter): 52–67.

———. 1982. *Never Done: A History of American Housework*. New York: Pantheon.

M. K. Trimble and Associates, Inc. 1971. *Final Report of the National Pilot Program on Household Employment, January 16, 1967–March 15, 1971*. U.S. Department of Labor, Manpower Administration Contract No. 82-11-71-05. Washington, D.C.

U.S. Bureau of the Census. 1979. *The Social and Economic Status of the Black*

Population of the United States: An Historical View, 1790–1978. Current Population Reports. Special Studies, Series P-23, No. 80. Washington, D.C.: GPO.

Vanek, Joann. 1979. "Time Spent in Housework." In Nancy F. Cott and Elizabeth H. Pleck, eds., *A Heritage of Her Own: Toward a New Social History of American Women*. New York: Simon and Schuster, Touchstone.

TWO
TECHNOLOGY AND THE CHANGING SHAPES OF WOMEN'S WORK

5

DOROTHY REMY
UNIVERSITY OF THE DISTRICT OF COLUMBIA
and
LARRY SAWERS
AMERICAN UNIVERSITY

Economic Stagnation and Discrimination

Women and blacks have borne more than their share of the burdens in the recent economic transformation of the meat-packing industry. This has occurred despite militant, progressive union pressure and vigorous governmental intervention which together forced the industry to grant formal equality to minorities and women. The resulting tensions have weakened the union, leaving it a less effective instrument for protecting the economic position of any workers, white or black, male or female. We reach these conclusions through an intensive investigation of a single meat-packing plant in a large, industrial city in the northeastern United States. This investigation included observation within the plant; interviews with numerous workers, union officials and managers; and a statistical analysis of data drawn from the firm's personnel department files.

The last two decades have witnessed a dramatic technological and geographical restructuring of the U.S. meat-packing industry. The smaller independent producers left behind in the march to the South

This essay is based on research carried out under the auspices of the U.S. Commission on Civil Rights. The data used are with the permission of the commission. The analysis presented here is the sole responsibility of the authors. We have benefited from the initial research design of Heidi Hartmann and the assistance, through all stages of the data collection, of Beverly White. This is a revised version of a paper published in *Sunbelt/Snowbelt: Urban Development and Regional Restructuring*, edited by William Tabb and Larry Sawers, Oxford University Press, 1983.

and West have experienced considerable difficulties. Many have gone bankrupt or sold out; others, such as the one we studied, have hung on. The workers in these distressed firms have found their economic position steadily eroding.

We were invited into the plant of one of these hard-pressed, independent packers. Our goal, which we announced, was to examine the internal workings of the firm (which we call here the Square Deal Packing Company) in order to analyze racial and sexual discrimination. When the workers learned of our mission, their immediate response was: "The women's libbers, pencil-pushers in Washington who don't know the donkey's work of a factory" are responsible for women being pushed out of their jobs and out of the plant. Union officials and lower management gave us the same explanation.

Our research combined methods from anthropology, economics, and history. One of us—Dorothy Remy, an anthropologist—spent two months in the plant, observing the work process and talking with people as they worked. She had access to all parts of the plant and, with the union's general steward, observed disciplinary cases involving all levels of management. In addition, she and a black, woman field assistant administered a formal questionnaire to over twenty workers. These interviews often lasted several hours and were conducted in the workers' homes. Most of those involved with the research project also attended at least one union meeting. The union allowed us to examine their records and freely answered our questions.

The firm also granted us free access to everything their personnel department recorded about its employees—information on race, sex, wage rates, promotions, demotions, and layoffs—from the date of hire (1928 for the most senior worker) to December 1977 when the study was carried out. All this information was coded and punched onto computer cards. After these data were collected, the other of us—Larry Sawers, an economist—carried out the statistical analysis.

We also made considerable efforts to connect what we learned from the workers, their leaders, and their records to what has been written about the history of the meat-packing industry, especially on the role of technological change and the effects of racial and sexual segmentation of the work force. The international office of the Amalgamated Meat Cutters and Butcher Workmen of North America provided published reports and answered our questions. Local union files containing old contracts, letters, minutes of meetings, and clippings from area newspapers rounded out the picture. Our vantage point outside the factory, with access to the entire spectrum of people involved, gave us more information than any single group of participants and allowed us to draw conclusions that might not have occurred to many of the people we interviewed.

Before World War II, Square Deal openly discriminated against women by paying them lower wages than men and against blacks by refusing outright to hire them. In 1942 the union arrived and demanded that the company move toward equal pay for equal work. Almost simultaneously, the federal government refused to buy meat for its soldiers unless suppliers agreed to hire blacks.

By the end of the following decade, starting wages for men and women had been equalized. Until this point, the firm had hired only a handful of black workers. After the late 1950s, however, the firm virtually ceased hiring women and instead hired black men. The effect of this has been to pit black men against white women, with both groups feeling betrayed by their allies among white men. How could this have happened when both white women and black men were protected by a progressive union, a seniority system, and civil rights legislation? The following accounts offer an answer.

The Restructuring of the Meat-packing Industry

The growth of industrial meat-packing unions in the 1930s led to management attempts both to move the industry geographically to regions where unions were weaker and to simplify the production process to use ever more unskilled workers, thereby undercutting the economic position of the organized workers. The major companies built their own yards to lessen their vulnerability to strikes in the city-side yards, which had plagued the industry during and immediately after World War I. More significantly, after World War II, production in the north central region—traditionally the center of the meat industry—shifted from the eastern part of the region to the western. It declined on Ohio, Indiana, Illinois, Michigan, and Wisconsin; and it increased in Minnesota, Iowa, Missouri, North and South Dakota, Nebraska, and Kansas. A second shift occurred in the South. Before 1947/1948 hogs produced in the South were shipped north for slaughter. By 1960–1962 hogs produced in the north central states were sent south for slaughter. (Amalgamated Meat Cutters, 1961: 5). Packers reduced their labor costs in both cases by moving into areas where workers were not effectively organized.

Mechanization and reorganization of production in the industry at large, and at Square Deal in particular, began in the early 1950s. The general pattern was to reduce the skill level required of workers. One important change involved replacing, with an electric saw, the heavy cleavers used to crack the breastbone of the cattle. A second change was the use of on-the-rail processes in the cattle kill. Killing and skinning the animals became a less physically demanding and skilled job, and it increased productivity by up to 50 or 60 percent. New equipment and production processes were also introduced in meat processing, sausage manufacturing, ham curing, and bacon slicing (Amalgamated Meat Cutters, 1971: 10–11).

These innovations affected employment in general and that of women and minorities in particular. Total employment in the industry and at Square Deal declined even though output rose, but the declines were not evenly spread through the labor force. The new equipment and processes, and the job losses, were concentrated in the jobs held by women and blacks.

By 1960 the U.S. Department of Labor (1961) estimated, "at current production levels, new equipment and new technology have been eliminating about 7,000 meat packing jobs a year" (2). A breakdown of the sex and race composition of the work force in the departments where mechanization was most advanced indicates that these departments were also those with the highest concentration of black and female workers. Splitting cattle breastbones with the heavy cleaver, for example, had been a "black job." Blacks have also been concentrated in the ham-curing department, where injection of curing solution by machines replaced the delicate and highly skilled job of injecting the solution with a hypodermic needle into the main arteries. Sausage manufacturing and bacon slicing have been traditional "women's jobs." Their skilled labor was replaced by new machines that fed sausage into artificial casings and tied the links. Machines did not necessarily increase the speed with which bacon was packed, but they did eliminate the need to train and retrain the skilled packers. (Meat processing and the cattle kill—areas where mechanization also changed production processes—are less readily identified with a particular race and sex.) Women's jobs were rapidly mechanized as the union forced the elimination of sex differences in wages.

Black workers appear to have been disproportionately hurt by plant closings. Union studies of the effects of plant closings on employment concluded that workers were not being reabsorbed into the labor force. The new jobs created by mechanization were not being filled by former meat-packers. The effects of plant closings, which often accompanied mechanization, varied from city to city, with black workers in predominantly black cities being the least likely to be rehired (Amalgamated Meat Cutters, 1961: 12–15).

Changes in the 1960s and 1970s had to do with the reorganization of the market for which the industry produced and with the implications this had for the nature of competition within the industry. There were three major transformations. First, major chain stores began buying, slaughtering, and processing their own meat products. Chain-store control over both production and distribution enabled them to undercut the major packers. Second, the major packers themselves were bought out by conglomerates who saw investment possibilities in the food industry. Third, traditional forms of beef production and distribution were transformed by innovators within the industry. In highly mechanized plants located near feedlots, beef was prepared for direct retail sale in supermarkets and shipped in boxes, thereby eliminating any butchering within the retail store itself.

These transformations challenged the domination and control of the industry by the major packers. The proportion of red meat produced by the major packers declined from 40 percent in 1947 to 29 percent in 1967. The big food chains took a major share of their markets as well as some of their profits. In 1960, for example, the chains had a 12 percent profit rate as compared with 7 percent for the big packers. (Amalgamated Meat Cutters, 1961: 5–15). The supermarket chains had great economic leverage through their access to customers, the buying power of their billions of dollars, and their own distribution networks.

Major conglomerates also entered into the food industry. Wilson and Company was taken over by LTV, a Texas-owned corporation whose earlier specialization had been in aerospace equipment and electronic gear. The fourth-largest packer was bought by AMK and then subsequently sold to the United Fruit Company. Now all three are covered by a single corporate umbrella called United Brands, Inc. Armour and Company, itself a conglomerate, was eventually taken over by a huge multinational corporation, Greyhound, Inc. (Amalgamated Meat Cutters, 1971: 4–5).

The third new force in the meat industry, Iowa Beef Packers, Inc. (now known as Iowa Beef Processors, Inc.), began in Denison, Iowa in 1960. By 1969 it had become the largest slaughterer and processor of beef in the world. IBP has been joined by Missouri Beef and American Beef. All three companies have plants adjacent to cattle feedlots. They have large, single-storied plants (in contrast to Square Deal's seven-storied plant) with the most modern equipment. Some have built airstrips nearby to facilitate shipments of the boxed beef throughout the country. They hire a disproportionately large number of minority women as production workers. These new beef-processing firms have adamantly refused to agree to the terms of the master contracts between the major packers and the union. They argue that the work is less skilled and therefore should be remunerated at a lower rate.

The challenge of these three structural changes in the meat industry confronts both packers and organized workers. We look at the response of each in turn and then examine the effects of these changes on independent packers like Square Deal, and their workers.

Beginning in the early 1960s, the major packers responded by reorganizing their production along lines of those developed by the beef processors. In 1961, for example, they spent ninety-five million dollars for a new plant and equipment (U.S. Department of Labor, 1961: 2). Single-level plants designed to facilitate the uninterrupted flow of products from one stage of processing to another replaced the multistory factories of the earlier periods. The new plants, located near centers of animal production, attracted workers for whom the largely unskilled work represented a steady source of income, not the loss of status it would be for workers with a history in the industry. The major packers have also been increasingly resistant to wage increases and other proposals submitted by the union in contract negotiation.

The unions have responded in three ways. First, the various unions representing packing-house workers have merged and then in turn merged with the Retail Clerks Union. Second, there have been considerable and protracted strikes. A third response has been the attempt to organize presently unorganized workers.

The small independent packers left in the older industrial cities experience enormous pressures. Competition from boxed beef, chain stores, and the traditional giants of the industry now owned by conglomerates threaten their profits and continued existence. Their labor force has long been accustomed to influencing wages and conditions of employment. Both companies and the union feel pressure to adjust to new demands by the federal government for compliance with health and safety regulations, sanitation inspection laws, and affirmative action legislation. Both sides feel victimized by external forces over which they have little control.

Square Deal is now the last firm in its city that both slaughters and processes pork. Square Deal eliminated its beef-slaughtering operation because it could not compete with the major packers or the new beef-processing firms that now sell boxed beef to local grocery stores in the city. Other operations have been eliminated, and technological innovation and speedup have reduced the work force still further, from a peak of over eighteen hundred in the 1960s to about one thousand at the time of the study.

The Impact of Retrenchment on Women

The dramatic deterioration in Square Deal's market position that led to a nearly 50 percent drop in the work force has hurt all categories of workers. Nevertheless, as the remaining workers believe, women have borne the brunt of the firm's retrenchment and been pushed out of the plant. Our purpose here is to explain why.

Women at Square Deal first received the same starting wages as men in 1959. The company had made it clear the year before that "with the equalization of male and female rates, separate male and female seniorities had been abolished."[1] The union opposed the abolition of sexual job designations, and their view prevailed, at least for a time. The Civil Rights Act of 1964, however, outlawed dual seniority provisions, and the men's and women's seniority lists were merged in 1967.

The push to reduce the discrepancy between the starting wages of men and women began when the union first organized Square Deal in 1942. Parity was reached in 1959. The company and the union had a series of meetings in 1958 to clarify the subject of male and female seniority. In the first meeting the union president said that "in September when male and female rates are equalized in the plant, it is rumored that the company is planning to eliminate females whenever they can." The company replied, "There are some jobs that are presently filled by girls which will be given to men should the present occupants leave the employ of the company. In the case of layoffs the company would

1. The issue of seniority lists is discussed in minutes from a meeting on November 21, 1958, between representatives of the union and the company.

not resort to subterfuge to eliminate girls but neither would they be given preference because of their sex."

Management at Square Deal wanted to eliminate women because men's greater physical strength makes them capable of performing a greater variety of jobs than women, and this flexibility is highly valued by management in a period when it is laying off many workers. To explain this fully, we must first explain the workings of the seniority system.

After an initial thirty-day probationary period, a worker's access to jobs, to work in other departments, and to promotions is determined by seniority. In the event of reduction in the labor force, the person with the least seniority is the first laid off and is the last to be recalled. These general principles of seniority serve both management and workers, but in somewhat different ways. From the workers' perspective, use of seniority as the primary allocating mechanism for jobs, promotions, and some benefits inhibits arbitrary behavior on the part of employers. The employer benefits to the extent that seniority creates a stable and they hope loyal work force. At Square Deal as at other packing plants, there is a combination department and plant seniority. After thirty days a person acquires seniority in a department, but only after a year does he or she acquire plant-wide seniority. A person maintains departmental seniority until such time as written confirmation of transfer to another department is filed. Thus a person may work on a temporary basis in one department while maintaining seniority in his or her original department. Job openings within departments are filled on the basis of departmental seniority.

Once a worker has acquired plant-wide seniority, he or she has the right to displace workers in other departments with less seniority when there are layoffs. Plant-wide seniority provides protection against "going on the street" but not against forced transfer to another department. Within departments, however, the hierarchy of skills and degree of unpleasantness of the different jobs is ordered by departmental seniority, not plant-wide seniority. The job that the senior worker takes when he or she bumps a junior employee out of a department is thus normally at the bottom of the department's skill hierarchy.

This combination of plant and departmental seniority provides strong incentives for workers to remain in their original department. Even if one has many years of plant seniority, one's ability to bid on the better jobs within one's department as well as a host of lesser privileges, such as choice of vacation times and even who gets to punch out first at closing time, depends on departmental seniority. From the perspective of management, departmental seniority encourages the development of a labor force experienced in the operations of a particular unit of the company and familiar with its machinery and tools. Indeed, a seniority system without some form of departmental seniority would create havoc for management. With every layoff, the most junior workers would leave while the remaining workers engaged in an enormous game of musical chairs, with seniority determining who got the best seats. With the entire work force reshuffled every time there was a layoff, the plant would be in chaos.

The nature of the seniority system has a number of implications for the status of women and minorities at Square Deal. For example, even though the contractual seniority agreements apply equally to men and women, white and minority, the departmental system reinforces and perpetuates any discriminatory effect of initial job placement by discouraging transfers between departments. A department may offer little room for advancement or may have unpleasant or unhealthy working conditions for all of its workers. But remaining within the department with much seniority may still be preferable to moving to another department where one will necessarily have the least seniority. Thus women and blacks become locked into their original departments even if they have undesirable jobs.

Of far greater significance, however, is that these rules governing seniority have motivated management to cease hiring women. The reason for this is that, when layoffs occur, senior workers end up with the worst jobs in their new department because it is these jobs which the most junior workers who are being bumped have held. The worst jobs are also most often the most physically demanding jobs. The women are either physically unable to perform these arduous tasks or do so only with grave risk of injuring themselves. The typical man is stronger than the typical woman and thus can perform a greater range of activities. This flexibility is especially valued in a production system like Square Deal's where there is great daily, monthly, and seasonal variation in both products and quantities produced. Flexibility becomes critical to management when layoffs are frequent, because of the widespread reshuffling of jobs that overflows the cushion of departmental seniority. Thus, in management's view, women were paid the same wage as men for the same job but could not be moved to the variety of jobs that men could and still be expected to physically perform. Thus, management chose to virtually cease hiring women.

Half the white male production workers in the plant in 1978 were hired after 1957, and two-thirds of their black counterparts were hired after that date. In contrast, only 5 percent of the white female production workers in the plant were hired after 1957. Of the workers hired between 1943 and 1952, 29 percent were women. If women had been hired and retained on the payroll after 1953 in the same proportion as they were in the ten years before 1953, there would now be 128 women workers (black and white) at Square Deal hired since 1957. Instead there are 18. There "should" be 2.3 times as many women workers at the company as there now are.

Some of the women attempted to fight back by petitioning the union and the government for redress. Four filed grievances through the union but were told they did not have a grievance because none of the contract provisions had been violated. At the union's suggestion, these four visited lawyers at a women's legal rights clinic in the city. They were told that the union should fight for them. The general steward went with the four to city- and state-level conferences on women's rights in an effort to get help, but to no avail—no law had been broken and the contract had not been violated.

The women forced out of Square Deal's labor force in the 1960s and 1970s found themselves most likely in difficult economic straits. Our study examined only the workers still at the factory in 1978, and thus we have only indirect evidence about those severed from the firm's payroll. Square Deal was located within the central city of its metropolitan area, and that city, like central cities throughout the north, has experienced slow growth, loss of jobs to the suburbs and the Sunbelt, and rising unemployment problems. The typical Square Deal worker is embedded in an ethnic neighborhood with a tight-knit and supportive social structure. Finding a job within a reasonable commuting distance was thus not easy.

The difficult employment situation of the laid-off women was compounded by the fact that by 1978 Square Deal was the only packing house left in the metropolitan area. Branch plants of the major packers as well as other independent packers had all closed their doors in the 1960s and 1970s. A few grocery stores still employed their own butchers, but this was little help, for those laid off from Square Deal were not journeyman butchers. They thus entered a labor market with a high level of unemployment where their skills were not valued. Older women in their forties and fifties indeed faced a bleak prospect.

The Cost of Layoff

In addition to permanent layoffs and failing to replace normal attrition, Square Deal also reduced its labor force by a substantial increase in temporary layoffs of workers who continued in the firm's employ. These temporary layoffs of workers were very unevenly distributed by sex and race for the same reasons that women were permanently laid off. Since we have no direct information about those who have left the firm permanently, we can only make qualified guesses about what their job loss might have cost them. But for those whose layoffs were temporary and who are still with the firm, we can estimate the costs of those layoffs with some precision.

Table 1 shows the average number of layoffs by race, sex, and seniority of production workers on the payroll in January 1978. At every seniority level except the last period, when only two women were hired, white women averaged more layoffs per worker than white men. For instance, for every ten white men hired in the mid-1950s, one has been laid off once during his career at Square Deal. By contrast, the average white woman hired during the same period has been laid off more than twice and thus is twenty times more likely to have been laid

TABLE I AVERAGE NUMBER OF LAYOFFS AND AVERAGE MONETARY LOSSES FROM LAYOFFS AND DEMOTIONS FOR PRODUCTION WORKERS, JANUARY 1978

			Average dollar loss per worker		
Senority (first hired)	*Number of workers*	*Layoffs per worker*	*All economic reverses*	*Layoff*	*Demotion*
1928–1937					
White: Males	10	.40	101.00	0	83.18
Females	2	1.67	0	0	0
Black: Males	0	—	—	—	—
Females	0	—	—	—	—
1938–1942					
White: Males	31	.09	368.10	0	260.78
Females	—	.37	170.65	9.97	160.68
Black: Males	1	0	30.68	0	30.68
Females	0	—	—	—	—
1943–1947					
White: Males	44	.26	357.00	29.62	296.58
Females	24	.42	242.95	35.23	207.73
Black: Males	13	.50	511.82	4.92	499.40
Females	0	—	—	—	—
1948–1952					
White: Males	75	.09	417.21	2.65	366.92
Females	32	.50	197.91	12.59	165.96
Black: Males	7	0	582.14	0	537.38
Females	0	—	—	—	—
1953–1957					
White: Males	71	.11	268.26	13.10	151.52
Females	10	2.27	3865.60	3595.60	269.80
Black: Males	28	.04	223.61	0.53	223.09
Females	0	—	—	—	—
1958–1962					
White: Males	46	.83	406.30	71.55	119.20
Females	1	4.00	1024.70	625.62	399.07
Black: Males	11	1.08	286.63	131.67	154.96
Females	0	—	—	—	—
1963–1967					
White: Males	54	.66	371.93	18.13	286.42
Females	0	—	—	—	—
Black: Males	27	.65	290.82	28.03	232.10
Females	0	—	—	—	—
1968–1972					
White: Males	73	.66	461.86	119.29	190.26
Females	1	6.00	4670.90	4670.90	0
Black: Males	38	.62	368.85	49.98	250.28
Females	4	2.50	730.17	625.46	104.71
1973–1977					
White: Males	57	1.53	1660.30	1385.10	10.09
Females	2	1.00	389.13	163.69	225.44
Black: Males	24	2.54	2196.30	2112.10	51.50
Females	0	—	—	—	—
F statistic			12.45	19.56	1.98
Significance			.0000	.0000	.004

off as a comparable white man. The one white woman hired in the late 1950s has been laid off six times. The few black women hired in the early 1970s have also suffered many layoffs; the four of them experienced altogether ten. The contrast between black and white men is much smaller than the differences between men and women; black men are slightly more likely to have been laid off than white men. Of the men hired since 1942 (when the first black was hired), whites averaged 0.56 layoffs and blacks, 0.82. Women, and to a lesser extent blacks, experienced not merely more layoffs but also longer ones.

We have measured the length of the workers' layoffs and the wages that they would have earned had they remained in the company's employ.[2] Table 1 shows that losses from layoffs and demotions vary widely according to seniority and confirms our perceptions of the differential impact of the firm's retrenchment on its workers. The average white woman's losses from layoffs are larger than the average white man's at every seniority level except the most recent (when only two women were hired). White men hired before 1973 averaged only $31 per person in wages lost from layoff during their entire career at Square Deal. The white women, however, have a dramatically different experience. For those hired before 1952, career losses are quite small—$35 or less depending on seniority. But for women hired in the mid-1950s, losses from layoffs are much larger, nearly $3,600 per worker. The one white woman hired between 1963 and 1973 lost over $4,000. We argued earlier that in 1958 management, since men's and women's wages were about to be equalized, decided to stop hiring women and not to protect the jobs of women remaining in the plant when retrenchment occurred. Women hired before 1953 apparently had enough seniority that, by the time the layoffs started in earnest in the 1960s, their jobs were protected. But the newer women workers were not, as the data forcefully show. The losses of the four black women hired between 1968 and 1972 are substantially greater than those of men with the same seniority. The black women's career losses amounted to $625,

2. This is not an entirely straightforward calculation. If a laid-off worker had remained on the payroll, he or she would have been granted the annual step increase in wages granted all employees as stipulated in the union contract. Since many of the layoffs were quite lengthy, the failure to include these step increases in the calculations would lead to an underestimation, possibly serious, of the loss in wages.

These calculations are based on straight-time wages and do not reflect fringe benefits, overtime, night bonuses, and so on. We have also excluded from our calculations of monetary loss any unemployment compensation, public assistance, food stamps, or other transfers received while unemployed. Furthermore, we have not adjusted our data according to the date of layoff. Prices have risen steadily, and thus earlier losses should have carried a greater weight than current ones. Similarly, we have not adjusted these calculations for what economists call the time discount or different preferences for when workers might have had the layoff. This calculation would have taken into account that most people would rather have the layoff later than sooner. This implies that the estimates we have made of costs of retrenchment are underestimated, but the relative ranking of the four race-sex groups would probably change little if time discounts were taken into account since the layoffs and demotions were experienced at roughly the same time.

while the men averaged $95. Black men's losses were roughly the same as white men's except in the most recent period.

The figures for losses from demotions also offer some interesting comparisons. Because of discrimination in placement within the plant, women were rarely promoted into the higher grade, better paying jobs. When the firm's reverses began, they did not have as far to fall down the job hierarchy as the white men who held the better jobs in the plant. Except for those hired in the mid-1950s, white women's losses from demotion were smaller than comparable white men's. The white men hired in the 1940s and early 1950s suffered losses in the vicinity of three hundred dollars, but those hired later experienced much smaller losses. (Some of these relatively high losses for white males hired before 1952 are probably "voluntary." Older workers, as their physical strength declined, frequently bid for lower paid but less strenuous assignments.) Black males as a whole suffered the largest losses from demotion of any group. Black men who had the greatest loss were hired around 1950, and their loss averaged about twenty dollars per year since they were hired.

All of the workers have been hurt by Square Deal's economic reverses, but the women, especially the older white women, have suffered the greatest losses. The men and women hired before 1952 have emerged relatively unscathed in the process we have been describing. They have experienced little loss from layoff and only moderate losses from demotions. For example, the white men hired between 1938 and 1942 have averaged about ten dollars per year in losses from both sources since they began working at Square Deal. After 1952, the picture changes remarkably. Women's economic losses mounted dramatically, mostly because of layoff.

These calculations do not pretend to be a complete estimate of the cost to the workers of the firm's retrenchment. For example, if the firm had not been experiencing economic reverses, it is likely that many of its workers would have received a promotion instead of a demotion. In addition the local union acceded to management's demands for across-the-board wage increases below those mandated by the union's national contract because of the distressed situation of the firm. Indeed, these negotiated "give-backs" have continued, occurring again during the winter of 1982. Furthermore, these calculations include only straight-time wages, not fringe benefits.

The white women hired in the mid-1950s averaged nearly four thousand dollars in losses from layoffs and demotions since they were hired. Most of these losses were incurred between 1968 when the egg-candling department was closed and 1973 when the night sausage department was closed. Four thousand dollars spread over two decades would have been considerably less worrisome than that amount concentrated in one or a few years. An interesting contrast can be drawn between the losses from layoff and demotion and the benefits from the equalization of wage rates that the union brought to the women. In 1942 when the union arrived at Square Deal, the women's starting wage was 73 percent of the men's. If women had continued to earn 73 percent as much as men between 1959 (when parity was reached) and 1978, the average full-time woman worker would have earned nearly forty thousand dollars less than she actually did. The equalization of wage rates played a prominent role in the process which led to women's bearing the brunt of the firm's retrenchment. This equalization brought *gains* to the women who were able to remain in the plant. These gains in monetary terms far exceeded the losses incurred by the women which resulted from the way in which management responded to sexual parity in wage rates. Of course, from the women's (and our) point of view, they deserved both wage parity and continuous employment.

Nonmonetary Costs of Retrenchment

There are a variety of other costs to the worker that are also spread very unevenly along sex and race lines. As Square Deal closed unprofitable operations, mechanized, increased the pace of work (speedup), and reorganized the production process, the company reduced its labor force by nearly one-half. Workers with lower plant seniority were discharged, but remaining workers were frequently squeezed out of their home departments to find work elsewhere in the plant. Since women, and to a lesser extent black men, were concentrated in departments which were closed or in jobs which were abolished, even those who were not laid off bore more than their share of nonmonetary costs. First, the most senior worker in a department can bid on jobs that he or she prefers and also has first choice of vacation time.

Second, job and department change frequently result in injury or stress-related disease. Most of these are simple muscle strains from performing the new task. Others are from knife cuts that result almost inevitably as new operations are learned. Still other medical problems are associated with the stress of changing one's job and the effect this has on preexisting arthritic or hypertensive conditions that are common among the firm's workers. Considerable physical stress comes from moving between departments with very different temperature and humidity conditions. Some butchering operations are carried out in what amounts to giant refrigerators, while many others are performed in a hot and steamy room where the newly slaughtered carcasses are scalded.

The most severe injuries were to women who attempted to do heavy laborers' jobs beyond their physical strength. The cases of particular women (for example, those who attempted to lift heavy loads unassisted and injured their backs) were frequently raised with the investigator during the time she spent in the plant. Several of these women were injured severely enough to require months away from work. These injuries or the threat of injury forced many of the women to accept temporary or even permanent layoff.

Third, there are the psychological effects on the way people think about themselves. As jobs were eliminated or mechanized, old skills were devalued, threatening a loss in self-esteem. Movement to a new department or new shift meant old friendships and work relationships were disrupted or lost. A more intensely stressful impact is felt by those men and women who spend lengthy periods without a job or even a department that is permanently theirs. There were workers from the 1973 closing of the night manufacturing department who had not signed into a new department five years later when our fieldwork was conducted. No sooner had the worker adjusted to a new department when she was again bumped into another department, continuing her odyssey about the plant. Such workers can never set down their roots, build new relationships, and hone new skills.

The Subtleties of Sexual and Racial Oppression

Both management and union officials were trapped by their sexism and racism and failed to respond to the conditions of women and blacks, thereby exacerbating an already bad situation. Both managers and labor leaders believed they bent over backward to fulfill their obligations to women and blacks. Indeed, if the company had suspected that any of its managers were discriminating in any way, it would not have permitted our study. The insensitive response of both management and union has embittered the women and contributed to a marked decline in the local union's militance. We describe here three situations in some detail to illustrate their racially and sexually discriminatory patterns.

June (not her real name) was about fifty-five in 1973 when the night manufacturing department was closed. She was physically small—only a little over five feet tall and weighing about one hundred pounds. Her story was told often in the women's locker room to illustrate the unreasonable demands placed on displaced women. One job assigned to her on the day shift was to push meat carts weighing over one thousand pounds. Another job was to insert gambrels in the hind legs of hogs as they came out of the scald tanks. She hurt her back badly attempting to do this work. At the time of the study, she had a relatively light job of inserting plastic bags of meat into a machine that created a vacuum, but the work forced her to reach above eye level and to remove her hands before the machine lid returned. She found the work difficult and was frustrated by her inability to perform it well; "I guess I'm too old to learn a new job," she said. "I'm not as fast as before, I must be getting old." "I can't be a spring chick anymore." The other women attempted to reassure her, but each effort was met with a reply about her age.

Phil was one of the men incorporated into the consolidated cut-and-kill gang. The slaughtering and initial butchering, performed in extremely hot and humid conditions, is followed by placing the carcasses in a cooler overnight. The next morning the remainder of the butchering is carried out in a refrigerated room. Formerly, there was sufficient demand to warrant slaughtering and butchering all day long, thereby allowing two different gangs to specialize. Now the workers are required to work in the cooler in the morning and in the hot, steamy cut room in the afternoon.

Phil was not used to the extreme heat of the cut room, especially when summer weather intensified it. The problem arose when Phil was out of work for four weeks for health reasons. When the doctors authorized him to return to work, Phil failed several times to show up when he said he would. In a meeting with a union steward and the plant superintendent, Phil assured them that medical problems which had caused him to miss work in the past were under control. His hypertension was controlled by medication, and he was participating in a program for alcoholics. The problem was, as the steward explained, "He didn't look forward to coming into the cut—he experienced sick feelings." The company management and the (male) steward agreed that this was a reasonable explanation for his repeated failures to come to work and that if he returned to the plant he could have a job in another department. The company and the union acknowledged in this meeting and at other times that some other men did not make the transition to the consolidated gang.

The contrast between June and Phil illustrates the sexist application of the seniority system. A male alcoholic who complained of "sick feelings" was allowed to transfer to a new department and a new job with union and management approval. A woman who was faced with the choice between risk of severe physical injury or layoff was told that the seniority system could not permit her to take a less demanding job.

A second example relates to union and management's differential perceptions of speedup in men's and women's jobs. A new frankfurter-stuffing machine was set in such a way that twice as many franks were hung on rods that in turn were placed on metal "trees" (to be taken to the smoking room) as with the machine it replaced. The women who lifted the rods of hanging franks as they came back from the smoke room were accordingly required to lift twice the former weight. One woman's doctor suggested she take an early retirement rather than continue to strain her back and arms. This new machine and a sausage-stuffing machine in the same department were now operated by four men, who replaced about twenty women who had held the best paying women's jobs in the plant. Both union officials and management held the machine responsible for the increased weight per rod. It was clear, however, that the machine could easily have been reset. This, then, was a classic case of speedup but was not acknowledged as such.

The response of both management and union was very different when men were affected by management's speedup: The line in the cut-and-kill room used to be set at 300 hogs per hour. At one point the company raised this to 426 per hour, but the room became too congested for safe, accurate work. After some experimentation, the rate was lowered to 320 hogs per hour. This rate was determined by negotiations among workers, union officials, and management. None of the individual men in that context was put in the position of publicly affirming physical inability to perform a job when the speed was increased. All could legitimate their objections by reference to very real safety considerations. But women had no assistance from the union in negotiating changes in the weight per rod. Their lesser physical strength was considered to be their own fault, about which nothing could be done. Where men had the machines adjusted down to their abilities, women were expected to keep up with the full speed.

A third example shows the subtle interplay between sexism and racism. One form of rationalizing production instituted in recent years has entailed use of production workers in quasi-supervisory positions. A leadman or leadlady oversees production procedures, functioning as a kind of "assistant foreman," but does not have the authority to directly order other workers. Leadpersons retain their position in the union but receive a bonus. The leadperson is regarded as having the most seniority in the department if issues such as bidding on a job, vacation selection, or layoffs arise. Management, of course, feels that they must be able to grant this seniority to the leadman or leadlady since production would be disrupted if an assistant leader who happened to be junior were transferred out of the department whenever fluctuations in output occur. Management's alteration of the rules of seniority, however well-intentioned, clearly creates a potentially explosive situation. In some departments, notably cut and kill, the lead position, in spite of the inherent tensions, has worked well. But in this and other situations, it has fostered divisiveness and hostility among workers.

Square Deal hired its first black women production workers in 1970. White and black workers knew that they were hired in order to comply with the Civil Rights Act. The women were accepted with little incident. One of them, Sally, was assigned to a traditionally women's department, the bacon room. Her white co-workers described her as a "wonderful worker to work with," a "good worker." The three black women, who had the lowest seniority, were the first affected by the 1974 layoffs. They were bumped into other departments and had to do the same work as the men. Sally could not afford a layoff; she had a child to support. She took hard jobs, including pushing carts of sausages weighing up to 2½ tons to the smoke room. The men would occasionally help, but mostly she did the work herself. Eventually, Sally was able to return to the bacon room. She refused an offer of promotion to foreman for the same reason some other blacks have refused the job: there is too much pressure associated with the foremanship, and there is no union protection if the company wants to fire you. Indeed, several black men who had been promoted to foreman in the company's attempts at affirmative action had been laid off and not rehired.

Sally was then offered the job of leadlady in her department. One of the reasons that she was asked was that there was a reassignment of foremen in the plant and the regular bacon-room foreman was now spending much of his time in another department. According to Sally, he left without teaching her how to use a new computer installed in the department. Sally took the books home with her and taught herself how to service the computer. She also learned to break down and assemble the machines, but here her work was always checked and double-checked by the foreman.

In many ways Sally was placed in a no-win situation. For a variety of reasons, the white women with seniority in the department resented her in her new role as their leadlady. According to the white women, the difference in Sally after her promotion was like that of Dr. Jekyll and Mr. Hyde. She became overbearing and bossy. The more serious problem, from the perspective of the older workers, was that she, who had less than five years seniority, remained in the department while older women with many more years of seniority were forced to be loaned out to other departments. Sally and the white workers agree that there was a work slowdown and that some attempts were made to discredit her as supervisor by turning out below-standard work. Sally confronted the resentment of the women workers with little or no effective support from management. During the crucial period when she was learning her new responsibilities and assuming a new role with regard to her co-workers, the department foreman was only infrequently present in the department.

The situation reached a crisis point. Higher levels of management became aware of what was happening and intervened to reestablish the active role of a foreman in the department. Sally lost the protected seniority of the leadlady position and once again became the person with the least seniority in the department. She soon was transferred out to another department where she once again was expected to handle essentially laborer's work. At least for some women workers in the department, the episode with Sally as leadlady has confirmed old convictions that black women are incapable of working in a supervisory capacity and that they can be expected to "take out their anger" on whites if they are put in a position of authority over them.

CONCLUSION

By 1960, Square Deal Packing Company ceased openly discriminating against women and minorities. With the merging of men's and women's seniority lists in 1967, both the union and the company gave the appearance of complying with not just the letter but the spirit of the Civil Rights Act of 1964. There were no gender-specific job designations or promotion ladders. The wages of men and women, blacks and whites with equal seniority were virtually identical. The traditional research methodology for uncovering discrimination would not have found any racial or sexual discrimination. But the in-depth interviews, the workplace observation, and the statistical analysis they inspired show that women, and to a lesser extent blacks, were indeed discriminated against as the firm retrenched.

The frustration and bitterness felt particularly by the women added to the general demoralization that blanketed the factory. The union, in which the women had formerly played a militant and spirited role, was considerably weakened without their enthusiastic support. The women's sense of betrayal goes beyond the factory gates. They believe that it was Washington politicians who prevented the union from saving their jobs.

> Women's lib is for those who have education so they can get the same pay as men, but not for those in factory work. It's for judges who have secretaries to work for them; not for people who have to do heavy work like us.

> Now the men have all our easy jobs and the women have the heavy labor jobs. Equal rights, [expletive]!

It is ironic that law intended to advance women's civil rights was used to eliminate a contractual provision to protect those jobs.

References

Amalgamated Meat Cutters and Butcher Workmen of North America. 1961. "Report on the Packinghouse Industry." Mimeographed.

———. 1971. "Meat Industry Collective Bargaining." Mimeographed.

U.S. Department of Labor. 1961. *Meat Packing*. Industry Manpower Surveys, no. 101. Washington, D.C.: GPO.

6

SUSAN PORTER BENSON
BRISTOL COMMUNITY COLLEGE

Women in Retail Sales Work: The Continuing Dilemma of Service

Retailing today is dramatically different than it was in the years before World War II. Transformed first by the war itself, then by the suburbanization of American life, and during the past twenty years by the introduction of computers, retailing has nonetheless continued to be a major employer of women (Table 1). The conditions and rewards of women's work in stores have deteriorated in the years since 1940, but ironically sales work still includes some of the features that made it attractive to women in the earlier years of this century.

Trends in Management

Certain key characteristics of retailing in the prewar period shaped the nature of women's selling work.[1] Perhaps the most important of these was the determination of most department and specialty stores to avoid self-service. Stores prided themselves on selling service as well as on a range of related services such as free delivery, charge accounts, and lavish public facilities such as lounges and restaurants. The cost of providing these services was enormous and relatively fixed. The store had to be staffed, maintained, heated or cooled, and lighted all year round, during all the hours it was open—whether during the profitable Christmas season or during the dull days of summer. Moreover, it cost

1. The discussion of management trends and worker responses before 1940 is based on my dissertation (Benson, 1983).

TABLE I WOMEN IN RETAILING

	Number	*Percentage of total work force*
Retail trade:		
1960	3,583,000	43.4
1970	5,089,000	46.1
1978	7,002,000	48.3
General mercantile:		
1972	1,495,500	69.6
1978	1,547,700	66.5
Department stores:		
1960	671,700	71.1
1970	1,083,100	69.4
1978	1,253,700	66.3

Source: Numbers from U.S. Bureau of Labor Statistics (1979: 753, 756, 757).

a store very little more to sell or deliver six blouses than it did to sell or deliver one. The profits on a sale involving more than one item could be as many as nine times the profits on a single-item transaction. Stores thus stressed more and larger transactions as the key to higher profits, and they placed the responsibility for these on the salesperson.

Managers were convinced that the appeal of their stores was firmly linked to the services they provided and were therefore reluctant to cut costs by eliminating "free" services and resorting to self-service selling. Instead, they intensified the work of their salespeople by urging them through training programs and various commission systems to engage in "suggestive selling," that is, to suggest additional merchandise to each customer and thus to increase the total of the average sale. In effect, the managers of these stores tried to train their employees to be *more* skilled rather than less skilled, to be more adept at sizing up and interacting with customers, to exercise more initiative, to be more knowledgeable about their merchandise. While workers in other industries were finding less opportunity to exercise skill on the job, saleswomen in department and specialty stores were encouraged to develop and expand their skills in the service of their employers' profits.

Like all managers, saleswomen's bosses used both the carrot and the stick to increase productivity. They were, however, much more directly dependent on their employees' good will than most managers and had thus to wield the stick more delicately. It mattered relatively little if a worker on a foot-press was in a good mood, but if a saleswoman was grouchy because of bad working conditions or angry because a supervisor bawled her out, she could ruin sales and drive away customers. To court their salespeople's good will, managers in many ways made stores more pleasant places to work than factories, providing comfortable employee facilities and such fringe benefits as discounts on store merchandise, paid vacations, and free health care. While such arrangements were unquestionably paternalistic and often condescending, they could make a woman's working life more pleasant on a day-to-day basis and sometimes had a real financial value as well.

The one carrot that managers were unwilling to use was money: saleswomen's earnings before World War II were almost always below those of women office workers and frequently below those of women in certain manufacturing industries, particularly the needle trades. Moreover, commission systems in stores worked in precisely the same way as piecework plans in factories: they were designed to increase productivity without a commensurate increase in pay, and managers invariably cut commission rates when saleswomen were earning "too much." Still and all, selling offered at least reasonably clean and steady work as well as the opportunity for variety and initiative.

While saleswomen in department and specialty stores thus enjoyed some advantages, those in five-and-dime or variety stores did not. They were paid at rock-bottom rates, received no benefits, and were expected only to keep their stock in order, to make change, and to wrap packages. Young, teenage women tended dime-store counters, seldom for very long, whereas selling in department and specialty stores attracted women of all ages and held them for a longer period. In all sectors of retailing, however, the Depression of the 1930s brought a change with grim implications for the future: the growth of part-time work. Frustrated at their inability to control the pace of salespeople's work because of seasonal, weekly, daily, and even hourly fluctuations in the volume of customers, managers introduced a variety of part-time schedules to save labor costs during slow periods. They particularly tried to recruit schoolgirls and college students as well as married women with children—groups which would form the backbone of the retail work force in the postwar period.

In the most general sense, this department store world has passed from the scene. Beginning with World War II, when personnel and merchandise shortages led to new selling arrangements, self-service schemes—those in which the customer has direct access to merchandise—proliferated. Virtually every department store in the country has implemented some form of self-service, sometimes eliminating human salesmanship by leaving customers to wander unassisted among open displays, sometimes using saleswomen as adjuncts to the displays.

When managers finally turned to self-service, they found many advantages in it. First, it led to a lowering of costs, as customers began to do work that had formerly been done by saleswomen. Second, in addition to balance-sheet advantages, self-service also lessened managers' social dependence on saleswomen. As one New England store manager recently confessed, "I spend half my waking hours trying to figure out ways to become less dependent on labor" (Bluestone et al., 1979: 164). Third, because the industry as a whole underwent a major postwar transformation, it was relatively easy to implement new operating practices in new settings. As a result of suburban growth, downtown stores declined while branches proliferated and even eclipsed their parent stores. In the mid-1970s Hochschild Kohn and Company closed its downtown Baltimore store and became a purely suburban operation; J. L. Hudson's of Detroit followed suit in closing its downtown store in early 1983 (Barmash, 1978; Cummings, 1982). Jordan Marsh, which halved the size of its Boston store in 1977, acknowledges that its Warwick (Rhode Island) Mall branch is now the company's "flagship" (Morgan, 1982). The new suburban stores were generally smaller, less grand, and less service oriented than the older palace of consumption. They dramatically intensified the trend toward part-time work, using housewives during the day and students in the evenings and on weekends. Fourth, self-service helped department stores to respond to competition from discount merchandisers during the 1950s, 1960s, and 1970s. Discounters' no-frills approach aimed to eliminate selling jobs entirely, relying on a supermarket-style checkout system. In response, department stores trimmed staffs and services even further.

Despite their conversion in practice to self-service, managers continued to write fervent tributes to skilled selling and service in the industry journals; typical was the trade association report which maintained bluntly in 1962 that "there is no substitute for good salespeople" (Store Management Group, 1962). Yet few followed in the footsteps of carriage-trade stores such as Saks Fifth Avenue and Bonwit Teller, which maintained their air of luxury and their tradition of service. By the middle 1960s most managers would probably have admitted in their franker moments that the model for the future was the self-service discount store with its salespeople reduced to mere stock handlers and cash register operators.

Within the last decade or so, however, the picture has again become more complicated. The revival and gentrification of central cities has sparked something of a revival of downtown retailing with an emphasis on elegance, high style, and service. Even Macy's, long known for serviceable merchandise at competitive prices, has redecorated its Herald Square store and added touches of style and luxury in an effort to vie with the likes of Bloomingdale's (Kornbluth, 1979). At first, it appeared that these central-city stores would rely primarily on dramatic display and decoration techniques—known in the trade as theatrical selling—to sell merchandise, but in recent years managers have begun to talk more like their predecessors in the years before 1940 (Ettore, 1979). They complain today about high employee turnover, lackluster selling efforts, salespeople's ignorance about their merchandise, and the enormous costs of doing business in today's economy. Moreover, they face a problem peculiar to the post–World War II period: the standardization of merchandise. Increasingly, they are reviving an early-twentieth-century solution to these problems: training employees in skilled selling. As one manager described the situation, "Since all stores carry the same goods today, the only difference is how well you help the customer" ("Retailers Discover," 1980). Today's manager is learning anew the important lesson that millions of dollars spent on elegant stores, displays, and advertising avail little unless they are backed up by an effective sales force. The message from customers also echoes that from decades past; a recent survey of the attitudes of women shoppers concluded that "efforts to attempt to change the 'salesclerk' to a 'professional salesperson' will be rewarded" (Burnett, Amason, and Hunt, 1981). The message is not entirely a welcome one, for it puts managers back in the uncomfortable position of depending upon the good will of the sales force. The switch to self-service was in some ways a retreat from defeat, as managers despaired of training saleswomen to be simultaneously creative and obedient.

A relatively recent development—the advent of the computer in retailing—is a counterweight to managers' renewed appreciation of skilled selling. Point-of-sale terminals, the beeping replacements for cash registers, enable managers to maintain closer control of staffing on a day-to-day and even an hour-to-hour basis, providing information that allows them to shift personnel to respond to fluctuations in customer volume. In addition they provide detailed and immediate information about what is selling, freeing managers from their dependence upon salespeople's shop-floor knowledge of customers' wishes and preference (Edgerly, 1979; C. H. Harrington, 1977; Morgan, 1982). Still, the computer can give only a partial picture of what happens on the selling floor; it cannot tell managers what a customer asked for but could not find, nor how saleswomen cajoled customers into buying more than they had intended. The most advanced computer system can only deal with quantitative measures and cannot compete with salespeople's qualitative judgment as the eyes and ears of managers.

Women Workers' Perspective

By standard measures, retail selling is not an attractive job. Full-time workers in retail trade earn less than three-quarters of the average wage for full-time workers in all industries. The low wage reflects in part managers' persistent unwillingness to pay for the selling skill they want their employees to display, as well as their tendency to hire those who command relatively low wages. Women are concentrated in the low-paying selling jobs in the industry and as a result earn, working full time, less than six-tenths as much as full-time male workers in retail trade. A large and growing proportion of workers in the industry is young (Table 2): in 1968 just over one-quarter were under twenty-five, but by 1978 four out of ten were (Job, 1980). Retailers have, however, been relatively reluctant to exploit black workers; traditionally the industry has bowed to racism in its effort to avoid offending white customers who control a disproportionate share of the nation's disposable income. Black women have made some inroads in retail selling

TABLE 2 AGE DISTRIBUTION OF SALESWOMEN, 1974

Age	*Salesworkers as a percentage of women workers in each age group*
16–19	11.4
20–24	5.6
25–54	5.8
25–34	4.6
35–44	6.1
45–54	6.9
55+	8.8
55–64	8.3
65+	10.7
66+	6.8

Source: *Monthly Labor Review* (1975: 6, 14, 24).

(between 1972 and 1980, for example, the proportion of black female salesclerks rose from 4.1 percent to 5.0 percent, while the proportion of black women in the female labor force declined slightly), but black women's representation among saleswomen is only half that of their participation in the labor force (Westcott, 1982).

Even more ominous than the grim outlook for full-time women workers in retail trade is the increase in part-time work in the industry (Table 3). The proportion of people working less than a thirty-five hour week in retailing increased from 29 percent to 35 percent between 1968 and 1978 (Job, 1980). In 1977, 40 percent of all female salesworkers were part-timers. Part-time workers of course earned notably less overall than their full-time counterparts, but they were also paid at a lower hourly rate.

Still, retailing[2] remains in some ways an attractive field for working women. Part-time work opportunities are important to many women, as are the relatively attractive and nonhazardous work surroundings. In some ways, the department store is a familiar and nonthreatening work environment; every woman was a customer before she became a saleswoman. Paid vacations are still more common in retailing than in factory work, and the prospect of a long summer layoff can be attractive to women with school-age children. But most often in interviews women mention the contact with the public, the greater variety and autonomy of sales work as compared to most factory or office work, and the opportunity to feel satisfied with one's work as the most positive features of their work.

2. Because my research has focused on women in department and specialty stores, I concentrate in this section on women in that sector of retailing.

TABLE 3 WOMEN'S PART-TIME WORK IN RETAILING, 1977

	Salesworkers	*Retail trade*
Number of part-time women	837,000	1,674,000
Percentage of all part-time women workers	11.8	29.7
Percentage of all women workers in category	40	32

Source: *Monthly Labor Review* (1978b: 6).

On the negative side, in addition to low pay and the difficulty of finding full-time permanent work, are the evening and weekend hours. Moreover, the joy of a saleswoman's life under some conditions can be its curse under others: while contact with the public can be a source of satisfaction and variety, it can also be oppressive when bad working conditions and customers' ill humor strain the nerves of the most patient. As saleswomen at Filene's put it earlier in the century, the customer was "our friend the enemy," and in all events the saleswoman has been vulnerable to being caught in the middle between her boss's demands and her customer's demands.

Women have dealt with the difficulties of work in retailing in a number of ways. The quietest, but perhaps the most common, has been simply to quit. Turnover, both historically and currently, has been high in the selling field and is presently estimated at 60 percent annually. In 1978, women in retailing had spent only about three-fifths as long with their current employers as had all women in the labor force (Job, 1980). High turnover throughout the industry has made it comparatively easy until very recently to move from job to job, and for many women work in retailing has been linked to the life cycle: a good way to work one's way through school or college, or a readily available part-time job during the child-rearing years. As more and more women have sought permanent full-time jobs even when they have young children, retailing has become a stopgap on the way to more lucrative employment.

While sex segregation works in retailing much the same as it does in other industries, locking women into low-paying dead-end jobs, it ironically forms the basis for a thriving work culture as well. There is ample evidence that, throughout the twentieth century, saleswomen have formed supportive work groups that framed and enforced a view of good selling and of a good day's work that was different from management's view. Emphasizing solidarity rather than competition among workers, these groups have, on the whole, countered management's efforts to raise productivity and have limited the work load to a generally accepted level. Women in numerous other occupations have developed a similar work culture, but the opportunities for on-the-job interaction among workers are greater in retailing than in most industries, and women's work groups in retailing have been particularly persistent under a wide variety of conditions (Howe, 1977). Although it cannot provide the protection of a union, saleswomen's work culture can on a day-to-day basis do a great deal to insulate the worker from the demands of customers and supervisors, while providing the warmth and support of a small group.

Women in retailing have sought to form unions since the early twentieth century. In the years before World War I, an independent department store workers' union, aided by the Women's Trade Union League, was active in New York City. Women were the driving force behind the widespread retail sit-down strikes of March 1937 and the organizing drive that followed. In the years after World War II, retailing unions were torn apart by internal strife and by red-baiting, and organizing efforts have been minimal since (M. Harrington, 1962; Kirstein, 1950). Although women are a high proportion of the members of the two major retail unions, and despite the fact that the Retail Clerks ranked second among unions in the number of women members in 1972, overall fewer than one in twenty women in retail trade are in unions (Table 4).

In addition to the low level of unions' organizing initiative, there are several other reasons for the reluctance of women in retailing to join unions. One is the so-called white-collar factor, or the tendency for white-collar workers to shun unions, but the desperately low wages of women in retailing go far to undermine whatever sense of privilege they might feel in this quarter. A second is the high turnover in the industry, unquestionably a major impediment to organizing. Nonetheless, there is good evidence that long-term female workers, both full time and part time, particularly older married women, have been strong union supporters. Third, retail unions have shared the tendency of all unions in the United States to be male dominated and to be relatively uninterested in pursuing issues of interest to women. For example, retail contracts customarily have provided a sex-based wage differential either directly or by stipulating wage differentials between departments staffed by men and by women. Moreover, they have placed long-term part-time workers (who are almost exclusively women) at a great disadvantage.

In some ways, however, the time is ripe for organizing women in retailing. In interviews with saleswomen, I have found many sources of dissatisfaction as well as signs of growing willingness to translate the solidarity of the work group into unionization. One major source of discontent is management changes. The recent merger movement has affected many retail stores, bringing changes in traditional management practices, layoffs, and shutdowns. Yet another is computerization. Point-of-sale terminals are frequently slow in operation and prone to breakdowns or errors, and the data they generate are often used to justify cuts in personnel and demands for increased productivity. A third factor builds upon the first two: many women have expressed their resentment of the fact that they are no longer able to serve their customers as well as they once were. They begrudge the loss of satisfaction in

TABLE 4 WOMEN IN RETAILING UNIONS

	Retail clerks	*Retail, Wholesale, and Department Store Union*	*All unions*
1956:			
Number of women	150,000	58,800	
Percentage of women	50	50	18.6
1966:			
Number of women	250,200	NA	
Percentage of women	50	NA	19.3
1970:			
Number of women	NA	70,000	
Percentage of women	NA	40	20.7
1976:			
Number of women	335,600	80,000	
Percentage of women	48	40	22.0

Source: *Monthly Labor Review* (1978a: 12).
Note: Since 1947, the average weekly earnings of nonsupervisory employees in retail trade have been lower than those of production and nonsupervisory workers in any other industry classification (U.S. Bureau of Labor Statistics, 1975: 254; 1977: 191).

a good job well done and also the loss of autonomy that the new practices have enforced. For many saleswomen, the visions of selling skill and of serving the customer well never waned. They almost invariably comment that they feel that management is standing between them and their customers, making it impossible to deliver good service because of store rules or merchandising policies. These comments echo those of teachers who say that school administrators are undermining the quality of education, or of nurses who maintain that hospital administrators and physicians limit their ability to give first-rate patient care. A woman retiring from a carriage-trade store after thirty years of selling comments that management is trying to turn the store into a copy of the city's largest popular-price emporium. Still, until the day she left the store, she maintained a large file of special customers to whom she gave personalized service, even though she was one of but four saleswomen on a floor where there had once been twenty-three (Interview with S. M., 1980). Another woman, after selling for nineteen years, transferred to a clerical position because a combination of management policies and personal circumstances prevented her from giving her customers the kind of high-quality service she demanded of herself and her store (Interview with C. E., 1981). Finally, as more and more women find that full-time paid work is necessary to their family's economic well-being, the low wages and part-time jobs of retailing have bred a new militancy and feminism among women in the labor force.

References

Barmash, Isadore. 1978. "Associated Dry Goods Shifting Its Retail Appeal." *New York Times*, December 22. D1.

Benson, Susan Porter. 1983. "'A Great Theater': Saleswomen, Managers, and Customers in American Department Stores." Ph.D. diss., Boston University.

Bluestone, Barry, Patricia Hanna, Sarah Kuhn, and Laura Moore. 1979. *The Department Store Industry in New England: An Analysis of Market Transformation, Investment, and Labor*. Harvard-MIT Joint Center for Urban Studies.

Burnett, John J., Robert D. Amason, and Shelby D. Hunt. 1981. "Feminism: Implications for Department Store Strategy and Salesclerk Behavior." *Journal of Retailing* 57: 82.

Cummings, Judith. 1982. "Once-Proud Store Has Its Last Christmas." *New York Times*, December 31, A7.

Edgerly, Leonard S. 1979. "Retailers Check Out Computers as Tools to Build Business." *Providence Sunday Journal*, July 8, F1.

Ettore, Barbara. 1979. "Stores Try Theatrical Selling Techniques." *New York Times*, January 23, D1.

Harrington, Clyde H. 1977. "Outlet Co. Installing $3 Million Computer System in Its Stores." *Providence Sunday Journal*, November 6, F1.

Harrington, Michael. 1962. *The Retail Clerks*. New York: Wiley.

Howe, Louise Kapp. 1977. *Pink Collar Workers: Inside the World of Women's Work*. New York: Putnam's.

Interview with C. E. 1981. November 7.

Interview with S. M. 1980. January 12.

Job, Barbara Cottman. 1980. "Employment and Pay Trends in the Retail Trade Industry." *Monthly Labor Review* 103: 40–43.

Kirstein, George G. 1950. *Stores and Unions: A Study of the Growth of Unionism in Dry Goods and Department Stores*. New York: Fairchild.

Kornbluth, Jesse. 1979. "The Department Store as Theater." *New York Times Magazine*, April 29.

Monthly Labor Review. 1975. Vol. 98, no. 11.

———. 1978a. Vol. 101, no. 8.

———. 1978b. Vol. 101, no. 11.

Morgan, Gwynne. 1982. "Jordan Marsh 'Steps Up' Quality, Prices." *Providence Sunday Journal*, September 12, F1.

"Retailers Discover an Old Tool: Sales Training." 1980. *Business Week*, December 22, 51–52.

Store Management Group. 1962. *Speeding Selling Service*. New York: National Retail Merchants Association.

U.S. Bureau of Labor Statistics. 1975. *Handbook of Labor Statistics 1975*. Reference ed. Bulletin 1865. Washington, D.C.: GPO.

———. 1977. *Handbook of Labor Statistics 1977*. Bulletin 1966. Washington, D.C.: GPO.

———. 1979. *Employment and Earnings, United States, 1909–1978*. Bulletin 1312-11. Washington, D.C.: GPO.

Westcott, Diane Nilsen. 1982. "Blacks in the 1970's: Did They Scale the Job Ladder?" *Monthly Labor Review* 105, no. 6: 29–38.

Bibliography

Barmash, Isadore. 1983. "Selling—Retailing's Lost Art." *New York Times*, March 15, D1, D4.

Benson, Susan Porter. 1978. "'The Clerking Sisterhood': Rationalization and the Work Culture of Saleswomen." *Radical America* 12: 41–55.

———. 1981. "'The Cinderella of Occupations': Managing the Work of Department Store Saleswomen." *Business History Review* 55: 1–25.

Clark, William E. 1962. *What Part-Timers Think about Their Job.* National Retail Merchants Association, Retail Research Institute.

McNair, Malcolm, and Eleanor G. May. 1978. "The Next Revolution in the Retailing Wheel." *Harvard Business Review* 56: 81–91.

"Minorities and Women in the Retail Industry." 1974. *Economic Priorities Report* 5.

"Retailing: The Next Ten Years." 1977. Special issue of *Journal of Retailing* 53.

Stores, The National Retail Merchants Association Magazine. 1948–present.

U.S. Bureau of Labor Statistics. 1968. *Employee Earnings and Hours in General Merchandise Stores, June 1966.* Bulletin 1584-2.

———. 1978. *Industry Wage Survey, Department Stores, May 1977.* Bulletin 2006.

U.S. Domestic and International Business Administration. 1975. *Department Store Retailing in an Era of Change.*

7

ANNE MACHUNG
UNIVERSITY OF CALIFORNIA, BERKELEY

Word Processing: Forward for Business, Backward for Women

"The era of focusing on automating the secretary and clerical labor force is drawing to a close," David Liddle, office vice-president at Xerox recently announced, "and the emphasis now is on automating white-collar workers" ("Invasion," 1981). That is not how word processing companies see it, and it certainly is not how secretaries, bookkeepers, and bank tellers are experiencing it. In fact, the automation of the secretary, the typist, and the bookkeeper, which began in the 1970s, is growing apace. Almost every large corporation in the country now has installed its own word processing center or is looking into it. Word processors are popping up in small offices and private homes everywhere. Word processing, in fact, is big business. Worth only about $780 million in 1978, predictions are the word processing market will generate $5 billion in revenue by 1984, a growth rate of over 500 percent in five years (Morner, 1979: 76; Schatz, 1982: 69).

But word processing constitutes only a fraction, though a sizeable fraction, of the whole office automation market, a market that spawns such prosaic products as electronic copiers and electronic filing cabinets, as well as more exotic items, such as local area networks (LANs)

Research for this essay was supported by a Lena Lake Forrest Dissertation Fellowship from the Business and Professional Women's Foundation. I would like to express my deep gratitude to the foundation for its generous financial and moral support. The data and interpretations represent, of course, my own views and not necessarily those of the foundation.

and Ethernets which link it all together. Moreover, while word processing is big, office automation is so much bigger. With hardware costs dropping and sales increasing 40 to 45 percent annually, that market could exceed three hundred billion dollars through 1987,[1] a rate *Time* claims "dwarfs almost every other sector of U.S. business" ("Fighting," 1981: 66).

Word processing, however, is not quite the same as real office automation. Zisman (1978), in fact, distinguishes between word processing (or "mere mechanization") and "true automation." With mechanization, hand labor is replaced by machine labor, but with automation, mental processes are displaced and machines themselves exercise discretion. In the truly automated office of the future, the "paperless office" as it is often called, the computer not only will control office activities but will exercise judgment by performing tasks according to a preprogrammed logic. So, while it is often claimed that word processing is paving the way toward the truly automated office, with word processing we are still only halfway there.

All this is very exciting for business, equipment vendors, and systems analysts alike, but its consequences for clerical and managerial workers alike are somewhat less exciting. Computerization is visibly reshaping office work in America today, but how is not really known.

Historically, office work has been labor intensive. Indeed, the technology involved in the office changed little between the invention of the typewriter in 1883 and the development of microchip technology in the 1970s. A few simple machines were added, some for adding, some for xeroxing, some for affixing postage; but the typewriter, in the main, remained the backbone of office technology. The office, as a consequence, it is often said, is a remnant of the nineteenth century.

But the development of microchip technology in the 1970s and the emergence of computerized typewriters (or word processors, as they are usually called) promises to change all this, to bring the office into the twentieth century. In their simplest form, word processors are electronic typewriters that can store texts, display whole paragraphs on television screens, play back pages at high speeds, and print out multiple versions almost instantaneously. Moreover, by permitting small editorial changes—commas added, sentences deleted, paragraphs shifted around—to be made without retyping the entire document anew, word processing vastly speeds up the typing function. All this technology is fascinating to those weaned on the old-fashioned typewriter, where each new revision required the slow and tedious job of retyping the entire letter or document.

1. Estimates for the total size of the office automation market vary, but most range between two hundred and three hundred billion dollars by the end of the 1980s. Whatever their magnitude, the purpose of these estimates is all the same: to generate more excitement for the coming of the "information revolution." The three hundred billion dollar figure reported here comes from Frost and Sullivan, Inc., a New York market research firm (see Thoryn, 1980: 58).

The Technical-Managerial Mentality

By eliminating tedious retyping, word processing is also eliminating the tedium from many jobs, many believe. Indeed, showcase companies, such as Ball Corporation, a diversified manufacturer of food and beverages, claim to have eliminated many tedious jobs altogether. With word processing they needed only 82 secretaries/clerk-typists in 1980; but without word processing they would have needed 126—a "savings," that corporation estimates, of 44 employees. At the same time, productivity rose 643 percent; while a secretary averaged 143 pages a month in 1974, a word processing operator in 1980 averaged 1,062 pages a month. This, the company furthermore claims, is saving them $475,000 in labor costs each year (Jones, 1981).

Other trade journals are likewise filled with such success stories. Each month, for example, *Modern Office Procedures* carries a story showing how word processing pays off, increasing productivity while reducing labor costs. In 1975, before word processing, for example, the 108 secretaries at Michigan Gas and Electric served 310 principals and produced 8.3 million lines of type. Three years later 215 secretaries there served 821 principals and typed 25.9 million lines. Word processing made the difference. "To date," *Modern Office Procedures* concludes, "the word processing operation has obviated hiring some 70 secretaries at a total cost of $27,000 each, which incorporates the cost of salaries, fringes, furniture, and equipment, saving Michigan Consolidated a cost-avoidance figure of about $1.6 million" ("1979 Word Processing," 1979: 76). Exactly what it cost that company to install and maintain expensive computer equipment, redesign offices, and hire computer programmers and systems analysts to oversee the whole automation process is not reported.

Promoted by a vast media blitz, the business rationale for automating the office is clear: to increase white-collar productivity and lower white-collar labor costs. Numbering nearly fifty million workers in 1980 and proliferating faster than any other segment of the labor force, business sees the growth of the information sector contributing significantly to an overhead cost squeeze in the nation's offices ("America's Offices," 1981; "Information Processing," 1979). But by investing huge sums of money in automated equipment, business hopes to curtail this growth. Underlying this are huge advertising and sales campaigns by computer manufacturers to sell their products; the aim of these campaigns is equipping offices everywhere with desk-top terminals, first supplanting clericals, next "supplementing" managers.

Profit, of course, is the motive. By increasing the productivity of each office worker (clerk and manager alike), business hopes to restrict the size of the white-collar labor force and control aggregate wages. To managers, go personal computers; to secretaries, word processors. Word processors therefore constitute but one of the many kinds of computers designed to meet emerging business needs, but also one of the earliest. Word processing is thus helping transform the office from a labor-intensive to a capital-intensive venture.

What business journals do not make clear is that automated technology at the clerical level is also, in part, a response to management fears that clericals are about to unionize. While only about 19 percent of the clerical labor force is currently unionized (Gifford, 1982: 50), those who are earn about 30 percent more than their nonunion counterparts (Working Women, 1982: 4). Unionization would threaten the very low wage labor base that has long characterized clerical work and would set up countervailing organizations within business that oppose managerial interests. By automating the office before unionization occurs, management hopes both to restrict the number of clericals who might, in the future, have access to substantially higher wages, and to curtail any future limits unions might place on their right to automate as fully as they wish.

Word Processing and the De-skilling of Clerical Work

Word processing as such also needs to be distinguished from continuous-process technologies. In some cases, automation in the office is proceeding by reassembling the components of different jobs into one. One worker is put in control of a computer which has recombined into a single task a number of different and highly routinized procedures that used to be performed by different people. This is apparently how Citibank in New York City, another showcase company, automated its letter-of-credit department, transforming clericals into "front line professionals" (Matteis, 1979).[2]

But most of the automation now going on in the office does not, however, involve the reintegration of broken-down, de-skilled jobs into a single, more coherent entity. Just the opposite. Word processing technologies, through which most office automation has been introduced, differ from the automation of wholesale procedures in that they enable a relative uncomplicated task, that of typing a letter or manuscript, to be broken down into yet smaller components. In word processing centers, for example, the different components of typing a letter are divided up and assigned to different people: a supervisor to schedule and allocate the work; a word processing technician to key the material into the central memory; a printing operator to monitor the output process;

2. Matteis (1979) also reports that by automating the letter-of-credit operation, managers at Citibank reduced the size of that department from 142 to 100 people. Nobody lost her job, but no new jobs were created either. While such figures reassure management about their ability to gain control over labor costs, they frighten clericals with the threat of massive unemployment. What happens to those who leave by "normal attrition," when one-third of the labor force is leaving by attrition? To talk, then, about how automation benefits some clericals is to conceal what it costs many others. Jobs loss—and anxiety about job loss—is one such cost, but certainly not the only one.

a proofreader to catch mistakes; and a clerk typist to pick up and deliver the work. In this sense, word processing closely resembles classical de-skilling: a whole craft is broken down into ever smaller components, mental work is separated from manual work, and bit pieces of the remaining jobs are parceled out to "detail workers" (Braverman, 1974). Because of this, word processing centers in large organizations clearly resemble assembly lines in the factory.

Restructuring Sociability

From the vendors' point of view, the major problem involved in introducing word processing and fully automating the office is not raising the level of technology but gaining acceptance of that technology from managers and clericals alike. Achieving the high productivity gains promised by equipment vendors requires, it is often said, restructuring the office, transforming the traditional secretarial-managerial relationship, and eliminating the "inefficiencies" of human relationships, interpersonal contact, and irrelevant conversation. Indeed, the equipment is often sold as a way to "end the social office," as if sociability among office workers impairs productivity.

The classic (and now discounted) grand IBM plan of the early 1970s for introducing word processing, for example, called for dividing the job of a secretary into two separate portions: typing and administrative support. All typewriters were to be banned from the secretary's desk, and all typing was to be consolidated into a single word processing center. Secretaries then became administrative assistants, typists became word processing technicians, and bosses became principals. It was anticipated that this would dramatically reduce the number of secretaries needed; some would leave by normal attrition, others "voluntarily" would enter the word processing center, and those left would double up on the number of bosses they worked for.

While some organizations still follow this plan, many have abandoned it, mainly because of the adverse effects it had on personal relationships between secretaries and bosses. The plan has not worked well, but reasons for its failure are obvious only in retrospect. Having worked their way up the corporate hierarchy, managers have resented losing the convenience and status associated with a personal secretary. Accustomed to having her there, many have complained their typing is not done as well in an impersonal center—that turnaround time is slow, that important versus unimportant matters are not distinguished from each other, that personal idiosyncracies are not understood or appreciated.

Secretaries, on the other hand, have disliked losing some of the protectiveness that secretarial–managerial relationships offered as well as the chance to "advance" up the corporate ladder with their bosses. They have missed their typewriters, so it is said, along with the flexibility that a one-on-one secretarial–managerial relationship provides.

So, at least, goes the business explanation for their resistance. The real story is somewhat different; and this, untold, lies with word processing operators. The following observations, collected by interviewing word processing operators working in centralized word processing centers in the banking and insurance industries of San Francisco between 1978 and 1980 (Machung, 1983), indicate a quite different situation.

Working face to face with a TV screen all day long, operators, especially those in large centers, have few social contacts except with each other. Unlike secretaries, who are highly visible at front desks, word processing operators are virtually invisible. Isolated from the rest of the corporation by their dress (frequently more casual), their age (frequently younger), and their race (frequently minority), they work anonymously under fluorescent lighting in crowded back offices and windowless rooms. A supervisor usually handles all contact with users of the center; operators often never see the person whose paper or letter they have typed. Bosses are known only by their names, not by their faces, and sometimes operators are even assigned arbitrary initials to prevent favoritism from developing between bosses and operators. Unlike secretaries, who are known by their first names and friendly manners, word processing operators are virtually unknown. Many have taken these jobs to escape the stigmatization and subordination of secretarial work, only to find themselves even more faceless and nameless. Gaining autonomy has cost them sociability; some miss it, some do not.

Though first introduced in this centralized fashion, more recently word processing terminals have been installed at the individual secretary's desk rather than in one central location. Decentralized word processing is beyond the scope of this essay. Vendors claim, however, that decentralization eliminates many of the problems associated with centralized word processing centers. How true this is remains to be seen. While decentralization may reduce depersonalization, the woman–machine relationship still seems to remain paramount, as secretary–boss relationships increasingly come to be mediated through contact with computer terminals.

Word processing introduced in such a way indeed destroys much of the social fabric that formerly wove the office together, undermining bases of loyalty and interaction between clerical and managerial staff, dividing their social worlds from each other, and further segmenting these relationships, all in the name of increasing productivity.

Restructuring Productivity

In word processing jobs, the semblance of craft in the classic sense of that term is returned to clerical work. All documents produced in the center come out looking beautiful, and operators, initially at least, feel quite pleased with their work. But there the resemblance to craft ends. In fact, it takes fewer skills than ever before to produce a beautiful-looking document; skills formerly belonging to secretaries are now built into word processing machines. Editing facilities, for example, make typos so easy to correct that both typing speed and accuracy atrophy over time; dictionary-checking facilities eliminate the need to spell well.

Moreover, to speed up production (which is the main justification for using word processing equipment) all work, especially that produced in large centers, is standardized. Formats are determined in advance and precoded onto the machine; margins are automatically set at a certain width; and signature lines are placed just so. There is little variety in the task at hand, and few decisions to make, except which keys to press, which codes to call up. Discretion is eliminated from the job, and so are surprises. Interruptions in the routine are experienced as aggravating and disruptive, rather than as challenges to master new skills and techniques. People become problems that operators escape by facing the machine, and bosses become "users" or even "dictators."

The job also takes little time to learn. Most word processors fully master their machine within three months; most tire of it within six months—then go looking for another job and another machine to learn. Operators describe themselves as having learned a new skill yet respond toward their jobs like only the most unskilled and unattached workers. Interest in the job quickly peaks, then declines; and as interest declines, errors go up and productivity goes down. Supervisors face the dilemma of either encouraging top management to invest in new, more sophisticated equipment in order to retain the interest of their staff, or encouraging worn out operators to leave. Most often, however, it is not even necessary to encourage operators to leave; they have already quit, voluntarily, long ago.

But this is commentary not on women and their motivation for working but on the nature of their jobs. Word processing equipment is deliberately designed for simplicity of use and for speed of production, not to enhance the dexterity, skill, or self-esteem of the craftsman. Operators are seen as easily trained, replaceable, and interchangeable, not as highly trained, especially competent, or invaluable workers.

That this is so is made clear not only in interviews with word processing operators but also in reports of leading equipment manufacturers. Recently Thomas Kavanagh, president of NBI, quipped that his corporation manufactures word processors so easy to learn that "users can take someone off the street with typing skills and put them into word processing" ("How not to Exploit," 1980: 92). WANG laboratories also design their terminals with such "human engineering" in mind. That it now takes someone with minimal typing skills only a day or so to learn how to use a word processor attests to its increasing simplicity. Manufacturers are here speaking with forked tongue: simplifying their equipment so thoroughly that it takes almost no time to learn and selling it to large corporations on that basis, but encouraging women to leave secretarial jobs and enter word processing on the expectation of upgrading their skills and career opportunities. Large corporations are buying, not only the equipment, but the line as well.

PRODUCTIVITY COUNTS, QUOTAS, AND CONTROLS

Word processing operators also work under constant surveillance, but the surveillance comes not so much from their supervisor as from their terminal. "An additional advantage of word processing systems," explains Donald Vadnais of 3M Corporation, is that "business can finally monitor and measure the productivity of clerical function" (Thoryn, 1979: 74). This basically means that word processing operators work under heightened production pressures; each line, page, and document they type is counted and tallied, along with each error, day by day, month by month. Almost all centers maintain such counts, ostensibly to justify the cost of the equipment. Sometimes these measurements are expressed in number of pages typed per day per operator, sometimes in number of clericals needed to support the managerial staff (the "secretary–principal" ratio). But the purpose of such measurement is control: mechanized, depersonalized, industrialized.

Operators, though, are told such counts are kept solely to justify the cost of the equipment: is it producing as much as was promised? Driscoll (1980), however, reviewed office automation investments and found that not one of forty large office automation users had ever gone back to evaluate the economic benefits of using automated office equipment once it had been installed. Cost justification, that is, occurs only before installation, never after; productivity counts and quotas, it seems, are kept only to speed up the work.

Needless to say, word processing operators know they are working under intense speedups disguised as production quotas; keeping their jobs means keeping up with these quotas; getting a raise means exceeding them. Thus the job is extremely pressured, perhaps the most highly stressed job in the country today. The National Institute of Occupational Health and Safety recently found stress among some clerical VDT operators to be greater than that ever reported before for a single occupational group, including air traffic controllers. Of the VDT operators at Blue Shield in San Francisco, 80–90 percent experienced eyestrain or muscle strain; anxiety, depression, and fatigue were also common (National Institute for Occupational Safety and Health, 1981; see also Smith, 1981; Working Women, 1981). Social skills are also eliminated ("It doesn't take much to talk to a machine"), and machine skills (the willingness to withstand boring, repetitious, and routine work for long periods of time) are highlighted. Such constitutes the freedom of the new clerical worker.

Turnover is accordingly quite high (running as much as 100 percent a year in many centers) as operators change jobs looking for variety, slightly higher pay, and a little less pressure. Nobody expects to receive a pension—the thought is ludicrous—and many operators contemplate working for temporary agencies where job security is even lower but pay slightly higher. Word processing has indeed become the vanguard of the six-month worker; rare is the operator who has stayed at the same job for more than a year or two. Such high turnover, of course, is saving business even more money that might otherwise be expended in raises, job benefits, profit-sharing plans, or pensions.

It is difficult to understand vendors' claims, widely repeated as verities throughout the business and trade journal literature, that automation is creating "stimulating careers" and "eliminating the drudgery" normally found in offices (Eddinger, 1980; "Office 'Miracles'," 1978; Wohl, 1981; for example). At issue is whose career is being stimulated and from whose job drudgery is eliminated. Under office automation, some jobs are indeed gaining in autonomy and creativity, but many are losing. For managers, those who design, manufacture, sell, and administer the new technology, automation does mean more control over labor costs, faster and more complete information, and higher levels of expertise, responsibility, and salary. But for clericals, automation means something completely different: more routinized jobs, more standardized work, greater pressure, and less sociability. And most clericals are women.

Sexual Stratification and Technological Transformation

The effect of automation and computerized technology upon the labor force, that is, is sharply stratified by gender. True when data processing was first introduced into corporate and government offices in the 1950s, this is even more true today. Comparing, over time, keypunch operators (who do the least skilled and most routine computer jobs for the lowest pay) with systems analysts (who have the most challenging computer jobs and the highest pay) illustrates this point (Table 1). In 1960, for example, 73 percent of all keypunch operators were women, while only 22 percent of all systems analysts were; but in 1980, 95 percent of all keypunch operators were women, and still only 22 percent of all systems analysts were. Despite extensive affirmative action efforts, things hardly changed in data processing—except to grow more stratified.

But what about word processing? Word processing in some sense represents the intersection of repetitious typing with repetitious computer work. At present, it is impossible to say exactly how many word processing operators there are in the country or what proportion are women, since neither the Bureau of Labor Statistics nor the Bureau of the Census classifies word processing operators separately; they are supposedly counted as secretaries, typists, or computer operators.[3]

3. Vendors report that seven to ten million people now work with VDTs and that there will be one word processor for every three clerical workers by 1985 (Working Women, 1982: 11). But these are industry figures, and they vary widely; nobody really knows exactly how many people work at VDTs each day and for how long. The need for this kind of information in order fully to investigate and estimate the effects of VDT work is obvious.

TABLE I GROWTH OF COMPUTER-RELATED JOBS, BY SEX, 1960–1980

	The professional line			
	Computer programmers		Systems analysts	
Year	Number	Percentage female	Number	Percentage female
1960	8,140	26.7	3,280	22.0
1970	161,382	22.5	79,961	14.7
1980	341,000	28.7	201,000	22.4

	The clerical line			
	Keypunch operators		Computer-equipment operators	
Year	Number	Percentage female	Number	Percentage female
1960	161,067	72.9	1,928	65.2
1970	272,921	89.8	117,313	29.2
1980	266,000	95.3	522,000	61.6

Sources: Figures for 1960 and 1970 are taken from the U.S. Bureau of the Census (1973: Table 221). Since 1980 census data are not publicly available at this writing, the closest detailed approximations to census data are from the U.S. Bureau of Labor Statistics (1981: Table 23).

But in 1980, 61 percent of all computer operators were women, 99 percent of all secretaries were women, and 98 percent of all typists were women. If the tendency for women to get slotted into the most routine, repetitious, and least skilled clerical computing jobs continues, more and more word processors will be women.

Right now the seeming neutrality of the new word processing technology conceals this gender divide. Just as the earliest typists were called "typewriters" after the name of their machine, so many word processing operators today are called "word processors" just like the machine they operate. But just as the novelty of typewriting wore off and women rapidly got slotted into these jobs (Davies, 1974), so, I suspect, as the novelty of word processing wears off (and the work is seen for what it actually is), women, especially minority women, will be slotted into these new jobs.

I am not here advocating that more men become word processors and keypunch operators to equalize the invidious and widespread effect of job segregation on the labor force. Rather, the nature of work itself must be changed. Bad jobs are bad jobs, unskilled labor is unskilled labor, whether done by women or by men, by minorities or by whites. But if my observations of San Francisco banks and insurance companies and my analysis of long-standing labor-force trends are accurate, word processing—and its consequences for the destruction of jobs, the health of the worker, and the loss of job satisfaction—are preeminently a woman's issue.

Worker Resistance and Organizational Response

There is no doubt that breaking up traditional working relationships and destroying jobs is provoking deep resistance from executives and secretaries alike, and the word processor industry has long realized it is people who form the biggest barrier to swiftly automating the office. To many, the willingness of office workers to accept such changes in jobs and office organization and to "discipline themselves" to the new system is the major factor determining how quickly word processing catches on ("Office of the Future," 1975: 50). Accordingly, the industry is devoting itself to a two-pronged attack: "educating" top management on the advantages of the new technology and devising ad hoc procedures for undermining resistance from below.

Computerworld, for example, explains resistance to technological change as a normal reaction to change of any kind; adjustment to that change therefore follows a "five phase predictable process": "First is self pity (why me?), then denial (not me!), then anger (I'll get even.), then bargaining (I'll cooperate if you will . . .), finally comes acceptance (what change?)" (Gaffney, 1981). Ironically, each of these stages almost parallels Kübler-Ross's (1969) five stages of death and dying—denial and isolation, anger, bargaining, depression, and finally acceptance—but no mention of Kübler-Ross (or of death and dying) has been made. "Each individual," Gaffney (1981) instead continues, "moves through this process at his own speed and some may get stuck in one phase if not helped to move on." Rather than "helping" clericals to move on, most of the trade journals, though, devote themselves to selling the equipment to top management.

Still there is some concern, however limited, with the jobs of lower level clericals, for resistance from these people (expressed as high turnover rates, high drug abuse, and high absenteeism) can significantly lower productivity. Even a carbonated drink innocuously spilled on a terminal effectively kills it for a day or two. So each month *Modern Office Procedures* describes how one showcase company solved the "people problems" in its word processing center by retraining the staff, redesigning the center, establishing career ladders, and hiring an experienced supervisor. None of these solutions in themselves is fallacious, but none of them really improves the job either.

Take career ladders for example. Establishing career ladders in most centers means little more than creating minute gradations among word processing jobs. Operators enter as "word processing trainees" and move to "word processing technician I" and then "word processing technician II"; but for most, career advancement peaks when they become senior word processing technicians or specialists. While a few operators do aspire to becoming word processing supervisors, this job leads nowhere, pays little more than the operator's job, and is far more cross-pressured; most operators do not want it. Other operators hope to become marketing service representatives for various equipment vendors or computer programmers, but to do so often requires skills, expertise, and college degrees not acquired as a word processing operator. There really is no career advancement possible within the field, and most operators know this.

Hiring an experienced supervisor also means little more than bringing in someone with smooth personal and organizational skills to replace the social contact operators qua secretaries formerly had with bosses. An experienced supervisor is somebody who restores sociability to the center, but in limited amounts; someone who oversees the entire process without directly interfering; someone who praises and compliments her operators for a job well done; and someone who "runs interference" between her operators and the professional and managerial staff. Most often the first-line supervisor is also a woman. But she too, like her operators, is under corporate pressure to produce, and this in itself points to the amount of organizational control that has been gained by installing word processing equipment. Not only is the unstructured secretarial–managerial relationship controlled by reducing the number of secretaries hired and doubling up on the number of bosses served, but the amount of personalism possible in the supervisor–operator relationship is restricted and bounded by the productivity pressures of the organization to which the supervisor herself is subject. She has to meet her quotas too.

What Next? Automating Management

What has happened, however, is that word processing systems have not lived up to their promises. Office costs have continued to rise despite the introduction of word processing, and few offices have achieved the productivity gains promised by vendors. For every showcase company there are untold numbers of failing centers. As a consequence, management efficiency experts and vendors alike are beginning in the 1980s to look at the real source of soaring office costs: not clerical salaries but managerial salaries, not clerical productivity but managerial productivity.

Almost all efforts at introducing office automation technology, Abraham (1981) has noted, have been directed at improving the productivity of the clerical staff; yet productivity gains in the typing area account for only about 1.2 percent of all U.S. white-collar business costs. Moreover, in 1979, U.S. businesses spent three times more on the salaries of "principals" (managers, professionals, and executives) than they did on the salaries of clericals: $435 billion was paid to principals, $135 billion to clericals (21).

Noticing this, vendors are shifting from selling office automation equipment exclusively as a device to increase clerical productivity and are now selling it as a device to increase managerial productivity. Celebrating this technological revolution, *Time* in 1982 named the personal computer "machine of the year." "TIME's Man of the Year," the editors announced, "is not a man but the computer itself" ("Machine of the Year," 1983: 3). Meanwhile vendors fear the word processing market is drying up; essentially they consider the nation's 5.5 million secretaries nearly fully automated and the word processing market "pennies" compared to the one hundred billion dollar potential of the business professional market (Schatz, 1982: 66). Moreover, by 1986 low-cost word processors will have "penetrated 30% of the U.S. heavy duty installed typewriter base," its estimated saturation point ("White Paper," 1982: 52). Whither next is into management. But nothing really is different on the executive terminals, Driscoll (1981: 20) has quipped, except for their mahogany paint.

But something is fundamentally different in the way computerized equipment is used at the managerial level and the way it is used at the clerical level. When the First National Bank of Boston installed minicomputers for both secretaries and professionals, some secretaries lost their jobs and others were reclustered into a "secretarial services center"; but professionals kept their offices, their desks, and their jobs (Synott, 1981).

Rationales for using computerized equipment also differ between the two levels. At the clerical level, word processing is cost justified—does it reduce the number of secretaries needed and increase the number of pages typed each day? But for professionals, no such justification is wanted. Listen to William Synott (1981), senior vice-president of the First National Bank of Boston, tell it:

> When savings are expressed in "soft" terms affecting professionals, such as getting better information faster and more reliably, the benefits usually do not translate into savings in jobs; thus, the results become more difficult to measure with anything approaching reliability. Justification in these cases can only be in the form of testimonials given by satisfied customers. (13)

How typical the Boston bank case is cannot really be known yet since automation of the managerial sector has barely begun. I have already argued that reports of how word processing affects clerical productivity often overstate the truth, that word processing does not increase clerical productivity nearly as much as vendors claim. Synott's comments that cost savings at the managerial level need only be expressed in "soft" terms (such as getting him better information faster) rather than in "hard" terms (such as job elimination) may likewise overstate the truth. Privately, vendors are predicting that automation will eliminate as much as 30 percent of all midmanagerial jobs by 1990. Whether this is so also remains to be seen. But since the impact of office automation on managerial jobs is indeterminate at this point in time, any remarks at this stage on how automation divergently affects managerial and clerical jobs can only be tentative and exploratory, meant to raise issues rather than resolve them.

But these differences between clericals and professionals suggest, however, that professionals and managers do not have to work under the same kinds of speedups and face quite the same threats of job loss or skill reduction that secretaries and clericals experience as their jobs are automated. They further suggest that the purposes for automating the office are different at the professional and managerial level from those at the clerical level. At the managerial level, the purpose of automated equipment is to please and satisfy the "business professional"—to get him better information faster and more reliably. But at the clerical level, the purpose is something else.

Astute observers speculate that the real reason for automating the office is not so much to control clerical labor costs as to control clerical labor. Noble (1979) argues that technology is a means of social control in the conflict between classes in society; numerical control was developed over record-playback techniques in the machine tool industry, for example, not because it was more cost efficient but because it enhanced managerial control more. Likewise, Barker and Downing (1980) see word processing in the automated office as a mechanism to replace looser patriarchal forms of control (characteristic of secretarial–managerial relationships) with more direct capitalist forms: the move, they label it, toward the real subordination of office workers.

Whither Next?

So while vendors claim that automation is needed in the office to control rising labor costs, it is mostly jobs in the clerical labor force that are being controlled; managerial needs for information are being well fed and attended to. In the capitalist economy as developed in late twentieth-century America, corporate needs for information (regardless of the ability of managers to digest it) and control take precedence over human needs for interesting, challenging, and dignified work. "How not to Exploit the Hardware" (1980), the title of a recent article in *Business Week*, sums it up; the viewpoint that it is possible to exploit human beings with the new technology disappears from industry.

The defining characteristic of the managerial–technical perspective, then, is that it takes for granted the "needs" of the corporation—for higher profits, more efficiency, greater productivity, and tighter control—and does not examine how these conflict with and undermine more basic human needs—for meaningful, dignified, challenging, and rewarding work. It is therefore up to clerical women themselves to define these as basic human rights and claim them as their own.

References

Abraham, Steven. 1981. "Is Office Automation the Best Darned Thing You've Ever Seen? Maybe." *Computerworld*, September 28: 21, 23.

"America's Offices Enter a New Age." 1981. *Nation's Business*, July: 48–54.

Barker, Jane, and Hazel Downing. 1980. "Word Processing and the Transformation of the Patriarchal Relations of Control in the Office." *Capital and Class* 19:64–97.

Braverman, Harry. 1974. *Labor and Monopoly Capital.* New York: Monthly Review Press.

Davies, Margery. 1974. Woman's Place Is at the Typewriter: The Feminization of the Clerical Labour Force. *Radical America* 8:1–18.

Driscoll, James. 1980. "Office Automation: The Dynamics of a Technological Boondoggle." Working Paper for the Alfred P. Sloan School of Management, Massachusetts Institute of Technology.

———. 1981. "Is Office Automation the Best Darned Thing You've Ever Seen? No!" *Computerworld*, September 28: 20, 22.

Eddinger, John. 1980. "21st Century Office: A Paperless Wonder." *Nation's Business*, July: 65–66.

"Fighting the Paper Chase." 1981. *Time*, November 23: 66–67.

Gaffney, Carol. 1981. "Crisis in the Workplace: Selling the Staff on Office Automation." *Computerworld*, September 28: 11.

Gifford, Courtney C., ed. 1982. *Directory of U.S. Labor Organizations.* 1982–1983 ed. Washington, D.C.: Bureau of National Affairs, Inc.

"How not to Exploit the Hardware." 1980. *Business Week*, March 24: 90, 92.

"Information Processing and Tomorrow's Office." 1979. *Fortune* (special advertising suppl.), October 8: 31–62.

"Invasion of the Computers." 1981. *Newsweek*, December 28: 57.

Jones, Rebecca. 1981. "Food Firm Finds Automation Fortifying." *Computerworld*, September 28: 69–70.

Kübler-Ross, Elisabeth. 1969. *On Death and Dying.* New York: Macmillan.

"Machine of the Year." 1983. *Time*, January 3: 3, 12–32.

Machung, Anne. 1983. "From Psyche to Technic: The Politics of Office Work." Ph.D. diss., University of Wisconsin.

Matteis, Richard. 1979. "The New Back Office Focuses on Customer Service." *Harvard Business Review* (March-April): 146–159.

Morner, Maimee. 1979. "Why Word Processing Companies Are the Talk of Wall Street." *Fortune*, December 31: 76–77.

National Institute for Occupational Safety and Health. 1981. *An Investigation of Health Complaints and Job Stress in Video Viewing.* Cincinnati.

"1979 Word Processing Executive: Leadership, Cost-Effectiveness, Career-Enhancement." 1979. *Modern Office Procedures*, June: 74–79.

Noble, David. 1979. "Social Choice in Machine Design." In Andrew Zimbalist, ed., *Case Studies on the Labor Process.* New York: Monthly Review Press.

"Office 'Miracles' that Electronics Is Bringing." 1978. *U.S. News and World Report*, September 18: 76–78.

"The Office of the Future: An In-depth Analysis of How Word Processing Will Reshape the Corporate Office." 1975. *Business Week*, June 30: 48–82.

Schatz, Willie. 1982. "A Terminal on Every Desk?" *Nation's Business*, February: 64–69.

Smith, Michael. 1981. *An Investigation of Health Complaints and Job Stress in Video Display Operations.* Cincinnati: National Institute for Occupational Safety and Health.

Synott, William. 1981. "Boston Bank Takes Office Automation via Well-Travelled Word Processing Route." *Computerworld*, September 28: 12–14.

Thoryn, Michael. 1979. "Office Equipment: Electronics Empties the Typing Pool." *Nation's Business*, February: 70–78.

———. 1980. "Tomorrow's Office: Wired for Words." *Nation's Business*, July: 56–64.

U.S. Bureau of Labor Statistics. 1981. *Employment and Earnings*, January, 180.

U.S. Bureau of the Census. 1973. *Census of the Population: 1970*, vol. 1, *Characteristics of the Population*, pt. 1, "United States Summary," sec. 1. Washington, D.C.: GPO.

"White Paper: Word Processing in Transition." 1982. *Modern Office Procedures*, June: 51–60.

Wohl, Amy. 1981. "'Office of Tomorrow': What to Expect." *Computerworld*, September 28: 5.

Working Women. 1980. *Race against Time*. Cleveland.

———. 1981. *Health Hazards of Office Work*. Cleveland.

———. 1982. *Office Work in America*. Cleveland.

Zisman, Michael. 1978. Office Automation: Revolution or Evolution? *Sloan Management Review* 19:1–17.

8

MARY C. MURPHREE
CITY UNIVERSITY OF NEW YORK GRADUATE CENTER

Brave New Office: The Changing World of the Legal Secretary

Since its creation in the latter part of the nineteenth century, the modern office has been gradually transformed into an increasingly rationalized, factorylike environment. As a result of specialization and new office technologies, numerous clerical occupations have been either radically altered or phased out entirely (Barker and Downing, 1980; Braverman, 1974; Glenn and Feldberg, 1977; Gregory and Nussbaum, 1982; Lockwood, 1958; Mills, 1956). At risk in the most recent phase of office rationalization is the occupation of the secretary, one of the largest occupations in the entire U.S. labor force and the backbone of traditional female employment. Secretaries, some four million in number, account for approximately one-quarter of the female clerical work

This research was supported in part by a National Institute of Mental Health dissertation fellowship, 5-F31-MH05860-02; a National Institute of Mental Health training fellowship, 5-T32-MH16373-03; a U.S. Department of Labor, Employment and Training Administration dissertation grant USDL 91-36-78-18; and a grant-in-aid of research from Sigma Xi, Scientific Research Society of North America. The findings presented here, however, do not necessarily represent the positions or policy views of these agencies.

The research was made possible by the cooperation of many people. I am particularly indebted to the secretaries, lawyers, and administrators at Firm X who were willing to share their experiences and opinions with me. I am also grateful to Sarah Spink, personnel director of another large New York City law firm, Deanne Martinicchio, and Herbert Gans, each of whom gave unfailing support and cogent criticism. Special thanks also goes to Lisa Master, Maureen Barden, Laurie Bauman, Judith Gregory, Gaye Tuchman, Cynthia Fuchs Epstein, Eve Hochwald, Anne Machung, Debbie E. Bell, Eugene Litwak, Roslyn Feldberg, Evelyn Glenn, Karen Sacks, and Ruth Milkman.

force and at least one-tenth of all paid female labor. In offices throughout the nation, an increasing number of administrators, paraprofessionals, and clerical specialists—working with sophisticated electronic equipment—perform tasks once the sole responsibility of the secretary.

This essay examines the trend toward the reorganization of secretarial work, analyzing a historically elite and traditionally skilled subset: Wall Street legal secretaries. Specifically, it considers: first, the ever-narrowing scope of legal secretarial work, especially how technology has been used to decrease traditional sources of secretarial challenge, variety, and autonomy; second, newer, more specialized forms of clerical production emerging in large Wall Street firms; third, the persistence nonetheless of secretaries in these firms as specialists performing critically important, if undervalued, nonroutine tasks; and fourth, how certain forms of word processing, when implemented by managers exclusively concerned with cost effectiveness, may lend themselves to technological discrimination.

The data used in this essay are based on a multimethod, multistage research project I conducted in a single, large Wall Street firm (Murphree, 1981). This firm, Firm X, is one of the twenty largest law firms in the world. In 1978 it had a total staff of over five hundred people including attorneys, and gross revenues were well in excess of thirty million dollars. Since 1975 I have followed closely its organizational development and the work lives of its secretaries by sustained participation as a floating secretary over a three-month period, in-depth interviews with the firm's attorneys and management staff, a structured survey with 60 of the firm's 107 secretaries, and an ethnographic study of the firm's typing pool. The analysis also uses data gathered from interviews with attorneys, secretaries, and personnel managers in a wide assortment of other New York City law firms. Data drawn both from historical monographs pertaining to law firm administration and clerical education, and from oral history with retired legal secretaries also inform the research.

The Traditional Legal Secretary: Generalist and Office Wife

Wall Street legal secretaries have been an elite of clerical workers. Of approximately 153,000 secretaries working in 1977 as stenographer-typists to lawyers engaged in private practice, law firms of various sizes, government and the judiciary, private foundations, and the legal departments of private corporations, some 3,500 were attached to the thirty-three largest Wall Street law firms. Essentially private secretaries to some of the more powerful men in finance and law, this small and predominantly female group has enjoyed both the self-image and the reputation of clerical brahmins. Their image comes from pay that is generally much higher than that of most other clerical workers; the prestige associated with Wall Street; and their reputation for above-average verbal abilities, legal know-how, client savvy, accuracy, and typing and stenographic speed.

Essentially skilled "generalists," legal secretaries have traditionally performed a multitude of both simple clerical and housekeeping functions and complex administrative and lawyering tasks. Beyond taking shorthand and transcribing items for her boss's signature and beyond acting as his gatekeeper (screening and placing telephone calls, greeting clients), a legal secretary typically might edit corporate minutes, draft standard wills or petitions following boiler-plate forms, or check legal citations and references for her attorney. She might also monitor the court calendar or docket, handle the firm's bills and charges, and work with an outside accountant on firm taxes. All this has been in addition to filing, ordering supplies, handling the mail, typing endless copy from drafts, collating multiple final copies, and, of course, making coffee. In its brevity this account of necessity seriously underplays the slow, evolutionary process of specialization and the strong relationship between specialization, mechanization, and size of firm. The legal secretary as "generalist," even today, depends to a large extent on the size of the firm. (See Murphree [1981] for a full discussion.)

Legal secretaries traditionally have been generalists in another sense of the term. In *Men and Women of the Corporation*, Kanter (1977) refers to the "principled arbitrariness," or absence of limits on managerial discretion, that characterizes traditional boss–secretary relations and legitimizes the absence of any job description for secretaries. In this connection Kanter also describes the bonds of loyalty and the contingent status reminiscent of feudal lord–vassal patrimony that characterize boss–secretary relations. Together these elements typically make for male boss–female secretary dyads in which the secretary, often willingly, plays the role of nurturant and supportive "office wife." Consistent with the patrimonial nature of boss–secretary relations Kanter describes, most legal secretaries have performed a wide variety of personal tasks for their attorneys unrelated to office matters. Unprotected by any formal job description, legal secretaries, like many other secretaries, have often been expected to keep personal check books, pay spouse's bills, address alumni or wedding invitations, run personal errands (e.g., buy gifts for the attorney to give or pick up laundry), or even babysit.

In keeping with the office-wife role expected of her, the Wall Street legal secretary further has traditionally performed certain supportive and nurturant tasks as well. Covering for an attorney's mistake, lying about his whereabouts when it is helpful, listening supportively (and in confidence) to his career or family problems, coaxing him to remember a family member's birthday or to make a critical phone call, all are important tasks associated with her sex-stereotyped role as handmaiden or confidante.

While this stereotype of the legal secretary persists to some extent in the media and classified ads, research on Wall Street suggests it is an anachronism that seriously misrepresents her current work experience. In the following section I show how specialization and mechanization have affected legal secretaries in Firm X.

SECRETARIES IN TRANSITION: MOVING TOWARD THE LEGAL FACTORY

According to Mills (1956: 198–212) and Braverman (1974: 341–348), the process by which secretarial work is specialized and mechanized is key to understanding managerial efforts over the last century to use scientific management techniques to convert the office into a factory-like organization to maximize managers' control, raise productivity, and increase profitability.

In a chapter entitled "The Enormous File," Mills documents earlier phases of clerical de-skilling associated with centralized copy-typing pools, the introduction of transcription equipment, and the proliferation of numerous types of machine operators and specialized clerks. A quarter century later Braverman (1974: 374) developed Mills's thesis and showed how professional administrators are using centralized data processing systems to fragment secretarial tasks further and reduce secretarial employment by breaking down "the social office" where managers high and low each had a private secretary.

The evolution of office rationalization in Wall Street law firms to a large extent follows a progression similar to that outlined by Mills and Braverman. As early as 1934, for example, Stone (1934) observed a trend toward legal mass production: "The successful lawyer of our day more often than not is the proprietor or general manager of a new type of factory, whose legal product is increasingly the result of mass production methods" (36).

Since that time, in an effort to increase their revenues (by increasing the number of clients and the number of hours they bill), firms have diversified their operations even further, becoming huge full-service firms capable of offering their corporate clientele a wide range of specialized legal expertise (Smigel, 1973). Firm X, for example, mushroomed from a 4-attorney firm in the 1940s to a 110-attorney firm in the early 1970s, to some 225 attorneys today. In an effort to raise the productivity of their staffs, law firms have also invested in new and varied technologies believed to increase document turnaround time and cut nonlegal overhead ("Business Bulletin," 1978; Campbell and Reisner, 1977). By the 1970s, as a result, all of the successful firms had witnessed a proliferation of service departments, occupational subspecialities, and clerical technologies that made the firm-as-factory a reality for one and all, including the legal secretaries.

An analysis of how managers reorganized law offices in recent times foreshadows the ways in which they are likely to use new technologies in shaping the office of the future. From about 1950 to 1978 Firm X underwent a transition during which its managers redistributed many secretarial functions to specialized, often automated, departments throughout their firm. A shift in authority relationships accompanied this redistribution; secretaries became increasingly supervised, evaluated, and rewarded by a bureaucratic personnel department. By the time of my study, each of the thirteen nonlegal service departments, without exception, was performing lawyering, administrative, clerical, or housekeeping tasks formerly the responsibility of the legal secretary.

Loss of Lawyering Tasks

While dispensing legal advice and representing clients has always been a lawyer's responsibility, legal secretaries traditionally were permitted to try their hand at drafting documents, filing briefs with the clerk of court, and doing legal research. Specialization and mechanization have progressively deprived Firm X legal secretaries of many of these "lawyering" functions. Today, middle-level partners and associates create most of the firm's legal documents, including even the simple boiler-plate instruments secretaries often used to prepare.

A new and growing occupation—paralegal work—has absorbed the lower level research and quasi-clerical, nontyping tasks formerly performed by attorneys and their secretaries. In 1978 the total number of paralegals in the thirty-three largest Wall Street firms equaled approximately 914 people, up 88 percent since 1975 ("National Law Firm Survey," 1975). Firm X in 1978 employed over 65. Paralegals have tended to be young women with bachelor of arts degrees frequently earned from seven-sister colleges. Their work ranges from organizing case files for huge take-over and antitrust litigations (Murphree, 1981) to shepherding projects on an attorney's behalf through the various service departments. While some of this work may be routine and boring, it demands a high level of organizational and interpersonal skill.

Firm X is eager to hire paralegals whose time may be billed to clients at an average of fifty dollars per hour. In contrast, secretarial services are figured as overhead. Therefore any "lawyering" on the part of the secretaries would constitute a scandal—if unbilled, by depriving the firm of revenue; if billed, by cheating the clients of "expert" time. As one Firm X attorney explained, "Unlike in the old days when secretaries not only put together wills but taught the young guys how to do them . . . it's not their job anymore. In fact, it's inconceivable. . . . My secretary hardly knows the names of my clients, matters, or cases, much less any legal procedures." Secretaries thus lose an opportunity to learn and practice new skills as well as a sense of how their work fits into the larger context of firm practice.

Paralegals are not the only group who have taken over tasks traditionally the secretary's. A centralized office headed by a licensed managing attorney and a staff of court runners keeps the firm's docket or schedule of court appearances and serves and files papers at the different state and federal courts. This office also maintains an up-to-date litigation form file and renders notarial services—all tasks previously the work of top-notch secretaries. Likewise, library duties such as tracking down legal citations have been transferred to specially trained legal librarians working with sophisticated computerized data systems.

Loss of Administrative Tasks

Challenging administrative functions once performed by Firm X legal secretaries are now divided as well among a number of specialized service departments. A "professional" personnel director working with a staff of six assistants is responsible for the recruitment, record keeping, evaluation, promotion, and termination pertaining to all nonlegal personnel, from legal secretaries to mail room clerks. This department also oversees the physical plant of the firm, supervises all decorating and office refurbishments, purchases office equipment and supplies, and negotiates all service contracts.

Similarly, a staff of professional accountants supervises the firm's financial matters, once a responsibility entrusted to many legal secretaries. At the time of the research, for example, a fifteen-person accounting team used electronic data processing equipment to compute attorneys' billable and nonbillable hours and send out client invoices. It also handled all firm disbursements and kept track of social security and pension plan calculations for every partner and employee. The accounting tasks left to the secretaries as a result were merely routine clerical tasks involving neither decision-making nor client contact. For example, except for a few who handled personal finances for their attorney, most secretaries merely typed vouchers and requisitions at the instruction of their attorney and submitted them to accounting. Occasionally, a secretary was asked to draw up a bill for a client on an individual basis. Only a few, however, were allowed to keep track of (though never compute) time to be billed for attorney appointments, phone calls, conferences, lunch engagements, and the like. The majority had no responsibility for any "bookkeeping."

Loss of Clerical and Housekeeping Tasks

While lawyering and administrative duties have provided intellectual stimuli to legal secretaries over the years, these have by no means been the sole source of challenge, autonomy, or variety in legal secretarial work. Many secretaries have found such straightforward clerical tasks as speed typing, stenography, and proofreading to be rewarding and challenging activities in their own right. Progressively, however, even such fundamentally "secretarial" tasks as these have been either automated or taken away from individual secretaries at Firm X and divided up among a number of specialized service departments. The nearly universal use of the dictaphone at Firm X, for example, has dramatically reduced the need for secretaries to take dictation. From the moment young lawyers enter the firm, they are urged to use machines, not secretaries, for their dictation. As a result, many of the secretaries (especially new secretaries!) complained of fewer and fewer opportunities to practice their hard-earned stenographic skills—skills which, as one secretary commented, "make me feel like a professional, more than just a machine," and "allow me to compete with myself."

The development of a separate proofreading department at Firm X has pre-empted another important source of autonomy and variety for the secretaries. Some seven specialists share with attorneys and paralegals responsibility for all documents sent out under the firm's name. While secretaries are permitted to proof small jobs, such as one- or two-page letters, at their desks, the 1977 secretarial manual insisted that all larger jobs be turned over to proofreading. Centralized proofreading deprives secretaries of a sense of pride in their work insofar as they no longer feel accountable for any finished product. As one secretary put it, "I don't have to type very carefully anymore and I miss the challenge. Proofreading is always there to catch any mistakes. He [the attorney] doesn't think I'd catch them anyway—I've no brain, right?—So it doesn't pay to extend yourself . . . I just type it out and send it down."

Filing in and of itself was generally regarded by Firm X's secretaries as an extremely boring task. The structure of the task, however, has traditionally allowed secretaries access to knowledge, and in the paper world of the office, this knowledge has translated into power. In the past it has been the secretary's task to keep track of every incoming piece of paper, as well as every letter, document, or copy generated by herself or her attorney. This task not only kept her boss dependent on her but kept the secretary up to date and informed on cases, clients, and priorities. At Firm X those duties are now the responsibility of a filing department which works directly with paralegals and attorneys. At the time of this study, a dozen full-time file clerks trained and recruited from outside the firm worked in Firm X's central files, sorting, storing, and retrieving the paperwork of the various legal departments. The legal secretaries' only obligation was to keep a "chron file" of letters she typed and to note on the corner of the file room copies correct client–legal matter code names. In many cases attorneys and paralegals assigned the documents file codes themselves and routed them directly to the file room, thereby bypassing the secretary altogether. To the extent that Firm X secretaries are losing exclusive knowledge of the files and in fact are often bypassed entirely, an important source of responsibility and control for the secretary is on the wane. Those who no longer control the jobs also lose a sense of task identity, that is, an understanding of how the documents they produce fit into the larger process of firm practice.

Mail and messenger tasks, which in the past afforded secretaries some autonomy and variety, have also been institutionalized at Firm X into a separate department. At the time of the study, some twenty-eight full-time clerks posted, sorted, and distributed all incoming and outgoing mail. This department also provided porter service for carrying every kind of article from office supplies to heavy furniture and equipment. Its jacketed messengers also served as "escorts" for visiting attorneys or clients, carrying files, tape recorders, and so on. While relieving secretaries of most of their "go-for" duties, the mail and messenger service has, nevertheless, deprived them of their autonomy and freedom of movement. Where formerly a secretary—perhaps in need of a change of scene or curious to see the office of a client she knew by telephone—might grab her coat, hop a taxi, and make some delivery in person, today she *must* use the messenger service.

A large, centralized reprographics department, outfitted with the latest duplicating equipment has taken over the bulk of the legal secretary's copying responsibilities. While this is largely a welcome innovation, it has nonetheless robbed secretaries of an important source of variety.

Similarly, numerous housekeeping duties—which as Mills (1956) reminds us were once a part of the secretarial role—have been removed. Today, professional cleaning services under subcontract to the building management carry out all heavy-duty cleaning tasks. By night, a legion of secretaries is replaced by a legion of cleaning personnel, usually minority and immigrant women, vacuuming, mopping, emptying the garbage cans, dusting, and so forth. Similarly, Firm X contracts with a fast-food service to run its office canteen and make coffee for the firm. Even the rubber trees shading the various reception areas are tended by a specialized "plant doctor" subcontracted by the firm. As a result, the legal secretary typically may, at most, fetch food from the canteen for attorneys and clients, straighten an attorney's desk, or water the plants in his office.

The combined services of the typing pool and the word processing department provide the most dramatic evidence of how tasks traditionally the backbone of secretarial work are being subdivided and automatized. As in most large firms, the Firm X typing pool can be traced back to the first time a senior partner gave his secretary permission to hire a permanent extra typist to take over some of her own typing overload. Its institutionalization, however, as a separate department with specialized functions, procedures, supervision, recruitment, and training, dates to the 1970s.

Staffed by a group of eighteen women, headed by a supervisor and an assistant supervisor, in 1977 the Firm X typing pool regularly provided clerical help to some 150 persons: lawyers without their own secretaries (usually junior associates and summer associates of the firm), attorneys with secretaries in need of "supplementary" or emergency (back-up) assistance, paralegal-assistants, or any nonlegal department (e.g., personnel) in need of clerical help. In addition, its staff received and transmitted all the firm's telexes, cables, and telecopier messages.

On a typical day the pool turned out between sixty and eighty jobs of varying length. While much of this work was similar in content to that of the private secretaries (e.g., letters, short legal forms to be filled in from copy, affidavits, memoranda to files, corporate minutes, drafts or contracts or legal briefs), the pool also performed a large amount of the heaviest and most repetitious copy typing once the responsibility of the secretary. For example, pool typists, not secretaries, typed draft after draft of long law memoranda or the tedious single-spaced real estate deeds drawn up by different attorneys. Similarly, pool typists, not private secretaries, did dictaphone transcriptions of the many trial exhibits and discovery documents submitted by the paralegals.

The pool also provided temporary clerical service for the firm. Daily, anywhere from one to a half-dozen of the permanent pool employees were assigned out of the pool to substitute for absent secretaries (Murphree, 1981: 135). It also functioned as the firm's only clerical training unit. Secretarial recruits with little or no experience in large firms (e.g., summer secretaries) were routinely introduced to the firm's procedures and personalities in the pool before being sent out on assignment to any member of the legal staff.

Along with a twelve-person night staff, the pool was also in charge of all large-scale ("big case") production efforts. For example, where pool typists were originally used *only* to *assist* private legal secretaries in preparing trial documents, the 1977 Firm X pool handled a large bulk of the entire task, from early drafts to final copy. As a result, private secretaries were called on only to prepare the first draft of a document. The organization of materials, revisions, and shepherding of the job through to completion has increasingly become the responsibility of the pool supervisor working with paralegals and attorneys.

A new centralized and ever-expanding word processing department, working in conjunction with the typing pool, has absorbed an even larger part of the typing and stenographic functions traditionally considered the responsibility of the Firm X legal secretary. Indeed, in 1983 the typing and word processing pools were combined into one unit.

Until then, word processing at Firm X consisted of a supervisor, two assistants, a utility person, and *six* terminal operators (or "word processors"). The department was charged with producing revised and eventually letter-perfect copy of raw materials created by lawyers and paralegals. The system it used consisted of a laser-driven optical character input-reader (the scanner); two redundant computers, each with separate log and memory units; a high-speed printer and a low-speed printer; and six concurrent VDTs.

The process works as follows: A legal secretary or a pool typist, working at her own typewriter with a special scanner-justified golfball element (and a special scanner-keyed format), types up material either handwritten or dictated to her (on tape or face to face) by an attorney or a paralegal. The result, in turn, is forwarded with a special requisition to the word processing department. Here the material is electronically read (in a matter of seconds) into the system by a laser-driven optical scanner (monitored by the utility person or one of the two supervisors), where it is stored on a disc in the memory of one of the two computers. Once the input process is completed, any of the six word processing operators can then begin the revision process. In less than a second he or she can recall the document by "file name" onto the videoscreen of the terminal, where it is displayed page by page. Using normal English commands such as "insert," "delete," or "replace," the operator begins editing the copy according to corrections made by the attorney on the original ribbon copy. She or he can at this point pick up input errors, rearrange graphics, and correct spelling. When any revision is typed, the system automatically readjusts spacing, margins, and pagination.

Upon completion of the editing process, the operator can activate either a high-speed printer (which produces copy at approximately eight pages per minute) or a low-speed printer (which produces "high quality typewriter" copy at three hundred words per minute or 1½ pages per minute) and obtain an exact copy of the revised text.

That copy is then either returned to the attorney for further revisions or, if requested, sent to the proofreading department, where it is read for both content and mechanical errors. When further revisions are required (whether by errors picked up by proofreading or by attorney revisions), the document is sent back to word processing. Again, a terminal operator—though not necessarily the same one who revised it originally—retrieves the original file from the memory, makes the necessary changes, "saves" the revision on the disc, then signals the printers for the new output. This output is then sent back to the attorney or to proofreading until a perfect copy is achieved. Once this happens (and some documents go through dozens of revisions), the final copy is sent to the duplicating department for reproduction. This final corrected computer version is then transferred from disc to tape and stored in a permanent archive in the word processing library, where it can be retrieved after court or client consultation for further revisions or to produce a master or mark-up copy for the use of any firm attorney originating documents in a new but comparable legal matter.

At best, then, in this system the legal secretary is reduced to preparing a "quick and dirty" first draft, to be perfected and followed through on by others. Even the need to know legal terminology—a skill touted in vocational manuals as de rigeur for legal secretaries—is on the wane in big firms. As a Firm X secretary explained, "The only thing legal about being a legal secretary is the name. The guy I work for spells out everything; furthermore, I only do first drafts for [word processing]. What they don't catch, the proofreaders will." These trends notwithstanding, there nevertheless continue to be legal secretaries at Firm X.

Secretaries at Firm X Today: Specialists at Nonroutine Tasks

Despite the loss of all their lawyering and administrative tasks, and the loss of many clerical tasks traditionally the backbone of their craft, legal secretaries at Firm X today still have an important job to do. In general the persistence of their occupation can be attributed to the larger number of critically important *nonroutine tasks* the secretaries continue to perform: tasks entailing contingencies, idiosyncracies, and ambiguous aspects; tasks necessitating an affective posture; extremely simple tasks involving economies of small scale, especially those requiring everyday as opposed to expert knowledge; and time emergencies too costly to routinize (Litwak and Figueira, 1968).

An analysis of the Firm X data reveals that the persistence of boss–secretary dyads (or certain triadic variations of this relationship)[1] are largely a function of the important nonroutine tasks the secretary performs daily throughout the firm. One of the most important of these tasks is that of gatekeeper. At Firm X it is the secretary's job to place, answer, and field telephone calls; relay messages; monitor an attorney's whereabouts; and control access to him by others in and outside the firm. To this end, it becomes her responsibility to interpret requests to reach the attorney, evaluate these requests in terms of *his* priorities, and pass them along at the appropriate time. Such tasks, of course, involve a large number of contingencies, often of an ambiguous and idiosyncratic nature. For example, the secretary must decide whom to put through when and who rates as a wanted interruption on one day and not on another. To do this well, of course, demands a certain amount of knowledge of an attorney's private and business affairs. This in turn necessitates face-to-face communication and at least a semipermanent relationship. Similarly, a secretary with an ongoing relationship to an attorney is more likely to be familiar with and hence quick at deciphering an attorney's poor handwriting than is some newcomer or stranger attached to a distant typing pool or word processing department.

Firm X legal secretaries are also called upon to perform various simple but *unpredictable* clerical tasks, especially those involving time emergencies. For example, rather than wait for the duplication department to make a one- or two-page copy and return it via messenger, attorneys routinely send their secretaries to the satellite copiers spread throughout the firm. Similarly, it is more efficient during a meeting to ask a secretary to type a short last-minute rider to a contract than to request such a document from the word processing department two floors away and wait for it to be processed and returned by messenger.

Most important, legal secretaries at Firm X continue to carry out the various socioemotional tasks Kanter (1977) argues are essential to any

1. The traditional one-on-one (one secretary working for one boss) dyadic relationship is gradually being eliminated at Firm X. Just as Mills (1956) and Braverman (1974) predicted, a deliberate effort is being made by management to break down the "social office" based on such dyads. Increasingly, more and more of the secretaries are being forced to work in polyandrous arrangements for more than one attorney, often as members of small clusters or minipools in teams with other secretaries. While these new triadic or pool arrangements mean more work for each secretary and a weakening of individualist, patrimonial ties to a particular boss (and as such are deeply resented by many secretaries), they are nevertheless primary groups by my definition insofar as they involve small, face-to-face interactions and hence lend themselves to efficient performance of a variety of nonroutine tasks.

office. These include such nurturant and supportive tasks as functioning as a sounding board or moral support for a boss, reading his moods, feeding him important bits of information picked up through gossip and the office grapevine, prompting him effectively to call back a troublesome client or write up a tedious but important expense report, and lying about his whereabouts. They also entail coaxing certain jobs through the bureaucracy of Firm X, that is, knowing whom to call for what task, asking in a way that fosters cooperation, and so forth.

An important but frequently overlooked passive function of secretaries is prodding an attorney's productivity. Numerous Firm X lawyers confessed to me that merely knowing a secretary was outside their office for a limited number of hours expecting to receive work had a stimulating effect on their own output. Several, in fact, reported that their personal productivity declined whenever their secretary was away: "When she is away I find myself putting things off and getting behind. She's the key to my performance—just by being there."

In this connection, most Firm X secretaries also perform numerous purely personal tasks for their attorneys, both older top partners and junior lawyers. While asking a secretary to do personal work is increasingly off limits, many lawyers feel that their ability to perform efficiently in law-related matters hinges on being able to turn over time-consuming but critical personal tasks to their secretaries. For the secretaries, the issue is more complicated. As the scope of their job narrows, many prefer doing personal tasks to doing nothing. At the same time, they perceive these tasks as unprofessional, even servile (Murphree, 1981).

While it is theoretically possible that female paralegals working with attorneys in close, dyadic relationships may someday take over many of the nonroutine tasks mentioned above, to date at Firm X these tasks continue to be performed by legal secretaries.

No longer generalists performing a wide variety of challenging tasks, then, Firm X secretaries today perform primarily these nonroutine tasks that involve social skills, time emergencies, and multiple contingencies. The importance of these tasks has generally gone unrecognized and been seriously undervalued—by law firm managers, by society at large, and to an extent by legal secretaries themselves.

The most cogent explanation of this phenomenon is developed by Machung (1983), who views the undervalued status of secretarial work as rooted in the patriarchal relations and stereotyped division of a labor characteristic of offices since the late nineteenth century. This ranked division of labor assigns high value to social and interpersonal skills when associated with "professional" work (traditionally performed by men) and low value to the same tasks when performed by "mere secretaries" acting in an assistant capacity.

> Secretarial jobs are advertised on the basis of technical skills. . . . But more fundamental and more central to the job are personality, social and diplo-

matic skills (a knowledge of people and their problems) which are demanded but not ostensibly recognized, except in their absence.

> At the upper reaches of organizational hierarchies, such skills are labelled "diplomatic" and regarded as highly skilled labor. Being relatively rare in the professional and managerial (and largely male) labor force, they are highly esteemed and amply compensated for. . . . But in a feminized labor force, this kind of labor is routinely expected and seldom [acknowledged]. . . . [S]tructurally it has paid companies not to recognize these emotional qualities as skills . . . not to dignify them by paying them, either in terms of salary or in terms of respect. (Machung, 1983)

In the archtypically patriarchal institution of Firm X, the know-how legal secretaries bring to their work and the working knowledge (Kusterer, 1978) they accumulate on the job count for very little in the reward system where the legal staff carries off the lion's share of both economic and symbolic rewards (Murphree, 1981: Chap. V). Much like housework, secretarial work at Firm X continues to constitute "invisible labor" unacknowledged and undervalued by those it serves.

The ever-narrowing scope of secretarial responsibilities and the continued devaluation of her remaining tasks have diminished many secretaries' work satisfaction and consequently the Firm's ability to retain a top-notch support staff (Murphree, 1981: Chap. VII). As a result management is looking more and more to the electronic office and the "miracle of word processing" to solve its myriad clerical problems.

In the following section I discuss how law firms generally are using different types of word processing to further departmentalize and specialize support operations, and I speculate on how these changes may affect different secretaries in the future.

Word Processing Cuts Many Ways

The cost of simultaneously supporting fleets of private secretaries and ever-burgeoning word processing departments began receiving great attention in Wall Street law firms during the early 1980s economic recession. An increased supply of lawyers, a leveling demand for legal work, and tougher corporate customers, forced more and more firms to look for ways to reduce their operating costs (Brill, 1982). The secretarial staff is a prime target for such reduction, despite considerable resistance from individual attorneys.

Vendors make fantastic claims for what is loosely called "word processing" as a system that will help firms raise productivity, reduce clerical costs, circumvent the shortage of skilled and willing secretaries, and make high turnover an asset by allowing firms to hire cheap, part-time, and hence nonunionizable labor requiring few benefits. Word processing, however, is not a monolithic phenomenon. The experiences of many different Wall Street firms suggest there are many different types of word processing systems—systems with contrasting implications for the degree of variety, autonomy, responsibility, respect, privacy, and even pay legal secretaries can expect from their work in the future.

At the crudest level of analysis, one can differentiate between centralized and decentralized word processing. This refers to the placement of work stations in the physical plant of the firms and, correspondingly, to the extent to which these arrangements predispose authority relations between operators and bosses to be either very bureaucratic, oriented toward a primary group, or quasi-bureaucratic in nature. These relationships can be represented in terms of a continuum. A word processing center represents the extreme case of centralization and bureaucratic control. Satellite work groups, on the other hand, combine decentralization with primary-group control. In the middle are satellite groups or minipools obligated to report simultaneously to individual attorneys and to a centralized personnel department. They will no doubt experience the costs and benefits of supervisory ambiguity described elsewhere for Firm X secretaries (Murphree, 1981). I discuss here the two extremes.

The Word Processing Center

A centralized system locates all of its word processing functions in a single work site in the firm, often called the Word Processing Center (WPC). Like the typing pools of yesteryear, the WPCs tend to be situated in windowless, fluorescent-lit space in the deep interior of giant skyscrapers. In most cases, terminals are lined up in long rows, desk-to-desk, or situated in modular work stations. Each is connected to a central computer. The WPC is overseen by a chief supervisor and several assistants. The supervisor, in turn, answers to the personnel department or to the executive committee of the firm.

Production in the center is factorylike in a number of ways. All input, copy typing, and text editing is highly paced and monitored. Control by supervisors is instantaneous and complete. Rules and regulations are explicitly stated and exceptions are rare. In addition to clocking in and out, operators are required to work on their terminals full time except for rigidly defined breaks. In some instances they have quotas to meet: they must complete a certain number of pages, lines, or even characters—all of which are computed by the machine. Much as on the assembly line, tasks and personnel are largely interchangeable. Supervisors may freely "interact" or electronically inspect any job going on at a terminal. Movement of the operator is more or less restricted to the "shop floor," or in some extreme cases, to the individual work stations.

While the experience of working in a centralized WPC resembles that of working in a typing pool, the electronic capabilities of the WPC allow for a degree of work monitoring and supervision far exceeding that exercised over pool typists. For example, using company facilities to do personal clerical tasks for family and friends has been a long cherished perk of office work. This practice, however, has been largely checked in the centralized, interactive centers where supervisors can control access to the computer memory and monitor the nature of the work on and off line. In an earlier era of word processing, operators often had moments of relaxation as they waited for text to be displayed on their video screen. Today vendors boast of eliminating the "folded arm" position and extol the pace-setting control made possible by "machine prompting," whereby new tasks are spit out onto the screen the moment old ones are completed. Key-stroke counting, production quotas, and piecework compensation are other forms of control on the horizon.

Work is often submitted to a WPC in a form that makes it meaningless and hence monotonous to a worker. For example, a large part of an operator's time may be spent inputting bits and pieces of draft material including long, tedious transcriptions from dictaphone tapes from a variety of anonymous lawyers. Operators have few, if any, ongoing or direct contacts with attorneys, and they may be pulled off different text-editing jobs (often the most substantive and skilled aspects of word processing work) at a supervisor's whim. Not uncommonly, a re-edit is worked on by a number of people, each of whom has no understanding of how this task fits into the larger scheme of legal practice, and therefore little incentive or accountability for the accuracy of the product. In addition, centers with advanced electronic filing capabilities tend to restrict access to a system's library to the supervisor and the legal staff. As a result, opportunities for operators to gain knowledge of the files or experience any task identity is severely curtailed.

The Satellites

Decentralized word processing, on the other hand, represents a different pattern of work organization being implemented in large firms. "Decentralized" refers to a system where VDTs are dispersed physically throughout the firm at a series of satellitelike work stations. These stations may either be electronically independent units that stand alone with their own computer and printing capabilities or units whose terminals and printers are dependent on a central computer some distance away.

The most distinctive form of decentralized word processing is one characterized by a primary-group social organization. As in the traditional (and patrimonial) attorney–secretary model, operators here usually work in close proximity to attorneys, who are the primary supervisors of their work. The work groups are small and involve continuous face-to-face interactions of a somewhat permanent nature. In general these work groups are set up around generic, substantively related areas such as a legal speciality (e.g., litigation department, corporate department, real estate department) or task (e.g., take-overs or an antitrust suit). A group may be as small as the attorney–secretary dyad or as large as four operators, two paralegals, and six or seven attorneys.

Relationships—depending on the size, nature, and personality of the individuals—are more or less affective and personal, with operators to some extent identifying with management. Attorneys and operators often collude as an individual team against the bureaucratic dictates of a centralized personnel department that threaten them as a primary group.

Although satellite machinery may be interactive throughout the firm, ability to monitor the operator is low in the decentralized system and impossible in its stand-alone variation. Secretaries in the latter case have full control of their machine memories, including space to do private work. High-status secretaries (those working with empowered attorneys) can expect to be granted access to space reserved for the attorney. Most will create and organize their own filing system, regaining an important source of knowledge and control. Even given variations in attorney status, personnel administrators have much less incentive to spy on decentralized operators than on WPC operators. Setting production quotas for attorney-directed operators, for example, is impossible without intimate knowledge of an attorney's legal team's work needs. Technically, word processing equipment already permits attorneys whose terminals are interactive with operators' terminals to monitor output, but the fealty or loyalty component inherent in face-to-face primary-group structures makes this, too, unlikely. On the contrary, most attorneys working in the decentralized system will grow increasingly dependent on the operator–technician, just as they formerly did on private secretaries. This, of course, is already true for the great bulk of attorneys who have no word processing skills themselves. I believe it will also be true for young attorneys who, even though they can do their own word processing, will stop once the fun-and-games aspect of the new equipment wears off. In environments where word processing has been around for a while, evidence suggests that except for those professionals who compose on terminals, the more tedious input tasks are relinquished as soon as possible to word processing operators.

In contrast to the WPC, task and personnel interchangeability at the satellites is relatively low. This is particularly true insofar as operators working for more than one attorney in cost-cutting cluster systems are called on to perform large numbers of the nonroutine secretarial tasks described earlier (see n. 1). Depending on the size of the work group, these tasks may well include a few of the lawyering and administrative tasks secretaries have been losing. As legal word processors regain some of these tasks, in addition to their new technical skills and always-underrated diplomatic skills, the combination of skills is going to raise important comparable-worth problems. Freedom of physical movement for operators is likewise the greater for those working at the satellites, as nonroutine demands from time to time provide reasons to move around the firm.

Life at the satellites, of course, is not necessarily a bed of roses for all secretaries. The primary-group nature of their association with attorneys may well encourage the same sexist and autocratic patrimony that characterized the former attorney–secretary dyads.[2] Nevertheless, in comparison with the factorylike WPC jobs, secretaries at satellites are generally better off.

The Trend toward Technological Discrimination

Despite potential advantages of a decentralized system for legal secretaries, centralized systems seem to have greater appeal to those who make management decisions. These are largely corporate "numbers men" who make their careers by focusing on short-run savings and cutting costs quickly through high-tech innovations, staff reductions, and tightened line control—all attractive components of centralized word processing. If adopted widely in Wall Street firms, a purely centralized model will mean the end of the special status and prestige these secretaries have traditionally enjoyed.

Secretaries assigned to the centralized sweat shops will fare badly indeed. Their sense of professionalism—feeble at this stage of transition but still intact—will be the first thing to go as machine monitoring replaces trust and loyalty as the incentive to perform. Rigid rules and quotas will trap women workers in unhealthy environments, forcing them to work hazardously long hours at VDTs. Job opportunities, along with benefits, good pay, and job security, will decline for most women employees as managers assign more routinized work to temporary and part-time workers (Feldberg and Glenn, 1983).

Management will nevertheless retain some women to work at satellite stations. Here, word processing technology will be used to enhance the secretarial job, providing higher status and better pay, and creating opportunities to learn more skills and take over new responsibilities—including even paralegal tasks. Job security will be increased as an operator acquires greater knowledge of the legal process, including the files, and becomes adept at challenging tasks like text editing and citation research. The number of these first-rate jobs will be small indeed, however, especially insofar as managers set up *de*centralized minipools or clerical clusters where secretaries have to answer simultaneously to individual attorneys and to a centralized personnel department whose demands are often contradictory.

Who will staff the jobs made possible by the new technology? Past and present practice indicates that an insidious kind of technological

2. The patrimonial attributes Kanter (1977) delineates as characterizing the boss–secretary office-wife structure are strikingly similar to the primary-group structure analysis I present here. They include the importance of loyalty and fealty, engendered by face-to-face relations to an affective, noninstrumental nature; the contingency of the secretary's status to that of the boss and the implicit need for permanence and reciprocity in the relationship; and finally, the absence of limits on managerial discretion, since the relationship is essentially diffuse rather than particularistic. The difference, however, in the two analyses is that the primary-group structure does not demand hierarchically organized relationships, whereas Weberian "patrimony," which inspires Kanter's analysis, assumes a superordinate–subordinate ranking scheme.

discrimination will exacerbate the castelike distinctions already present in large firms. More and more men and privileged women, disproportionately from the white upper and middle class, will get the so-called professional–technical decentralized word processing jobs; the inferior, factorylike jobs in the large centers will go to lower-middle-class and working-class women, especially blacks and minorities or older unskilled women entering the labor force for the first time.

The new technology is sure to be blamed for this discrimination. In fact, technology is neutral. Discrimination comes from the choices office managers and planners make in implementing and staffing word processing. The sex, race, and class typing of bad jobs is a human decision. Those intent on managing organizations "scientifically" will embrace centralization for its short-range profitability and control despite the toll it will take on worker morale and long-range productivity. The drive for profit will create bad jobs. Prejudice will determine who gets them.

References

Barker, Jane, and Hazel Downing. 1980. "Word Processing and the Transformation of the Patriarchal Relations of Control in the Office." *Capital and Class* 19: 64–97.

Braverman, Harry. 1974. *Labor and Monopoly Capital.* New York: Monthly Review Press.

Brill, Steven. 1982. "Surviving the 80s Shake-out." *American Lawyer* (November).

"Business Bulletin." 1978. *Wall Street Journal,* August 24, 1.

Campbell, W. J., and E. J. Reisner. 1977. "Will Your Next Partner Have a Magnetic Heart: Computer Assistance for the Practice of Law." *Case and Comment* 82, no. 5: 18–30.

Feldberg, Roslyn L., and Evelyn N. Glenn. 1983. "Technology and Work Degradation: Effects of Office Automation on Women Clerical Workers." In Joan Rothschild, ed., *Machina Ex Dea: Feminist Perspectives on Technology,* 59–78. New York: Pergamon.

Glenn, Evelyn N., and Roslyn L. Feldberg. 1977. "Degraded and Deskilled: The Proletarianization of Clerical Work." *Social Problems* 25, no. 1: 52–64.

Gregory, J., and K. Nussbaum. 1982. "Race against Time: Automation of the Office." *Office, Technology, and People* 1, nos. 2, 3: 197–236.

Kanter, Rosabeth M. 1977. *Men and Women of the Corporation.* New York: Basic Books.

Kusterer, Ken C. 1978. *Know-How on the Job: The Important Working Knowledge of the "Unskilled" Worker.* Boulder, Colo.: Westview.

Litwak, Eugene, and Josefina Figueira. 1968. "Technical Innovations and Theoretical Functions of Primary Groups and Bureaucratic Structures." *American Journal of Sociology* 73: 468–481.

Lockwood, David. 1958. *The Blackcoated Worker.* London: Allen and Unwin.

Machung, Anne. 1983. "From Psyche to Technic: The Politics of Office Work." Ph.D. diss., University of Wisconsin.
Mills, C. Wright. *White Collar.* 1956. New York: Oxford University Press.
Murphree, Mary C. 1981. "Rationalization and Satisfaction in Clerical Work: A Case Study of Wall Street Legal Secretaries." Ph.D. diss., Columbia University.
"National Law Firm Survey." 1978. *New York Law Journal,* September 18, 14–17.
Smigel, E. O. 1973. *The Wall Street Lawyers.* 2d ed. Bloomington: Indiana University Press.
Stone, Harlan F. 1934. "The Public Influence on the Bar." *Harvard Law Review* 48: 1–14.

Bibliography

Blackburn, Norma D. 1971. *Legal Secretaryship.* Englewood Cliffs, N.J.: Prentice-Hall.
Davies, Margery. 1974. "Woman's Place Is at the Typewriter: The Feminization of the Clerical Labor Force." *Radical America* 8: 1–18.
Driscoll, James W. 1982. "How to Humanize Office Automation." *Office: Technology and People* 1: 167–176.
Edwards, Richard. 1979. *Contested Terrain: The Transformation of the Workplace in the Twentieth Century.* New York: Basic Books.
Garrison, Carol Reed. 1974. "The Background, Current Status and Future Role of Legal Secretaries in Illinois." Ph.D. diss., Southern Illinois University.
Grandjean, Burke, and Patricia Taylor. 1980. "Job Satisfaction among Female Clerical Workers." *Sociology of Work and Occupation* 7, no. 1: 33–53.
Leslie, Louis A., and K. B. Coffin. 1968. *Handbook for the Legal Secretary.* New York: McGraw-Hill.
Levy, Beryl Harold. 1961. *Corporation Lawyer: Saint or Sinner? The New Role of the Lawyer in Modern Society.* Philadelphia: Chilton.
Manikas, W. J. 1975. "A Paralegal Is not a Lawyer in a Wheelchair." *Manpower* (October): 11–14.
Menzies, Heather. 1981. *Women and the Chip.* Montreal: Institute for Research on Public Policy.
National Association of Legal Secretaries. 1974. *Manual for the Legal Secretarial Profession.* 2d ed. St. Paul, Minn.: West.
National Commission on Working Women. 1979. *National Survey of Working Women.* Washington, D.C.
National Law Journal, May 1979.
Oelrich, Elizabeth S. 1968. "The Position of the Female Secretary in the U.S. from 1900 through 1967: A Historical Study." Ph.D. diss., University of North Dakota.
Strong, K. D., and A. O. Clark. 1974. *Law Office Management.* St. Paul, Minn.: West.
U.S. Bureau of Labor Statistics. 1979. *Women in the Labor Force: Some New Data Series.* Report 575. Washington, D.C.: GPO.

U.S. Department of State. 1975. *Secretarial Task Force Report*. Washington, D.C.: GPO.

Werneke, Diane. 1983. *Microelectronics and Office Jobs, The Impact of the Chip on Women's Employment*. Geneva: International Labour Office.

Zuboff, Shoshanna. 1983. "New Worlds of Computer-mediated Work." *Harvard Business Review* (September–October): 142–152.

9

LEIGH S. ESTABROOK
SYRACUSE UNIVERSITY

Women's Work in the Library/Information Sector

Until recently, the field of librarianship was clearly defined. It encompassed those workers—clerical, technical, and professional—employed in formal organizations known as libraries, the principal types of which are academic, public, school, and special. Although the clienteles, organizational settings, collections, and services may differ, the tasks within are similar. They essentially involve the collection and organization of graphic and visual materials and the provision of access to them.

Social and technological change during the past ten-to-fifteen years has significantly altered library organizational structure and patterns of service. Computerized information storage and retrieval have been incorporated into libraries and also into many corporate units outside libraries. Commercial organizations have extended their internal information systems. They have also become involved in selling information as products to other companies and to individuals through mail, cable, or computer systems.

This essay examines the effects of these changes on the structure of work, women's pay, working conditions, training and job opportunities, and the efforts women in librarianship have made to improve their situations through collective action, organizations, and litigation.

The Changing Structure of Work

Three interrelated developments are changing the structure of library/information-sector work. First, corporate involvement in and appropriation of library activities has intensified. Second, much library work is becoming automated. Third, libraries are under increasing pressure to be more productive.

Corporate Involvement

Corporate involvement in and appropriation of library activities is wide ranging and multidimensional. Briefly, information has become big business. Within companies, the management of internal information systems such as personnel or inventory records has become more centrally important to decision makers, making information-management and information-systems positions organizationally important. Managers have also become increasingly concerned with obtaining information about the environment that might be useful in their work. Special market research publications on industries (priced at fifteen hundred dollars for one hundred pages of information, for example) or economic forecasting services are two examples of how this concern for information has been made profitable. The information industry now encompasses organizations that produce and distribute information, those involved in the telecommunications industry, and those who manufacture computer hardware or software to support information systems. The impact of this industry on library-sector work has been substantial, and there is evidence that it will produce dramatic changes in the way library services are developed and delivered.

Library work has become the domain of many different types of organizations and divisions within organizations. Information brokers now offer in-depth reference service, organization of information services, and other library work on a contractual basis. This makes it possible for organizations to maintain a library with a smaller professional staff or a less skilled staff who can perform day-to-day functions. Specialized tasks are then contracted out.

Within corporations, the onset of the so-called information age has led to the development of numerous different information positions including information manager, information intermediary, information operations coordinator, and information-systems specialist (Debons et al., 1981). Many of these positions are technical and require specialized training in computer science or systems design. Within organizations, the corporate library may be supplemented by a technical information center, a records management division, an archive, or other sections whose primary function is to provide organization of and access to information. At the same time, there is increased emphasis within corporations on information management. In many corporations, technically trained workers have been moved into managerial positions because of a lack of appropriately trained personnel. In others, individuals from schools of management, public administration, and library science are being hired.

Library schools have responded to this expansion of information functions within organizations by broadening their curricula. As of

1982, two accredited library schools (Syracuse and Denver) had developed specialized programs in information management, and others have been investigating this type of program.

As a result, there is increased territorial competition within universities for the training of information managers. Within library schools and librarianship, a dual-career structure is emerging, with the more aggressive and ambitious students directed toward information management, and others, toward work in traditional library settings. A small but significant number of people who identify themselves as librarians now work in the information industry (Sellen, 1980). This has affected professional education and placement, research in the field, and the structure of library and other professional associations. The structure of the field of librarianship has become less clearly defined.

The growth of the information industry has also affected the structure of work within libraries. A relatively small but growing market for the information industry has been the home information market. A number of services developed for home use compete with traditional library services (e.g., Dow Jones News Service and *The Academic Encyclopedia*). In some communities, libraries find themselves in competition with the home information market (Estabrook, 1981b).

More important is the increasing privatization of information. Over 50 percent of data bases currently produced now are proprietary. Libraries, which for years asserted that their mission was to collect and disseminate all relevant information, are forced to contend with the fact that much corporate information is simply unavailable and that which is can often be obtained only at very high cost. Both academic and public libraries have found that the only means of offering certain types of specialized services is through fee-based services to users. In libraries in which this has happened, there is now a two-tiered client structure—paying and nonpaying—and a consequent professional division between those who work with the two types of users. Preliminary evidence from research in this area indicates that paying users receive better service (Nielson, 1983).

Automation

Pressures from the corporate sector have also affected the second major change in libraries: automation of library processes. Libraries have been important purchasers of hardware and software systems that can substitute for the human library labor force. Both technical and public services have become increasingly automated in libraries in the past ten years. Although no empirical studies have been conducted, there seems to be evidence that the result of this transition has been a general deprofessionalization of librarianship. Increasing acceptance of available computerized cataloging records has all but eliminated the position of professional cataloger in many libraries. On-line bibliographic data-base searching has become one of the more professional reference tasks in that it allows the librarian to assume a unique role of intermediary between the user and computerized information. This upgrading of role appears to be transitory, however, as data-base producers are seeking to develop user-friendly systems to which users can obtain direct access without the assistance of a librarian. There are other changes occurring. The number of professional, relative to nonprofessional, staff is reported by some librarians to be decreasing; and the actual variety and range of tasks being performed by nonprofessionals is increasing while those of professionals are decreasing.[1] For example, in some academic libraries, clerical workers find themselves responsible for many decisions about how to input data into the computer. Before automation (and the consequent need to use computer time efficiently), these kinds of decisions would have been handed over to professionals.

The introduction of computers into libraries has been in part a response to pressures from computer producers. It has also been necessitated by economic pressures on libraries that have forced library managers to attend to the productivity of their organizations.

Pressure for Productivity

As in other organizations, library labor costs have risen as computer costs have decreased. Changing the way in which library procedures are carried out has been one way to control costs. A second method has been to shift the types of services offered. Labor-intensive activities such as community outreach or adult and children's programming have been curtailed (White, 1983). Lending of best selling books has been reemphasized. A service of this sort has a known and responsive clientele, requires relatively little staff time, and has a recognized measure of success: circulation. Libraries, as noted, have also instituted fee-based services; these have taken the form of charges for bibliographic searches for individual users. Libraries have also begun more extensive information service to businesses, which pay an annual fee in return. Overall, there has been a significant shift in organizational priorities within libraries toward services most likely to help the institution survive (Estabrook, 1979).

It seems likely, then, that the next two decades will find the following changes in the structure of work in libraries: First, a diffusion of library activities within nonlibrary organizations; second, an assumption of the more profitable library activities by private industry, for example, cable companies; third, a decreasing number of professional activities within libraries, leading to increased division between labor and management within these organizations; fourth, increased competition between the private sector and libraries for control of access to information; and fifth, a diminution of the societal role of libraries. This

1. The author has recently begun interviewing both professional and nonprofessional staff in academic and public libraries to ascertain the extent and nature of this development. Part of the framework for this analysis is laid out in Estabrook (1983).

generally pessimistic view is not subscribed to by many within the field, but it is important to note that many of the more optimistic views are based on an assumption that the relationship between the nonprofit and the for-profit information sectors will be mutually beneficial (National Commission on Libraries, 1982). Those who hold the more optimistic views do not see competition as destructive to library survival; I do not agree. Effective workers and profitable services are likely to be skimmed off by industry, leaving public, academic, special, and school libraries with services too costly to support in a long-term economic decline. In fairness, it must be stated that little research to support either position has been done. Discussion of future directions follows.

Women's Opportunities in the Library/Information Sector

To understand opportunities for women in librarianship, it is necessary first to clarify the nature of women's library work. The designation *librarian* denotes one who holds the professional degree in librarianship and who works in a position in a library classified as professional. Almost 50 percent of those who categorize themselves as librarians, many of whom are employed in school libraries and almost all of whom are women, do not have the designated professional degree (Heim, 1982). These people may consider themselves professional librarians, but those conducting research in librarianship may not. Within the library/information sector, there are also people classified as technical or clerical workers who are not considered professional employees and who are usually excluded from any study of the library profession.

What may seem somewhat like hairsplitting to those unfamiliar with librarianship is in fact important, for it affects both the research about the field and the opportunities for women within it. Librarianship is a clearly stratified profession, one that insists on the differences between professional and nonprofessional workers. Only in exceptional cases can a person without the required credential obtain a professional librarian's position. The importance of this stratification becomes evident when one begins to examine women's opportunities and actions in the library/information sector.

Of the approximately 160,000 people classified as librarians by the U.S. Bureau of Labor Statistics (1975), 84 percent are women, and 92 percent are classified racially as white.[2] Women and minority library workers are represented disproportionately in public and school library

2. These statistics are based on 1970 census data and include all those who consider themselves librarians. The data are thus not limited to "professional" librarians. More recent data indicate that these percentages have remained relatively stable in the intervening years. See the annual survey of placement and salaries published in *Library Journal*.

positions. In all types of libraries, except school (where approximately 10 percent of new male graduates are placed each year), male librarians command three times the number of professional administrative positions expected were such positions distributed randomly (Heim, 1982). A recent survey of library association members found 49.6 percent of the men held administrative positions compared with 30.4 percent of the women (Heim and Estabrook, 1983). Salaries for male library school graduates in 1980 were 4.3 percent higher than for female graduates, and the salary differential increases for librarians who have been active in the field for a number of years (Heim, 1982). In part, this salary differential can be accounted for by the differences between men and women in managerial responsibility and types of employment; but when these and other variables such as publication rate, professional involvement, and date and level of professional degrees are held constant, gender differences in salary still obtain (Heim and Estabrook, 1983: 35–36).

At present, some women appear to be optimistic about the effects of current changes in librarianship on their pay, working conditions, promotion, training, and job opportunities. The handful of women who have succeeded in their own information-brokerage businesses and the several hundred who have assumed responsible and highly paid information positions within corporations are offered as examples to those newly entering the field. The book *What Else You Can Do with a Library Degree*? (Sellen, 1980) is a best seller to placement officers, young professionals, and those who have found their jobs offer no mobility. The 1970s buyers market for librarians even seems at this writing to be shifting to one in which there are more job listings and fewer graduates competing for these positions (Van House, Roderer, and Cooper, 1983).

There is little evidence, however, that working opportunities will improve for most of those currently employed in libraries. To the contrary, there is much to suggest that, for many women, opportunities—particularly professional opportunities—will not increase in the next decade or two (Van House, Roderer, and Cooper, 1983). This analysis is based in part on the trends I projected in the first section, including the projected transition in on-line searching positions, the continued decline of professional cataloging openings, and an expected increase in automation of other library activities.

Opportunities for librarians outside of libraries may increase (although one may have to face the question When is a librarian not a librarian?), but the structure of these jobs make them particularly susceptible to discriminatory practices. They are, first of all, isolated. Women have little collegial support, and many of the jobs at this time are offered through the old boy network. The jobs are also ill defined. A recent study of information professionals (Debons et al., 1981) found no correlation between a person's job title and his or her responsibilities in a position. It can be expected that women who enter these jobs will have difficulty interpreting to management the nature and function of the "librarian's" responsibilities.

A preliminary investigation of human resource issues of information-systems personnel (Center for Information Systems Research, 1981) revealed other problems particularly salient for women who may move into this area: lack of any formal mentor systems, uncertainty about career path, and lack of clear opportunities for promotion. There has also been some evidence that women in these types of jobs are being segregated into user services and are generally excluded from technical-systems positions. It should be noted that the emerging fields of information-systems management and the information industry are very much male dominated. At recent (1981) meetings of the Information Industry Association and the Conference on Information Systems, over 90 percent of the participants (and an even higher percentage of the speakers) were men.

Training opportunities do not appear to offer a solution to this continued segregation. For those currently in the field of librarianship, continuing education has been limited by financial pressures on libraries. Moreover, female librarians receive less release time and less financial support for training than their male counterparts (Heim and Estabrook, 1983: 31). Loss in real wages has also made it increasingly difficult for librarians to support additional education. Blumberg's (1980) study of various occupational groups found that between 1967 and 1977 librarians lost 10.3 percent in real earnings. This study, based on Bureau of Labor Statistics data, includes all those classified as librarians, both professional and nonprofessional. A recent analysis of members of the American Library Association found that between 1970 and 1979 there was a loss in earning power of 25 percent for members of the professional association. For women in the association, the loss was 29 percent (Estabrook and Heim, 1980: 658).

Formal education in library schools appears to support the trend toward education for jobs outside library organizations. Public library and children's services courses have minimal enrollment. In several library schools, faculty positions in these areas have been replaced by positions in information systems. Placement officers look toward information management in private industry for their students. Training, both formal and informal, seems to support the diffusion of the field into nonlibrary organizations (Van House, Roderer, and Cooper, 1983) and is thus reinforcing the trends I have identified. It does not appear to offer opportunities for increased achievement by women in librarianship.

Collective Bargaining by Librarians

There are no reliable statistics on the percentage of librarians formally affiliated with labor unions or professional/staff associations. In 1975 it was estimated that less than 20 percent of professional librarians were affiliated with a unit responsible for collective bargaining for the group (Weatherford, 1976). No estimate of affiliation of nonprofessional workers is available. Unionized librarians are drawn primarily from public and school libraries and also include some from academic libraries, principally at large state institutions. Virtually no special librarians or librarians in information-management roles have union affiliation. Membership in bargaining units is diffused among numerous different unions.

The American Library Association (ALA), the association that accepts as members all who are concerned with libraries, has avoided representing its members except on issues of intellectual freedom. It did, however, adopt a policy in January 1980 that stated that "the American Library Association affirms the right of eligible library employees to organize and bargain collectively with their employers, or to refrain from organizing and bargaining collectively, without fear of reprisal." Within ALA is the Library Union Task Force; and several state library associations, including New York and Massachusetts, have sections devoted to issues of collective bargaining or staff organization and union activities of the membership. Each of these has as its primary activity information sharing among the group's membership. The Library Union Task Force, for example, with coöperation from Simmons College Graduate School of Library and Information Management, is collecting examples of union contracts to assist its members. Although each of these associations has a primarily professional membership, both ALA and the state associations have considered issues of concern to professional, technical, and clerical employees.

The one library association that has made an attempt to represent the collective interests of its membership in a more active way is the National Librarians Association (NLA). With a membership of about two thousand, NLA is less than one-tenth the size of the ALA. It recently announced, however, its affiliation with the Quincy, Massachusetts–based Hospital, Library and Public Employees Union.

The small percentage of librarians affiliated with unions, the diffusion of affiliated members among a number of bargaining units, and the nonactivist stance of the major professional association can be attributed in part to librarians' ambivalence toward the labor movement. As striving professionals, librarians may see collective action as undermining professional autonomy or expertise (Estabrook, 1981a). Affiliation with a movement associated with working-class members may seem to conflict with the status concerns of librarians. Many professional librarians are classified as management and as such are excluded from bargaining units. Even those librarians who have been members of bargaining units are uncertain about how they should proceed. Those affiliated with large units have expressed concern that they are not getting adequate service in grievance procedures and contract negotiations from their representatives. Librarians often feel lost in larger units. Professionals also become ambivalent when they find their salaries converging with those of nonprofessionals, as has happened in some recent negotiations. It should be added that there are some structural factors that contribute to these concerns and problems. In some libraries the bargaining unit includes all employees—both professional and nonprofessional—except those who are explicitly classified as management. In academic libraries many librarians who do not consider themselves management have faculty status and by the *Yeshiva* ruling are thereby ineligible to affiliate with labor unions.

Despite these hesitations, there is some evidence that union involvement of librarians is increasing and that librarians are becoming willing to assume a more activist stance (Peace, 1982). Librarians in San Jose, California were recently part of a successful job action. In 1980 at the Public Library of Youngstown and Mahoning County, two unions, Service Employees International, Local 627, representing clerical and maintenance workers, and the Public Librarians Association, representing the professional librarians, struck after a breakdown in contract negotiations. This strike lasted for almost three months before the professionals reached a final agreement, and it took even longer to settle with Local 627.

Whether the NLA and its small union will make any progress in organizing professional librarians or whether larger unions will succeed in improving their representation is unclear. Equally uncertain is the extent to which affiliation with labor unions can be used by librarians—both professional and nonprofessional—to improve their working situations.

Action through Library Organizations

Working conditions of women in librarianship have also been addressed by several specialized groups. At the national level, there is the Committee on the Status of Women in Librarianship, part of the ALA. It recently received two research awards: one to study the status of women in librarianship (Heim and Estabrook, 1983) and one to work on issues of pay equity (Peace, 1981). The product of the second award was a packet of information for library workers entitled *Pay Equity: Comparable Worth Action Guide* that provides guidance to individuals or groups seeking to achieve readjustments in pay scale based on comparison with other groups within an organization or community. The Office of Library Personnel Resources, directed by Margaret Myers, was a major contributor to this work and in 1980 began a clearinghouse on comparable pay issues. It has also conducted studies of minority representation in the field and provided important support for projects on women in librarianship.

State associations also have committees and round tables that devote themselves to promoting women's issues and informing members and the public about women in library work. Other associations with a large library membership have been less successful in forming committees to address women's issues. Most significantly, the American Society for Information Science and the Special Library Association—

the two organizations that most directly address issues relevant to librarians in the corporate sector—do not have committees to address issues of women in the profession. At the summer 1983 Special Library Association meeting, the women's caucus was unable to achieve formal committee or task-force status. One of the major arguments by those opposed was that an association comprised of a majority of women did not need a specific group to investigate women's issues.

Those organizations that include librarians who are working in the information sector, such as the Society for Information Resource Management, have not yet developed subgroups to address women's issues.

The one organization actively involved in the interests of nonprofessional library staff is Women Library Workers. In 1980 this group began the *WLW Journal: News/Views/Reviews for Women and Libraries*, an expansion of a newsletter the group had already published for four years. It has recently been investigating possible changes in structure to represent feminist librarians not currently represented by other organizations (Heim, 1981).

Legal Action

Within librarianship there have been few legal suits by women or on behalf of women. There has been some litigation to determine bargaining units for librarians. There have also been several affirmative action complaints, and recent court decisions may encourage librarians to litigate more frequently. In April 1983, for example, thirty-seven female librarians at the University of Minnesota were awarded $905,000 after data indicated discriminatory salary differences between male and female employees ("In the News," 1983).

Informal Networks

An outgrowth of a conference on women in librarianship held at Rutgers University in 1974 has been the development of a strong, if informal, network of women who have attempted to act as mentors to one another, to students, and to employees. A directory of women willing to help other women (*SHARE*, 1980) is in its fourth edition, and a second women's conference was held in 1980. The bonds developed in these contexts are remarkably strong and are perceived by a number of women to have enhanced publishing, research, and job opportunities.

Within librarianship, the major factor inhibiting progress through collective action of any sort is the rigid stratification of the profession and the continued strength of the belief that "professionals" are not subject to the same workplace dynamics as other workers (Norman, 1982).

Conclusion

The social and economic factors affecting the profession of librarianship are the same that affect other women's occupational groups. One important difference is the connection between library work and the information sector—an economic sector that is expanding perhaps more rapidly than any other at this time. From the evidence available, it would seem that women's opportunities in this changing field are not going to be significantly altered, except for the small percentage who are employed as information managers. Even in this area, the gains may be short term.

Important research has been conducted on the status of different groups of professional women within librarianship. Many areas remain for investigation. What is happening to the types of jobs held by both professionals and nonprofessionals, and how exactly have their functions changed? How are these changes affecting the relationships between the two groups—professional and nonprofessional? Is the evidence of de-skilling and specialization of work some have reported representative of structural changes occurring throughout the library field and in all types of libraries?

The diffusion of librarians into various organizations increases the difficulty of answering some of these questions. The resistance of professionals to acknowledge their worker status may restrict their ability to understand the impact of various changes on their jobs. But just as economic changes are affecting women's willingness to take collective action, so too are they pushing librarians toward a greater willingness to examine openly some of these very difficult questions.

References

Blumberg, Paul. 1980. *Inequality in an Age of Decline.* New York: Oxford University Press.

Center for Information Systems Research. 1981. *Human Resources Policy.* Cambridge: Massachusetts Institute of Technology.

Debons, Anthony, Donald W. King, Una Mansfield, and Donald L. Shirey. 1981. *The Information Professional: Survey of an Emerging Field.* New York: Dekker.

Estabrook, Leigh S. 1979. "Emerging Trends in Community Library Services." *Library Trends* (Fall): 151–164.

———. 1981a. "Labor and Librarians: The Divisiveness of Professionalism." *Library Journal* (January 15): 125–127.

———. 1981b. "Productivity, Profit and Libraries." *Library Journal* (July): 1377–1380.

———. 1983. "The Human Dimension of the Catalog: Concepts and Constraints in Information Seeking." *Library Resources and Technical Services* (January/March): 68–75.

Estabrook, Leigh S., and Kathleen M. Heim. 1980. "A Profile of ALA Personal Members." *American Libraries* (December): 654–659.

Heim, Kathleen M. 1981. "Women in Librarianship." In R. Wedgeworth, ed., *ALA Yearbook, 1981.* Chicago: American Library Association.

———. 1982. "The Demographic and Economic Status of Librarians in the Seventies, with Special Reference to Women." In Wesley Simonton, ed., *Advances in Librarianship*, Vol. 12. New York: Academic.
Heim, Kathleen M., and Leigh S. Estabrook. 1983. *Career Profiles and Sex Discrimination in the Library Profession.* Chicago: American Library Association.
"In the News." 1983. *American Libraries* (June): 337.
National Commission on Libraries and Information Science. 1982. *Public Sector/Private Sector Interaction in Providing Information Services.* Washington, D.C.: GPO.
Nielson, Brian. 1983. "The Impact of a User Librarian Responsiveness: An Examination of Online Bibliographic Searching and Reference Practice." Ph.D. diss., University of North Carolina.
Norman, Nigel. 1982. "Librarians and the Dilemmas of Professionalism." *Information and Library Manager* 2, no. 3: 64–67.
Peace, Nancy. 1981. "Library Personnel: Collective Bargaining." In R. Wedgeworth, ed., *ALA Yearbook, 1981.* Chicago: American Library Association.
———. 1982. "Library Personnel: Collective Bargaining." In R. Wedgeworth, ed., *ALA Yearbook, 1982.* Chicago: American Library Association.
Sellen, Betty Carol. 1980. *What Else You Can Do with a Library Degree?* Syracuse, N.Y.: Gaylord Professional Publications, and New York: Neal-Schuman.
SHARE Directory. 1980. Women Library Workers. Privately published.
U.S. Bureau of Labor Statistics. 1975. *Library Manpower: A Study of Demand and Supply.* Bulletin 1852. Washington, D.C.: GPO.
Van House, Nancy A., Nancy K. Roderer, and Michael D. Cooper. 1983. "Librarians: A Study of Supply and Demand." *American Libraries* (June): 361–370.
Weatherford, John W. 1976. *Collective Bargaining and the Academic Librarian.* Metuchen, N.J.: Scarecrow.
White, Lawrence J. 1983. *The Public Library in the 1980's: The Problems of Choice.* Lexington, Mass.: Lexington Books.

Bibliography

DeWath, Nancy V., and Michael D. Cooper. 1980. "1981–82 Library Human Resources: A Study of Supply and Demand." Rockville, Md.: King Research, Inc. Mimeograph.
Guyton, Theodore Lewis. 1975. *Unionization: The Viewpoint of Librarians.* Chicago: American Library Association.
Heim, Kathleen M., and Carolyn Kacena. 1981. "Sex, Salaries, and Library Support . . . 1981." *Library Journal* (September 15): 1692–1699. (Earlier reports by Heim and Kacena appeared in *Library Journal* in 1979 and 1980 and by the series initiators R. L. Carpenter and K. O. Shearer in *Library Journal* in 1972, 1974, and 1976.)
Nielson, Brian. 1980. "Online Bibliographic Searching and the Deprofessionalization of Librarianship." *Online Review* (September): 215–223.
O'Reilly, Robert C., and Marjorie O'Reilly. 1981. *Librarians and Labor Rela-*

tions: Employment under Union Contracts. Westport, Conn.: Greenwood.

"Placements and Salaries." 1973–1982. *Library Journal*. An annual survey published in successive years.

Schiller, Anita R., and Herbert I. Schiller. 1982. "Making Information Private." *Nation*, April 17: 461–463.

Schlacter, Gail. 1973. "Quasi-unions and Organizational Hegemony within the Library Field." *Library Quarterly* (July): 185–198.

KAREN BRODKIN SACKS
BUSINESS AND PROFESSIONAL WOMEN'S FOUNDATION

Computers, Ward Secretaries, and a Walkout in a Southern Hospital

Today, there is a widespread movement for equal pay for work of comparable worth. This is a strategy for closing the gap between men's and women's wages under conditions where jobs are very much segregated by sex. It seeks to have jobs where women predominate paid at the same level as jobs at a comparable level of skill and responsibility that are held mainly by men. Because it has involved reevaluation of job skills, the comparable-worth movement has focused national attention on the fact that much of women's so-called unskilled labor requires definite, identifiable skills. Unfortunately, this movement has given too little attention to systematic racial segregation within those occupations classified as "women's work" and to the additional racist undervaluation of jobs that black and other minority women are assigned by employers.

At New South, as at other hospitals, the work force is overwhelmingly female and is occupationally segregated by race as well as by sex. Here, ward secretaries are mainly black women, whereas secretaries and medical secretaries are overwhelmingly white. Before they walked

---

Some of the ways that many ward secretaries contributed much to this analysis will be obvious to readers. I would like to thank them and wish it were possible to do so by name. I hope I have portrayed their ideas, feelings, and actions accurately. My thanks to Kay Day, Evelyn Nakano Glenn, Dorothy Remy, and Carol Stack for their help does not have to be anonymous. All names of people and the name of the hospital have been changed. The ethnographic present is 1980.

out, ward secretaries' pay was two grade levels below that of secretaries, a reflection of New South Medical Center's (NSMC's) view that their skills were far from equal. In addition, very few black women were at a higher pay level than ward secretaries. For white women, administrative secretary (two grades above secretary) was the top of the ladder for all but a handful of nonprofessionals. After the walkout, ward secretaries' pay was raised to the level of secretaries', and they became key organizers for a union whose bargaining unit was to include, and was supported by, many secretaries.

At one level, this essay is about *how* and *by whom* jobs are defined and about the relationship of job definitions to pay and working conditions. At another level, it is about the specific devaluation of black women's jobs and about the initiatives they took to force upgrading of their jobs, pay, and working conditions. In what follows, I first describe the work of ward secretaries, highlighting the "invisible" aspects of the job. In the second section I deal with how ward secretaries' awareness of their skills generated a militant action that forced NSMC to grant official recognition of and pay for those skills. In the third section, I deal with the all-too-common fact that these victories are not secure: that New South has been slowly and persistently undercutting many of their gains, necessitating continual activity by ward secretaries just to maintain the fruits of their efforts.

"Invisible" Work

I learned about "invisible skills" accidentally, in the course of trying to understand the process by which ward secretaries organized this successful collective action. I interviewed Denise Thompson and Evelyn Beasley, two senior secretaries who were central activists, and wrote a draft analysis. Fortunately, I showed it to Evelyn, who in turn showed it to Denise and to her sister-in-law, Felicia. When I saw them next, they had all read and discussed it. They agreed that it was awful. "Too one-sided; it sounds like a leaflet," said Evelyn. I was puzzled that someone who had been an activist would find my critical portrayal of working conditions objectionable, particularly since that was the way it was presented to me. I did not stay puzzled long. Evelyn told me: "When I read this, I felt I must be some kind of fool to stay here if that was all there was."

I had detailed what was wrong, the reasons for taking action. Evelyn's comment raised a more immediate pair of alternatives: collective action versus the individual action of quitting. Ward secretaries must have walked out *because* the job was worth fighting for. I think that the walkout was possible and successful for many of the same reasons that ward secretaries stayed on and enjoyed their jobs in spite of some very oppressive conditions. "You need to talk with more people and get the whole picture," Evelyn told me. She, Felicia, and Denise then gave me a list of twenty or so secretaries on different wards, services, and shifts and with different views on the world. They called Violet and Alice, explained my research, and sent me over to them. From that point on, I was passed along people's kinship and friendship networks, as well as to people who were selected because of a particular experience that someone thought I should learn about.

When I realized that ward secretaries were cooperatively organizing my research and teaching me, I also realized that they were doing the same thing with inpatient health care delivery. Coordinating and teaching people is a central and exciting, though stressful, part of their jobs. It is also one of the invisible skills not recognized by New South's administration. The informal ward secretary networks I was passed along are also significant and invisible attractions of the job. They are sources of social life, workplace support groups where ward secretaries can affirm their worth and the worth of the work they do, as well as bases of trust strong enough to sustain collective action and confrontation.

Hospital wards are intimidating places for the uninitiated. Most people gravitate toward the large counterlike desk somewhere in the middle of the hall, hoping to find a person to guide them. This is the nurse's station or ward desk. Sooner or later everyone who has business on the ward will be there—for a while. The desk is permanently staffed by one or two ward secretaries whose job it is to coordinate and organize patient care information, orders, and tests for all patients on the ward. They convey the care plans and orders that are doctors' ideas about what a patient needs, to the nurses, lab personnel, and people from the dietary department who put various parts of it into practice. They link the wards where patients "live" to the departmental people who take an active role in a particular aspect of their care. Ward secretaries have to mesh the schedules of many people, often with diplomacy and some firmness.

Denise Thompson is a gregarious heavy-set black woman. Not yet thirty, she has been working at New South for about ten years. During this time, she has thought about taking other jobs and has been active in efforts to improve wages and work life at the hospital, but mainly she enjoys her work and the people she meets. Denise works days on a small ward. Normally, she covers the ward with another secretary, though as often as not I have seen her alone, or with a trainee. This morning her co-secretary was working elsewhere because they were short staffed, and Denise's new trainee was sitting with her books on her lap, watching the activity. It was very busy, too busy for anyone to pay much attention to her. Denise was on the phone most of the time—actually on two phones—together with paging nurses and aides on the intercom to go to one or another patient's room. As a woman in a nightgown and robe walked by her desk, Denise hailed her to ask if she had brought her chart back from the test she had just had. She had not and apologized with some embarrassment. Denise told her not to worry, that she would phone down to have it sent up. At the same time, a man, about to be discharged, stopped at the desk to pick up his return clinic appointment and prescriptions, which his doctor was supposed to have given him. After some searching, because this was the first Denise had heard of it, Denise found them at the desk. She suggested to the man that he wait in the back room for a bit because the intern was supposed to talk with him before he left. The man pointed out that both his doctor and the intern had walked by him twice and waved without stopping. Denise paged the intern to have him come up as he was supposed to do. The intercom buzzed. A patient wanted a nurse to come to her room to open a can of soda. This is a private ward. Denise rolled her eyes, turned to an LPN at the desk, and said, "Would you?" The nurse answered "No" but went anyhow. I felt conspicuously idle, when Denise took advantage of a break in the action to ask me what kind of work I did when I was not hanging around the desk. I told her *that* was my work. "Oh," she replied deadpan, "nothing."

Though ward secretaries do not phrase it this way, I see two aspects to their job. One has to do with coordinating and organizing the records of medical care. The other has to do with coordinating the actual people involved in this care. These two aspects require different kinds of skills, and successful ward secretaries need to use both kinds. NSMC administration recognizes the second not at all and only part of the first.

In the hospital bureaucracy, there can be no planning for treatment without a record of what has already been done by a variety of people who may never see each other. Every real act has its paper or computer image. Ward secretaries keep these records for all patients on their ward. They also communicate with all hospital personnel performing services for patients on the ward and schedule these services. Their job puts them at the hub of inpatient care.

NSMC is becoming increasingly computerized. The computer system allows the ward secretary to register information at other locations via teletype, thus allowing direct recording at a distance. For ward secretaries, this is perhaps the computer's single most time-saving and appreciated use. Each communication involving data terminals produces multiple copies of a printout of the transaction. Printouts of some transactions—test and procedure results—go into patient charts; others, requisitions for tests for example, are printed in the relevant labs. One copy of all printouts on the ward teletype is kept by the ward secretaries or their supervisors to keep track of all work. This is the paper image of work.

Alice Dixon began working as a ward secretary before there were computers on the wards. After stating emphatically, "I would *not* like to go back to the manual requisitions!" she explained that the computers were a very positive step on two counts. First, they eliminate a most time-consuming piece of drudgery: having to write a never-ending number of requisition slips by hand. Second, computers provide a record of who did what work. Paulette pointed out that the responsibility as well as the drudgery was greater under the manual system. The consensus among those who have worked both systems is that computers allow ward secretaries to do the routine work faster and with less chance of error. It also protects them from being scapegoated for errors of others.

The first computer system decreased the load on ward secretaries, but since they were the only people on the wards trained to use the complicated codebooks, no one else could help them out with their work in a pinch. This monopoly of skill proved advantageous when secretaries walked off their jobs in 1974. The newer computer system prints operating instructions directly on the screen and requires no special training to use. "Now if a secretary isn't there, the nurses can sign on and do what they want themselves," according to Robert, one of the few male secretaries involved in this walkout. While Robert thought that the walkout might have spurred New South to get this system—so that ward secretaries would not be able to paralyze the hospital again—Evelyn saw another side. Yes, she said, the new computer provides easier access, "But you don't know how unhappy the nursing staff is. Nurses don't know how to use the computer because they didn't want to learn. We still have to teach them, and they don't want to know." From the nurses' perspective, learning to use the computer opens the way to adding an additional dimension to their already full workday.

Management has also used the computer's speed as an opportunity to add new tasks to the work of ward secretaries. Until recently, nurses and ward secretaries' supervisors used to order supplies for the ward from the central supply department. Each ward has a fairly routine shopping list of things that need to be kept in stock, from intravenous supplies and antiseptics to soap, lotion, and paper, as well as not-so-routine items that need ordering from time to time. Before the hospital began to computerize ordering, central supply workers came to the wards, checked the supply carts, and restocked them. As computerization proceeded and central supply pulled out of restocking, nurses and supervisors found they were spending the better part of a day ordering. Hospital administration shifted the job to ward secretaries, who are finding out that not only are they expected to do the ordering but they are also expected to run around and find out what needs to be ordered.

The record-keeping aspect of the ward secretary's job is the only aspect given formal, national recognition by hospital administrators. The U.S. Department of Labor and the American Hospital Association jointly published *Job Descriptions and Organizational Analysis for Hospitals and Related Health Services*, a compilation of standardized job descriptions and hospital organization gathered by an extensive survey of hospitals. According to this source, the job of ward secretary requires a high school education and no previous experience (as at NSMC). Under the heading of "worker traits" it stresses the abilities to understand procedure routines and verbal instructions, do arithmetic, and maintain clerical detail. As "interests" ward secretaries should have "a preference for established routine in keeping patients' charts, preparing schedules, and verifying supplies." They should be able "to carry out repetitive operations under specific instructions and in accordance with established procedures." This description focuses on the secretaries' relationship to charts and requisitions; it says nothing about their relationship to people.

Almost all the ward secretaries agree that they are "the nerve center of the ward" and that the job "is a real mental strain." Sally put it more forcefully: "To be honest and truthful, ward secretaries run New South Hospital." As I listened to secretaries describe what they do, and as I watched them do it, I began to realize that they were not only clerical or data processing workers but also administrators and that this aspect of the job produced most of the stress. When Beverly elaborated on the tension of the job, people loomed large: "Ten people talking to you at once, the phone is ringing, and the teletype is jammed. Doctors talking to you like you're supposed to know everything."

Secretaries orchestrate the activities of specialists at all points on the medical center hierarchy, but they do so in a context that is a setup for stress and conflicts. Administrators, with their high pay, status, and formal authority, have an easier time telling people what needs to be done than do ward secretaries. But secretaries have to do a significant amount of this type of work with no authority, low pay, and low status in the hospital's chain of command. There is plenty of talk about teamwork and the "New South Family" by hospital administration, but there is no recognition that health care teamwork encompassing many departments needs on-the-spot coordinating. So far as I can tell, that job falls to secretaries, who have to do it without bossing or ordering because some personnel—particularly the doctors—would not take it well.

According to the formal job description, ward secretaries do not have patient contact and have no direct role in patient care. In reality, they play an important role as informal intermediaries between patients and the mass of specialists charged with different facets of patient care. Some of them take a strong interest in learning all they can about the medical aspects of the ward. Yvonne works on a research ward and finds that she has picked up a good bit of knowledge about pediatric respiratory diseases that helps her treat her children. As a teenager, Sally spent the better part of a year in the hospital. For her, there is a "purpose to be in the hospital. I enjoy helping others because I know how it is." It is often the ward secretaries as well as the nurses who organize parties for patients' birthdays or homegoings. Perhaps because they have no formal role, ward secretaries are often the main people to think about hospital patients as people with human needs for conversation, rest, and cheer.

This is also true when it comes to scheduling tests or procedures. Doctors might ask for a particular patient to be scheduled for a number of tests. Tanya explained that she had several things to consider when she did so. First, she needs to know how long each test is likely to take. A liver scan, for example, can take three hours. Some departments are known for canceling a patient's test if the patient is not on the floor when called. While diplomacy may help in stalling for some time, it is better not to schedule too closely. Second, and more important, doctors seldom consider whether or how much a particular test or series of tests can fatigue a sick person, or about how tiring being wheeled around a large, crowded hospital can be. Tanya tries not to schedule anyone for more than two or three things in a day because most of her patients were exhausted by more than that. Ward secretaries often need to exercise their judgment to mesh doctors' plans for treating an illness with the state of a sick person's constitution at any given time.

Teaching is another unrecognized and unrewarded job that ward secretaries perform. Primary care and responsibility for each patient is given to first-year interns. The work load of ward secretaries shoots up each July when new interns come on the job because they do not know many of the hospital's procedures, and they do not know their way around the hospital. Some tests and procedures can only be scheduled by the interns, who often do not know this. New interns also have to be taught to write out reasons for procedures they want the ward secretary to schedule. Here, teaching often consists of a time-consuming paging of the intern. Robert noted matter-of-factly, "New interns are indoctrinated to get all they can from the ward secretaries." Sally added that one of her biggest hassles was trying to read doctors' writing and to get them to write legibly. "If you can't read it, you've got to page them to come up and decipher it before you can do anything with it."

Teaching people who are overworked, high up on the hospital's status hierarchy, and who have not been told that they are being taught is a difficult and often thankless assignment. Because it is not part of their job description, ward secretaries get no support from hospital administration; house staff do not recognize it as a necessary part of their training and seldom appreciate it either. Indeed, secretaries often complain about the abusive way doctors treat them and about how the whole burden of resisting and "straightening them out" falls on their shoulders. Problems are multiplied both by the number of interns who have patients on the ward and by the number of doctors involved in the care of each patient.

Mary pointed out that even routine work involves directly coordinating people. The phones ring fairly constantly; "mostly it's people wanting to know where a patient is and what they've had done. Some things can't be done before others. If a patient needs four tests in one day, I'm on the phone for fifteen minutes getting each department to tell me when they're through so I can have a messenger pick them up and take them to the next place."

Ward secretaries also help coordinate nursing. As they come on duty each shift, nurses get a care plan for each of their patients. In the past, nurses came to the desk to find out what the orders were. Maybe it is the nursing shortage, which, together with a high turnover rate, is acute at NSMC, but, "Now they expect to be called and told." Beverly said that she does this, even though she really does not have the time and resents the extra work, because "it's a pain to have the doctor asking if the test is done and to have to say you don't know [because the nurse hasn't picked up her orders]. I'd rather initiate the procedure by calling the nurse and telling her."

I have often watched nurses, house staff, and medical students ask a ward secretary to phone someone for information for them when they were standing next to the phone. They continued to stand there during the conversation, to clarify their question to the secretary in response to a query she relayed from the party on the line, and to wait for the answer from the secretary when she got off the phone. Patricia sighed and agreed that both doctors and nurses often interrupted her work to ask her to do something for them that they were quite able to do for themselves: "To keep peace, a lot of the time I go ahead and make the phone call." Too, some doctors write their orders piecemeal, "and that keeps us hopping."

There are concrete skills involved in coordinating and maintaining cooperation from people whose jobs and places in the hospital's hierarchy of power and prestige often put them in conflict, while forcing them to work as a team. For the most part, ward secretaries learned these skills from each other and in their own families; and they shared them among themselves informally along lines of friendship, work socializing, and on-the-job training.

Ward secretaries have to deal with two kinds of perennial problems. The first is the interpersonal problem of maintaining working relationships with higher-ups who belittle ward secretaries, while resocializing those higher-ups to the realities of ward secretaries' jobs. The second is the institutional problem of the low pay; grievances over scheduling, staffing, and other working conditions; and the low esteem in which NSMC holds ward secretaries. The institutional situation, of course, encourages abusive behavior from doctors, supervisors, and nurses. Ward secretaries have been fighting on both the interpersonal and the institutional fronts, but in different ways.

The interpersonal battles sometimes seem like a series of unconscious catch-22s. Offensive behavior from doctors, supervisors, administrators, and nurses seems to come from an unspoken belief in their high prestige relative to ward secretaries and also from an institutional view that ward secretaries just do routine paper pushing. For secretaries to be successful, however, they have to get those they coordinate, especially higher-ups, to stop acting as if they were commissioned officers ordering enlistees and to start behaving like part of a team. The catch is that many of the "officers" they coordinate do not know that there *are* coordinators or that coordination and teamwork is really how health care gets delivered. Instead, they tend to equate teamwork with their giving of orders. Helen observed, "They don't think the ward secretary position is important 'til they don't have one; then they run on like a chicken with its head cut off." Jane spoke for many secretaries:

> Their attitudes are really, really nasty. You have to count to fifty. Sometimes I just walk away. I don't like being yelled at. I'm an adult; I'm grown. If you can't speak to me without yelling, don't speak to me at all. Often they yell about something the ward secretaries don't know about. It's really the big ones that think you're, excuse the expression, shit. What they're saying is that they think you're ignorant; and they never apologize when they accuse you wrongly. They don't try to learn your name; they call us "hey you." Very few say "good morning." It takes everything I have to keep this job.

For some doctors, tantrums and loud abuse were an automatic response to anything other than instant gratification; they acted as though they had a *right* to yell without regard for anyone's feelings and felt no obligation to apologize when they were wrong. Some doctors are racially prejudiced, and some ward secretaries felt that this was why doctors disregarded their feelings and were blind to their capabilities. Ward secretaries regard the kind of behavior Jane described, as well as less offensive acts—like asking them to make phone calls that the doctor or nurse could make just as easily—as a way of pulling rank. Doctors and others used their high status to belittle ward secretaries, to reinforce managerial and institutional views of their "worth" in the hospital ranking system and of their capabilities as both workers and adults.

Institutional ranking systems and interpersonal rank-pulling are inextricably bound up with racist attitudes and institutionally racist patterns of job allocation. With very few exceptions, doctors and RNs are white; most ward secretaries and LPNs are black. These are about the top of the pay scale for all but a few black women at New South. Many ward secretaries see racism not only operating against them directly but also working against black patients. Several women discussed their frustrations with racist staff. One ward secretary, who was the only black person on her ward at the time, told of a group of white doctors who referred to black people by a variety of derogatory names. When she called them on it, they just laughed at her. She said that it was hard to confront a bunch of doctors, harder still being the only black person on a ward. Another woman wrote up a doctor for calling a black patient a "subhuman animal." She got no results from hospital administration, but she was not surprised. The consensus was that ward secretaries had no help from management in stopping racist behavior; they were on their own and had to help each other.

But sometimes victims cannot help themselves, and racism kills. One ward secretary who worked the night shift told of a black woman patient who "turned bad" (started dying). Both LPNs and the ward secretaries tried to get the RNs to call the doctors. They refused, claiming that she was not really sick. In despair, the LPNs rolled the code apparatus (equipment for dealing with cardiac arrest) right to the woman's door. Finally, one black LPN called the doctors. By the time they got to her, the woman had died.

In part because the formal education of higher-ups in general leaves them ignorant or misinformed about the realities of social relations and about the people they work with, and in part because ward secretaries are in the center of activity so that everyone comes to them, the burden of initiating on-the-job remedial training in social relations, or "manners," falls to them. New South's formal rules and medical education both encourage rank-pulling and hierarchy, but the nitty-gritty of medical care needs to be carried out by a different set of behavioral rules. Though most secretaries dislike snobbishness and arrogance, I do not think they are making a fundamental challenge to the existence of the formal hierarchy. Instead, they are telling doctors and others that insisting on the privileges (real and imagined) of rank can make it almost impossible to solve problems and resolve conflicts so that people can continue working together. Almost all secretaries indicated that they had to set these ground rules. This is a concrete skill that takes time to learn. In general, senior ward secretaries said that they had good relations with doctors, that they had learned to elicit "teamwork" behavior with a minimum of conflict over the issue. Younger ones, however, or newer ones like Jane, had more difficulties.

The line between interpersonal and institutional problems is not a hard and fast one. That is, the hierarchy and values embodied in formal hospital administration affect the way people act toward one another on an interpersonal basis. In this respect, ward secretaries have an uphill battle to reorient people's views of them, of the work they do, and of the way they are treated as individuals. So long as the institutional message does not change, they have to shovel sand against the tide, so to speak. This is because many of the personnel with whom they work, especially house staff and nurses, are constantly changing. Every doctor and every nurse has to be dealt with independently. On the other hand, to the extent that ward secretaries can change the institutional view and treatment of them, they have an easier time teaching the attitudes and behaviors that make it possible and pleasant to do their job.

From Potlucks to Protest

New South's definition of ward secretaries and their work has regularly sparked some form of collective protest. To a great extent the unity and shared understandings that are the necessary conditions for such actions are generated and sustained by ward secretaries' informal workplace and community social networks.

The administrative organization of work, that is, scheduling and rotations among different wards, tends to bring secretaries of a unit together and to establish communication across shifts as part of the daily work routine. Informal social networks are built on and reinforce these lines of communication, with secretaries and nurses on a ward, paired wards, or wards of a unit getting together for holiday parties, informal cookouts, picnics, dinners, wedding and baby showers, and lunches throughout the year. Depending on the constellation of people involved, almost anything from someone's leaving, to a patient going home, to doctors rotating off the ward can be the occasion for a social event. Some of these events, mostly those on holidays, are initiated "from above," for example, by a head nurse, by a supervisor, or by the attending physician in charge of the ward. But others, especially those outside the hospital, come from the initiative of a friendship network that often extends beyond the unit. Many ward secretaries were born and raised in the town and have ties of kinship, marriage, school, community, and church, all interwoven such that there are many workers in the hospital with whom they share some relationship. People tend to tell friends and relatives about job openings and to recommend them, so that ties of kinship, work, and friendship reinforce each other.

These relationships become part of the raw material that ward secretaries work with in creating social networks in the hospital and creating the close personal friendships and familylike ties that sustain their unity and spirit. New South is where many secretaries have made their closest friends; and most of these tend to be other secretaries and nurses with whom they work. Paulette and Patricia, though they are sisters and both ward secretaries, belong to different work-based social circles. Evelyn; her sister-in-law Felicia; Denise, whom Evelyn has known from high school days; and Denise's husband's cousin Nancy are all secretaries on the same service as well as friends who hang out together outside of the hospital.

While ward secretaries bring family *to* work, they recognize that friendships and familylike relations also come from and are created *at* work. Until recently, the bulk of ward secretary training took place on the wards. Senior secretaries were assigned trainees and given most of the responsibility for training them. Because supervisors and most senior secretaries worked on the day shift, most training took place then. After completing their training, however, new secretaries were assigned wherever there were vacancies, generally the evening or night shifts and on wards different from the one on which they trained. The relationships established between trainee and trainer are important in several respects: for passing on informal rules for handling the job; for communicating the ward secretaries' view of themselves and of the work they do, rather than a management view; and for establishing close personal friendships. Alice has worked on her unit for about eleven years and has helped train a fair number of secretaries. In the course of training Yvonne, they became friends. When Yvonne saw the house next door for sale, she knew that Alice was looking for a house and told her about it. Now they are also next-door neighbors and car poolers. In turn, Yvonne has maintained high school friendships with

Willa and Violet. Willa is a ward secretary on another service; Violet's good friend and co-secretary is Alice. Yvonne has become "best of friends" with her co-secretary on the ward where she now works.

Through a combination of training, school, and co-worker relationships, the ward secretaries of most of the wards on one unit, and those of an unrelated ward, make up a fairly tight group of friends. A similar situation exists on another unit; and each of these networks has ties to most of the other units' friendship groupings. This was also the case when ward secretaries walked off the job in 1974.

The major reason for the walkout, as well as the subsequent conflicts with New South's administration, is the nature and worth of the ward secretaries' job. The introduction of computers to the wards of NSMC was a catalyst. It focused their grievances and legitimated their views of their work: "The majority of us felt with all this new training they should offer us more money. Any time you work with a computer they should give you more. If you're lucky enough to get in research you could make much more out there than here." As events unfolded, ward secretaries asserted in words and deeds that their jobs were more complex, skilled, and responsible than New South would admit. They demanded pay, autonomy, and respect for their work as coordinators of patient care on the wards.

Pay and certification in computer skills were twin and linked concerns. The women resented the hospital's refusal to increase pay or to provide certification of their competence in using a computer system. One ward secretary phoned a hospital in another city and found that her counterparts there—mainly white women—started at higher salaries than senior ward secretaries were earning at New South. They found, too, that New South changed their plans for a new job title for ward secretaries (data processing technicians) when they had reason to believe that a technical classification might mandate more pay than a clerical one. Certification was important because ward secretaries saw it as helpful for getting better jobs elsewhere. "As they say in the computer room, New South will teach you all you want, but they won't give you that certificate." Without it you cannot move, and if you cannot move, they can pay you what they choose.

While there were many grievances over schedules and supervisors, some ward secretaries, including some of the more active, had few complaints besides pay. But the anger was deeper and more widespread than any particular grievance: "We just about run the hospital, but we're being cheated out of the money." Because money is a measure of respect as well as a means to buy bread, anger centered on the hospital's systematically demeaning their job and denying their abilities. This is why those with few daily problems got very involved: low pay, no certification, and personal abuse were visible signs of management's attitudes.

Consider, too, that most ward secretaries are black and that this is one of the better paying jobs black workers can get in significant numbers at this hospital. It is not easy to distinguish abuse generated by snobbish attitudes from abuse generated by racist attitudes. But the systematic underrating of a complex job by hospital administration could only reinforce racist ideas about the abilities of black women. The town had an active black movement from the late 1960s to the mid-1970s, and many ward secretaries were involved in some facet of it while in high school. During most of this time, the town's schools were segregated. "At New South was the first time I *saw* what they were talking about—whites on top and blacks on the bottom. Ward secretaries were considered dumb even though we were running things. Even if I hadn't been to freedom school, I couldn't take not being treated like a human being."

Several friends called a meeting at one woman's home. Some thirty ward secretaries turned out to draw up a petition centered around four demands: better pay; two weekends off each month and days off at regular intervals; more respect and an end to abuse from doctors, nurses, and administrators; more ward secretaries hired ("You worked a ward by yourself then").

There were a variety of meetings, including one with an administrator who was reported to have said that you could pull a ward secretary off the street anytime, that they were a dime a dozen. "That was supposed to stop us from walking out; but it had the opposite effect." Since New South promised nothing in response to their petition except to "work on it," ward secretaries held a second meeting, attended by perhaps 75 people—an impressive showing considering that there were probably no more than 150 ward secretaries at the time, and some of these were at work during the meeting. They decided to call in sick as a safe way of walking out in the absence of a union.

Ward secretaries agreed that their action was effective, particularly on the largest and busiest services, where supervisors and untrained administrators had a terrible time trying to cover the wards. They felt that both the hospital and the patients suffered as a result of inadequate coverage, but as one woman commented, "They use patients as an excuse to kill you—and they're robbing the patients blind." Another noted that the place was "a mess" when they returned and that it took a great deal of work to put it back together.

The walkout brought some real changes. "We said the only way we'll come back is if you don't fire anybody"; management hedged, "and we said we'd still be sick—so they gave in. We got uniforms the color we wanted. They wanted us to pay for it. They paid. We got respect. You know how doctors throw charts? Now they can't." Pay was raised from level three to level four the following January and has since been raised to level five, that of secretaries, and ward secretaries received an immediate twenty-cent increase and alternate weekends off. The unpopular administrator somehow disappeared. Lines of authority were clarified between nursing administration and ward secretary administration, so that ward secretaries were no longer in the middle. Nothing changed with regard to problem supervisors. The number of ward secretaries increased, ultimately by about 60, or 40 percent, though this seems to have been gradual and uneven over time and by unit. As a result of the walkout, "all of a sudden someone realized our job was important. Any time you have a walkout, it does tell somebody that something's wrong and that you do have the ability to organize." One woman who was not a central participant thought that the walkout gave all ward secretaries a "sense of accomplishment" both at communicating how responsible and important their job was and at their ability to organize to do something about their lot.

Finally, about eight months after the walkout, the hospital presented ward secretaries with computer certificates ("They just gave it to keep us quiet"), but even this seems to have required some additional meetings and organizing. One woman said that they got the certificates by having a meeting of their unit with supervisors and unit administration. The initiators were senior secretaries central in the walkout. "If they complained, others would follow suit."

Six years, and considerable numbers of new ward secretaries, later, the informal social networks are still in place. Patricia had told me that the ward secretaries on her unit had regular parties and dinners as well as a Christmas party, to which they contributed a dollar every two weeks, and that Beverly was the treasurer. Beverly explained to me that last February all the ward secretaries had agreed to contribute dues into a fund to rent a hall and buy decorations and refreshments for a dance this Christmas. Virtually everyone was involved in cooking food and selling tickets to people in the hospital. Posters throughout the medical center publicized the event as one given by ward secretaries for all hospital workers. It was a very clear display of solidarity and spirit.

I asked Beverly where all the organization came from. She told me that shortly after she began working at New South she gave a goodbye party at her house for a ward secretary who was taking another job. Since many of the secretaries on this unit knew each other from high school anyhow, they began getting together regularly for dinners every two weeks at someone's house. Beverly has been active in keeping them going. Together with other social events in and out of New South, this social network has been going for five years and includes just about all secretaries from all wards.

As ward secretaries and LPNs, black women are the main builders of ward and unit networks. While they put a good deal of effort into involving white women workers, the hospital's racially segregated hiring patterns together with those of the medical hierarchy reinforce color, sex, and class lines. Practical nurses—LPNs—are mainly black women. RNs are overwhelmingly white. Most of those I spoke with stressed that color did not separate them at work; some emphasized that both black and white workers on the ward—including RNs—were part of the dinners, picnics, and other events held at people's homes.

On one ward, however, where all the ward secretaries were black and all the nurses were white, the nurses took the initiative in organizing out-of-hospital parties and dinners. While the secretaries I spoke with praised the good relations that existed regardless of color at work, they also said that the black workers did not go to the parties outside of the hospital, even though "they [doctors and nurses] all get after us the next day for not coming." Every year the ward secretaries and messengers (also black) talked among themselves and declared, "If you go, I'll go," but they never did. When I asked why, one woman said that they were all afraid that they would not fit in outside the hospital—and that discovering it might jeopardize the good work relations they had. Another contrasted it with parties and showers in the hospital—where everyone goes and brings gifts "because everyone's here"—they belong and do not have to explain themselves. But both women also indicated that the root of this lay in the hospital's segregated hiring patterns. One said that if there were more black nurses, ward secretaries would be more comfortable going, for they would not have to hurdle both race and hierarchy barriers at once.

While the hospital's patterns of racially segregated occupational categories increase the difficulty of integrated social networks, black and white hospital workers put a fair amount of effort into overcoming them. The success of the ward secretary walkout indicates the importance of everyday socializing as a basis for both the trust and the shared understandings that any kind of collective action requires.

Eternal Resistance

All the ward secretaries with whom I spoke believe the walkout brought lasting benefits. They are equally unanimous about the need to do more. Alice on the good points of her job: "There's no harassment; we do things on our own and we communicate well. To me you couldn't ask for a better job." And on the bad points: "It's just the money." Violet: "We just about run the hospital, but we're being cheated out of the money." Mary acknowledged that she probably would make less money if she tried to find another job; at the same time, she feels that what she makes as a ward secretary "is not enough money for what I do." These two aspects of money make it the focus of ward secretaries' long-standing and widespread anger at New South's administration systematically demeaning their job and denying their abilities.

Two recent events have brought these issues to the surface again: New South's training program for ward secretaries and its implementation of a system of photo-identification badges. In the last year, the hospital has begun to change the training program so that it is more solidly under management control. Initially funded by federal money, the new program puts trainees in classes eight hours a day, full time, for six weeks before they begin to work the wards. Some senior ward secretaries were asked to work as teachers in the management-controlled program but refused. I discussed the new program with Beverly, Sylvia, Tanya, Mary, and Sally. There was consensus that trainees came through the program only "partly trained, but you have to train them on the ward. There are some things you can only learn on the wards." Sally emphasized the importance of on-the-job training for teaching shortcuts. Sylvia spoke about little things that they teach in class that are silly, for example, that nurses should verify secretaries' work, when it is much easier and faster for the ward secretary to check herself whenever she has time.

Probably the most important thing that ward secretaries passed along to trainees when they did the training was their mind set or consciousness of the job, one that is very different from a management view of them as routine paper pushers. Ward secretaries teach new secretaries how to assert themselves and to know that they have the responsibility for teaching cooperative styles of behavior, especially to higher-ups. Sylvia pointed out that all secretaries still "tell the new ones to speak up for themselves when you know what you want to say and can say it with a smile on your face and give a direct explanation." With the new program, ward secretaries still have to spend a good amount of time training, but now without even informal recognition by management that this is one more part of their job that has not been eliminated by so-called training programs.

More than the work is involved, though. Management-controlled training undermines ward secretaries' abilities to pass along their sense of dignity and consciousness of what their job involves and how to do it—and replaces it with the administrators' idea of the job and appropriate attitudes. Mary told me that the person running the program has only three month's summer experience as a ward secretary; that teachers in the program earn far more than secretaries; that they teach courses about "attitudes, psychology, and other crap. Then these girls hit the wards with no knowledge of how to do anything, and they feel they know more than the ward secretaries. We have to train people who think they know." Most ward secretaries are angry at the lack of any significant pay differences between a new trainee and a ward secretary with seven or more years experience. They see it as New South's way of telling them that it is an unskilled job and that experience and ability are not worth anything.

A similar bone of contention underlies secretaries' dissatisfaction with the identification badges they have been given. These have the person's picture, name, and job title or department. There was some initial grumbling all over the hospital about unflattering pictures, the hassles of remembering the badge, and the wrinkles the clips put in some clothes; but by and large, within a month almost everyone wore the badge, and the grumbling stopped. Except among ward secretaries. Six months later a good number of senior secretaries had pasted over the part of the badge that identified them as "ward support" personnel. In its place they had written "ward secretary, certified data technician." Other ward secretaries refused or "forgot" to wear their badges; and at least one refused to have her picture taken. Even though Beverly says it is "no big thing," it is a significant enough issue for the secretaries on at least two services to hold meetings with their administrators to try to get the badge changed.

While it is not a formal protest, it is pervasive and persistent. "We just get on the phone and talk about it," said Beverly. Sally saw that a friend on another ward had changed her badge, so she did likewise; and her play sister followed along with others on the unit. They had an unsuccessful meeting with the administrator of their service in an attempt to get the badges changed. Patricia said that the secretaries on her unit were also supposed to be having a conference with their administrator. Beverly and Evelyn say they have asked and have been waiting for a month for a meeting.

There is still another dimension to secretaries' frustration. There is nowhere to go, neither a pay scale nor a promotion ladder that recognizes increases in skill, ability, and experience. Evelyn expressed what many ward secretaries feel: "I love that job, but people just starting are making almost as much. You feel foolish doing nothing. I've got to find something at a higher level." Most often people feel conflicts between their need for more money and recognition and the fact that they would have to give up the sociability, real challenges, and responsibilities of their present job in order to get the money and recognition. Many, like Evelyn, Beverly, Mary, and Sylvia, oscillate between two strategies: actively organizing ward secretaries and workers elsewhere in the hospital to improve their wages and working conditions collectively, and seeking out jobs (together with the necessary training) that they hope will give them the best of both worlds. Interestingly, they gravitate to the first option, pursuing the second perhaps more intensively when the possibility of collective action looks bleak for the immediate future. Shortly after the failure of an organizing drive for a union, Mary applied to nursing school; Beverly enrolled in several business courses; Evelyn began to make plans to get a college degree and major in business; Sylvia is trying to become a medical secretary. Nevertheless, they fight even while hoping to switch. Said Evelyn, "Usually it's me and Denise calling people." Quite independently, Violet told me that when people seem dissatisfied, Evelyn and Denise usually ask Violet and Alice if they want to do something. She and Violet are central people on their unit, Alice figures, because they have been there longest. Sylvia also looks to Evelyn and Denise, and they in turn discuss things with Beverly.

Conclusion

Ward secretaries at New South were motivated to walk out because the administration systematically undervalued the nature of their work, particularly the level of skill and responsibility it required, and because the administration demeaned the people who did the job. Ward secretaries were *able* to act collectively because of the strength of their informal work-based social networks. These were the ties that carried their own understandings of their worth and the worth of the work they did. Social networks combined with on-the-job training helped make these understandings conscious and collective and provided bonds of trust strong enough to risk acting on them.

THREE
WORK AND RESISTANCE IN THE GLOBAL FACTORY

11

NINA SHAPIRO-PERL
UNIVERSITY OF CONNECTICUT

Resistance Strategies: The Routine Struggle for Bread and Roses

Manufacturers in low-wage, labor-intensive industries, like costume jewelry, achieve high productivity through expanding their operations and intensifying the pace of work itself rather than through wide-scale technological innovations. In the costume jewelry industry of Providence, Rhode Island, where 70 percent of the work force is female, workers feel the effects of capital's strategies through shrinking wages (eroded by "incentive" schemes like piecework) and deteriorating work conditions (speedups, expansion of duties without additional pay). Conventional notions about women workers tell us that jewelry workers accept their lot with passivity, being preoccupied, as women supposedly are, with their families and domestic roles. The virtual absence of unions, strikes, or other signs of militance in the jewelry industry seem to reinforce this view and to suggest that worker resistance to these conditions is altogether missing.

In six months of fieldwork in a Rhode Island jewelry factory as an ordinary production worker, I learned that women workers have a wide range of strategies of resistance—both individual and collective—to the oppressive conditions in which they work. This essay considers several: pacing, wherein workers selectively hustle and idle in the course of a workday and thus regulate their output to serve their

I wish to thank Susan Porter Benson for her careful reading and creative suggestions on an earlier draft of this essay, and Karen Sacks for helping me clarify some of the major themes.

economic interests; griping and antics, commonplace shop-floor behavior in which workers collectively protest the work situation and safely (i.e., without fear of individual retaliation by supervisors) challenge management's control of the shop floor; and quitting, a final and serious act of resistance to oppressive work conditions whereby workers withdraw their labor, sometimes defiantly, from the work process but in so doing also rob the shop of its militant leaders.

In the second half of this study I focus on the cleaning struggle, a series of efforts by which workers protested an expanded work load (a cleaning detail) and struggled to preserve their original jobs and, in the process, their sense of dignity. The resolution of the cleaning struggle highlights the limitations of the low-risk, low-gain strategies I examine here.

Through these examples of shop-floor resistance, I show that workers, as part of their daily work routine, wage a struggle for "bread and roses," though their struggle does not conform to traditional patterns of worker militance, namely, sit-downs, walkouts, and strikes. Examining everyday shop-floor behavior like pacing, griping, or quitting for the resistance embedded in it reveals two things: that the largely female costume jewelry work force is not, in fact, the passive and apathetic group it is reputed to be but is *already* engaged in a silent struggle with management over control of the work process, and that viewing worker fight-back only in terms of conventional measures of militance like strikes or walkouts results in overlooking the more informal but ongoing fight-back strategies that are enduring and creative and may contain the embryo of future worker organization.

These resistance strategies are creative acts made with purpose by workers who aim to limit, more than change, what management can do to them, while keeping their jobs. These strategies do not formally challenge management's power through a series of actions that, by their nature, involve more risk taking and historically have required collective action, formal leadership, and possibly, a guiding ideology. Rather, these resistance strategies are low-risk, low-gain plans, sometimes conceived collectively, but most often carried out individually to protect one's economic interests or personal sense of dignity. Ironically, these individual acts of economic self-interest are reproduced by worker after worker, side by side; and though performed individually, they nonetheless grow out of a shared class position.

Workers, when asked about their everyday behavior at work, do not use class terms, nor do they discuss their behavior as strategies of resistance to management. Instead, they often see their resistance as appropriate individual responses to get the most out of work economically from an employer who pays them poorly. When I asked one woman why she slowed down on a time study, she replied, matter-of-factly, "To get a higher price [piece rate]. . . . We have to play it smart like they [management] do."

The fact that workers do not talk about these behaviors as strategies or in class terms does not mean that they fail to understand the class relations that structure their workday. The point of this essay is to show that, quite the opposite, their conduct is no less than a calculated defense of class interests based on an experiential understanding of class struggle. I focus on workers' careful time calculations on and off piecework to illustrate how finely tuned their sensitivity to, and understanding of, exploitation really is.

At the same time, workers have internalized the legitimacy and prerogatives of management to "do what they will" with employees during the workday. This belief is absorbed in phrases one hears from fellow workers, like "That's the job" and "Factories are like that." This sense of employer prerogative is so deeply instilled in them that acts of resistance to management that workers engage in as part of their normal daily routine often do not appear to workers as what they are: class-based strategies to challenge management's control of the work process.

Viewing these behaviors as strategies of resistance helps to render explicit the antagonistic relations between workers and managers that are embedded in the capitalist labor process. Calling them "strategies of resistance" makes explicit what is implicit in workers' words, attitudes, and actions. In the process of considering these resistance strategies, the popular view of jewelry workers as passive women resigned to the grim life in jewelry may be altered, supplanted by one of jewelry workers as strategists, creators in an unglamorous daily struggle for bread and roses.

An Industrial Ethnography

In 1978 I did anthropological fieldwork in a large costume jewelry factory in Providence, Rhode Island. As a production worker with no prior factory experience, I was arbitrarily assigned to the setup and charge department upon being hired on by "H&B Creations."[1] H&B employs 350 people, many of them first-generation Portuguese immigrants, in a sprawling one-story factory in an industrial section of Providence. H&B typifies the larger costume jewelry firm of today, housing separate departments for different operations and methods of jewelry production (electroplating, toolmaking, polishing, casting, lost wax, footpress, setup and charge, etc.) under its one roof. The majority of its work force is employed in jobs classified and paid as unskilled or semiskilled, though these labels often bear little relation to the actual skills required of workers on the job (Bookman, 1977: 124). Over 60 percent of the workers are women, the majority of whom are steered into jobs said to require the "feminine" traits of nimbleness, dexterity, and patience. At the time of my work, the women's wages generally started at $2.70 per hour (minimum wage then was $2.65), whereas men,

1. The name of the company, the identifiable characteristics of the workplace, and the names of the people have been changed to preserve their anonymity.

directed into "heavier" jobs, started at $3.00. Most workers train for less than one week on the job. Toolmakers, a local of the International Association of Machinists, are the only organized group of workers in the plant.

H&B promotes itself as a progressive employer offering a variety of fringe benefits, including piecework. The company's cheery paternalism—"It's teamwork that got us this far!"[2]—wears thin when workers daily confront an employer that pays meager wages and provides no sick leave, no job security, no functional job descriptions, and no system of awarding raises. Workers express resentment at management practices of eroding piecework earnings; handbag and lunchbucket searches on leaving work; and serious violations of health and safety standards.

Workers in the setup and charge department produce jewelry through a method of soldering. A setup and charger assembles (sets up) raw pieces of jewelry and solders (charges) them together according to a pre-thought-out process on precut heat-resistant boards. When completed, the boards, which are stamped with the design impressions of the jewelry style, are fed into ovens, where they are carried by conveyor belt through high heat for several minutes. The furnace solders the pieces together and "jewelry" emerges from the other end. The jewelry is dumped into boxes for inspection before being routed to other departments for electroplating, polishing, and so on. The boards are recycled to workers.

At full capacity, the setup and charge department at H&B has forty production workers who sit on high-backed stools at four-foot-wide, waist-high benches arranged in two parallel rows; each row holds ten facing benches. At the end of the two double rows are three anhydrous ammonia gas ovens. Atop the pyramid of the all-female work force of thirty-odd production workers and four supervisory personnel is the only man in the department, the foreman, Fred. Second in command is the "floor lady,"[3] Bea, who carries Fred's directives to the "girls" (production workers). Assisting Bea are two first-generation Portuguese "floor girls," both fluent in Portuguese and English. Bilingual floor girls are crucial to a department that is over one-third Portuguese, the rest being a mixture of Afro-Americans, first- and third-generation Italian-Americans, and third-generation Irish and Anglo-Saxon Americans. The floor girls are responsible for the direct supervision of the setup and chargers and in both cases were recently promoted from bench-

2. One of the owners of H&B Creations introducing a profit-sharing plan to an assembly of workers.

3. The power relations between management and workers are built into the language of the shop, capturing differentiation even within management ranks: foreman, floor lady, floor girls, girls. The term *girls* used by managers and workers alike to refer to production workers is common parlance in work situations where women are concentrated into low-status jobs. Parts of this essay reflect the colloquialisms of the shop.

work. Their highly stressful jobs paid thirty cents per hour more than benchwork.

Resistance Strategies over Work Structure

Nowhere is the struggle between jewelry management and workers as sharp as it is over wages. H&B management capitalizes on the low wages in the industry as a whole by setting up a two-pronged structure of work time within the plant: day rate and piece rate. Day-rate jobs start at five cents above the minimum wage, regardless of the amount the worker puts out. Piece-rate jobs pay by the amount of work produced at a given rate of pay, rates determined by management. Piecework holds out the promise that a worker's high output will be rewarded in payments that go beyond the (implicitly) meager wages otherwise earned in jewelry, and management correctly assumes that jewelry workers will go after piecework. In workers' own words, piecework offers them the only real chance to "make money" in jewelry. For management, piecework not only assures high rates of productivity; it is also a lever of social control that can be used to reward, threaten, or punish workers with "good" and "bad" jobs.

Floor supervisors have unlimited powers to assign workers jobs that pay by the day rate or piece rate. To the worker, this means for days or weeks on end, one might be "stuck" on a day-rate job, while favorites might be on piecework indefinitely. Since the pay earned from "good" piecework jobs can sometimes be twice that of day-rate earnings, workers' livelihood was at stake, and tension over piecework assignments pervaded the shop floor. The presence or absence of piecework invariably set the mood of the department. When there was a supply of piecework, workers talked and joked as they sped along. One fun-loving worker would cheer-lead other pieceworkers on with the chant: "Make money, make money." But when there was little or no piecework, or piece rates were particularly low, workers employed various resistance strategies to protest the situation and assert some control over the conditions of their work.

The mix of day-work and piecework jobs under the control of management and thus open to favoritism produced a resistance strategy among workers that I call "pacing."[4] As I am using it here, pacing is a strategy of time calculation where, in the course of a day, workers will selectively "hustle" and "idle" when it serves what they perceive to be their best interests. On a day-rate job of inspection, for instance, a jewelry worker may take frequent breaks and "forget" to inform her

4. Pacing, of course, is not new. Ever since the nineteenth century, workers in labor-intensive industries have practiced pacing (formerly called "systematic soldiering") "to keep some time for themselves, to exercise authority over their own work, to avoid killing 'gravy' piecerate jobs . . . to stretch out available work. . , to 'make-out' on 'stinkers.' . . , and to express hostility to management" (Noble, 1979: 31).

supervisor that she has run out of supplies. She will give as little of herself as possible, lacking, as she does, a sense of loyalty to an employer that gives so little in return. Alternately, on piecework, setup and chargers generally work at the greatest speed they are capable of, demanding more supplies as soon as they run out, so as to maximize their own time on piecework.[5]

Pacing is the result of a process whereby jewelry workers make a careful study of their own time and motion on the shop floor. Workers study their own time and motions, not the way management does—where the workers are objects with parts to be controlled—but as self-conscious actors protecting their interests in a work process. Just as capital has transformed time into something it owns during the workday and has devised two methods to pay labor for its work (day rate and piece rate), so too does the worker attempt to take back control of her work time. She transforms her workday into what can be abstracted as "time zones." She works "for the company" on day rate, "for herself" on piece rate, for piece rate shifts the responsibility for production levels from management to the worker and affords the worker some measure of control over her wages.[6] This finely tuned self-consciousness results in behavior that palpably changes when she goes from day-rate to piece-rate jobs.

When workers pace, they exploit every possible "pore" in the workday. This is seen in worker's elective use of nonscheduled breaks. On piecework, for instance, the setup and charger rarely takes breaks. Said one woman, "You *know* no one has to go to the bathroom on piecework." But, on day-rate jobs like inspection and repairs, workers take their "little trips to the bathroom" frequently. This is a constant source of aggravation to supervisors, who can do little about it. Not only do the supervisors themselves enjoy their smoking breaks in the toilet, but restricting people's access to it would damage the company's image of itself as a progressive employer. Workers saunter back and forth from scheduled coffee breaks and lunch when the work awaiting them is day work. Lost production time is not their problem. "Those girls can walk really fast when they want to," said Bea, the floor lady, as we walked behind some workers slowly returning from lunch. Deliberate stalling in such instances became such an irritant to management that new rules were enforced to insure workers were at their benches on time. Over time, workers subverted these rules too.

In contrast, when production time was of the essence, pieceworkers *demanded* supplies from the floor girls. Waiting sometimes two or

5. Workers do not always speed on piecework. Given the structure of the piecework system itself, where management sets the rates squarely in its interests, pieceworkers develop a new logic of time-motion calculation (see Shapiro-Perl, 1979).

6. Or at least *appears* to shift responsibility for output to the worker. Pieceworkers quickly learn that management never really gives up control over the piecework system. Management still sets the rate of payment and has unlimited power to step in and bust a rate at any time. In this way, management can exact high outputs but cut back on its payment.

three minutes for setup boards cut deeply into a pieceworker's time where her pay depended on her output for the time on the job. One worker demanded that she be given credit in terms of boards she could have completed in return for the wait she was forced to bear; another worker simply left work early when there were few boards available so she would not "lose" the piecework money earned up to that point. Another worker brought in a whistle and blew it loudly when she needed boards—an act everyone found hysterically funny. Yet when the same workers were on day-rate jobs like inspection, they would *wait* for supervisors to discover they had run out of supplies. When one infuriated supervisor demanded to know why a particular worker had failed to tell her she needed more work, the woman replied in a classic demonstration of passive resistance, "I forgot."

Once *on* piecework, time calculation assumes a new logic. As I have discussed elsewhere (Shapiro-Perl, 1979), pieceworkers regulate their output by manipulating their own time and motions in reaction to management's manipulations of the piece rates. They slow down on management's time studies to make sure they get a good price; they speed up, once the price comes in, to maximize their earnings. They force themselves and other pieceworkers to take breaks, thus holding back production in order to preserve a good rate. Sometimes pieceworkers slow down production collectively by restricting output to protest a bad piece rate and get it retimed. To workers, piecework does not present a unity of interests where "the company gets production and the worker gets to make money," as the company would have it. Nor does the pieceworker, as our nation's folklore would have it, work against the clock—a clock disconnected from its social context. Pieceworkers, by their actions more than their words, see piecework for what it is: a system of job time where the company predetermines that it will have to pay out very little extra in piecework wages. Rather than working for the company or against the clock, pieceworkers set their own clocks against management.

Before assessing how effective pacing actually is, let me briefly review other ways jewelry workers register their resistance to management's presentation of work. Griping and antics are sets of behavior so common to the shop-floor landscape that they easily go unnoticed as methods of fight-back. When unfinished jewelry was found in the toilet in the women's bathroom, it was plain to workers and supervisors alike that an anticompany act of sabotage had been committed. But it was much easier to miss the anticompany sentiment embedded in the griping in which workers routinely engaged. Workers griped continuously about being treated like children when, for example, personnel monitored the lunch line for workers who cut, or when someone's seat was changed for talking too much.

The piecework system itself generated the most persistent griping. Workers constantly complained about the low rates, or favoritism, or the absence of piecework altogether. Though workers sometimes blamed their co-workers for busting the rates, floor girls most often took the heat for the injustices, inconsistencies, and frustrations pieceworkers encountered. The morning after an intense day of griping over piecework, I met Gloria, a floor girl, in the factory parking lot. As we walked into work together, she spoke wistfully of the paradise of another jewelry plant where everyone worked day rate all the time. "I wish there were no piecework," she lamented. The stress of her job—representing the company's interests on the shop floor where the struggle over the paycheck was waged anew daily—was plain. While griping rarely led to retiming of a job (whereby presumably, workers might get a better rate), clearly it made life difficult for the supervisors. Because everyone griped, supervisors were disinclined to single out individuals in retaliation; and when facing this show of unity, they were cautious, anyway, of stirring up the wrath simmering beneath the surface.

Demonstrations of anticompany feeling sometimes had a lighthearted edge to them. One day during a fight over piecework, the humming of some pieceworkers grew into a well of voices as workers egged each other on to hum louder and louder. A cautious floor lady approached the bench and quelled the swell with the diplomatic warning "Singing is for the shower, ladies." Occasionally workers took to throwing jewelry at each other—a vivid display of anticompany sentiment (though carefully "aimed" at other workers) and an indication as well of the esteem workers had for the goods they turned out. Supervisors invariably tried to contain such antics by nervously joining in and putting a stop to them. Supervisors' behavior in such cases corroborates the view that everyday griping and antics, behavior that might otherwise be taken for granted, were collective strategies of protest against the work situation. Such behavior enabled workers to voice their resistance collectively and to engage management safely in a test of wills for control of the workplace.

Griping, particularly, chipped away at the social cement that held supervisors and workers together in a friendly, familial workaday spirit. Work life was stressful enough, riddled with the tensions of an uncertain paycheck and tight controls. For many, fighting about work only aggravated the stresses they routinely handled. The excessive smoking, indigestion, and general cases of nerves that supervisors and workers complained of were exacerbated by griping and fighting back. So while such strategies were effective in getting to the supervisors, workers often took the brunt of them. In this way the strategies often backfired on workers themselves. One woman complained that the recent fighting made her "stomach tighten up the moment she stepped off the bus in the morning and entered the factory." However much she and others thought company rules unfair, she desired a workplace that was friendly, especially when she spent fifty hours a week there. Fighting back might help sometimes, but stirring up discontent was unnerving in itself.

Pacing, on the other hand, was a nonconfrontational strategy of resistance, for it existed in that realm of work life that defied tight controls and close monitoring by supervisors. It was part of that realm where workers could exercise a degree of control over their actions by manipulating that time and space that management reserved for humanness. By spending time in the bathroom, workers preserved a bit of room for themselves. On this level, pacing succeeded as a strategy of resistance to management's pervasive control of work. On another level, however, pacing behavior was turned against workers, for there is evidence that management actually makes use of workers' time strategizing. Not only is pacing not a secret, it appears to be anticipated by management. Contrary to its pronouncements about the unity of interests between workers and the company, management in fact presumes that workers act in their *own* interests. In light of the low wages, lack of benefits, and work conditions I have described, management knows it must cajole its employees into working in the ways it desires. This is, of course, the basis of scientific management, which both presumes and institutionalizes class conflict in the workplace. H&B Creations' payment system of day work and piecework is a case in point.

When H&B wants, above all, for workers to put out a lot of work, it builds the piecework incentive into that process and designates as piecework those jobs where jewelry is produced from scratch. Thus, when the setup and charger assembles thousands of raw parts into finished goods, she is paid on an incentive basis: by the piece rate. Lest the pieceworker turn out huge amounts of work but of poor quality (here management again anticipates a conflict of interests), H&B builds quality controls into the work process. Each setup and charger's lot of work is designated by her letter. Poor-quality work can therefore be returned to its "proper" owner. Piecework is the rule, then, when output is primary and quality secondary.

In contrast, when management deems quality and care to be more important than output, as in inspection and repairs of goods already assembled, it designates such jobs day work. That is, when management desires workers to proceed more slowly, it pays such jobs by the hourly rate. When I asked one supervisor why inspection was not piecework, she replied, "You think the work would get done on piecework?" implying that pieces needing inspection would be skipped over too quickly.[7] Lest workers inspect goods so carefully that little work is completed (again management anticipates worker fight-back through pacing), management measures output on inspection and repairs through the gross measurement of weighing goods turned out by each worker.

In sum, then, management anticipates pacing behavior and adapts

7. For a fascinating discussion of why management pays inspection by hourly rates, see Thompson (1917: 97).

this workers' strategy to its own purposes. When it wants work done carefully (and presumably the worker must go slowly), management designates such work "day work" and pays the worker by the hour, implicitly *assuming* the worker will slow down or idle on company time. Similarly, management *expects* workers to hustle on piecework when there is the chance to make more money than hourly pay, so it harnesses this incentive to jobs in which output is paramount by designating such jobs "piecework" and paying by the piece rate.

Management's co-opting of pacing illustrates the relative weakness of a strategy that challenges management's grip on the work process in piecemeal ways. By negative example it points out the immense power management wields and the seemingly infinite ways it can step in to squelch worker resistance or turn it to its own ends. It points to the need for worker strategies that *directly* attack the social relations governing production rather than the labor process bit by bit. Perhaps the strategy of pacing can be most effective in its educational potential, for it provides an excellent illustration of the conflict of class interests at the heart of the labor process. Organizers can use it as a mirror for workers to see themselves in the act of resistance and more fully appreciate the significance of their ongoing fight-back. Pacing (and its co-opting) lay bare the competing interests of workers and managers that any worker will tell one about, if not in words, then in deeds. Pacing provides the opportunity for such actions to be summed up.

The Struggle over Cleaning

Management's prerogative to have a worker fired for refusing a job is an unwritten rule that workers carefully observe. The narrative that follows illustrates workers' strategies for resisting expansion of their work loads when their supervisor capriciously decided to require setup and chargers to clean the department. In contrast to griping, antics, and pacing, workers' strategies here targeted management's treatment of employees as people rather than the structure of work itself. Workers confronted management on the issues of job description and dignity, although they went to great lengths to avoid direct confrontation. The cleaning battle shows the avenues unorganized jewelry workers took to resolve a grievance over job description in the absence of a union contract. It points to the need for union protection; but it also shows how the fight for dignity on the job goes on in the absence of unions.

Supervisors in the setup and charge department set out upon a new course one day by asking two workers to clean the department—to sweep the floor with large pushbrooms, dust the ovens and storage shelves, and wash down the thirty-five workbenches. Indignation swelled among the workers. Those selected to clean were chosen with care. They were both relative newcomers and presumed to be compliant. As one worker put it, "Something like this happened before. They just ask people who won't answer back and nothing happens." As the two swept, grumbling spread through the department. "I didn't get hired as a janitor," said one woman. "I got hired to set up and charge." Others had already absorbed their indignation into resignation: "Don't make yourself sick from worry about it. That's what factory jobs are like . . . especially nonunionized ones: they treat people bad."

The grumbling continued during the morning, throughout breaks and lunch. In fact, breaks proved to be an important time for workers to talk with each other and, significantly, to communicate their views, though not directly, to management. Carla, for example, "publicly" registered her resistance to the cleaning program by telling Geri and me in the bathroom that "they dare not ask me to sweep." When I naively pointed out to her later that she had said that in front of a worker tight with the supervisors, Carla said this was her intention. Through a strategically placed intermediary, Carla voiced her indignation to management while avoiding a confrontation with them. In a similar way, management squared off with workers by using the floor girls to communicate their views on the cleaning issue: said Mary, a floor girl, to a worker, "Look, if you're on day pay, what does it matter what you do?" Floor girls attempted to unite workers around management's view that the issue of cleaning was one of payment and not power. They tried to avoid at all costs, a confrontation with workers demanding some control over the conditions of their work.

By lunchtime, workers, who until then had not eaten together, crowded around a lunch table to discuss the situation and plan strategies. If asked to clean, one woman theorized, she would just leave work for the day, saying she had an appointment, and in this way avoid a showdown. Geri wanted to meet the issue head on and refuse to clean. She would later say, "After other times like this in other places, when you see we are all numbers in production and they don't give a damn—you realize there's just a certain amount you can take. You don't have to be ignorant or rude about it. . . . But you have to stand up for what you believe in." Linda was skeptical about sticking her neck out: "You never know what will happen when you finally stand up. Some say they're all with you—because they don't want to look bad when everybody's talking; but when it comes to the moment, forget it. . . . I've worked in jewelry shops before and I know." Lou-Ann thought we should go and complain at the personnel office before lunch was out, but Carla, appealing to other workers' sense of fair play, was convincing when she said, "In all fairness, we should talk to Fred [the foreman] about it first before going over his head."

So it was agreed that we would talk to Fred. But no one volunteered or was asked to be the spokesperson for the group.[8] When we returned

8. At times like this throughout my six months of fieldwork, the contradictions in my role of participant-observer were sharp. Of course I had a great desire to "organize" my co-workers' complaints into a plan of collective action, but I did not want my presence, particularly my potential leadership, to "change" the "normal" course of events. As the struggle unfolded, other leadership emerged. The strategies taken by individuals and the group are

to our benches, work began and the plan fell through. But the issue was hardly over. People adopted a wait-and-see attitude. Gloria, a Portuguese worker close to the supervisors, clearly did not want the cleaning issue to die. Before the day was over, Gloria floated a collective strategy: "We have to do *something*. We should all sweep under our own benches. That will give them the message." But Gloria knew "we'd need at least 50 percent of the girls with us" for it to work, for individual sweeping would go unnoticed unless done systematically. No one picked up on this suggestion. If anything was to be organized, more time was needed. At this point, the struggle was not even a day old.

The talk of cleaning lasted for a long time. Workers asked each other what their husbands had to say about the issue. Workers complained about being treated like a (time) "clock number" and of the many such indignities of working in a "joint like this." Lack of control over the conditions of work was at the heart of these complaints, and cleaning emerged as one indignity where the line had to be drawn.[9] For many, the time had come to say, "No more!"

During this period, however, there was no systematic strategizing going on. Basically, people were preparing themselves *as individuals* to deal with this issue, and for some this meant getting psyched to quit if necessary. As Rosemary said to me, "You learn these things. Not to get upset by this. Never take the job seriously. Just go from one factory to the next. Stand up for what you think is right. You wait for the right time to say things. You're young. You'll learn this."

That Friday, one week from the first cleaning episode, workers arrived to find a co-worker cleaning the department. Tension was palpable. Everyone waited for something to happen. Then Gloria started griping to Mary, the floor girl, and told her there was "no way" that she, Gloria, would ever clean when her turn came. Mary did not want to hear about it. A loud argument ensued. The floor lady, Bea, came over. Gloria yelled at Bea, "That's what you have janitors for! We weren't hired to do this." Now a group gathered around Gloria's bench. Geri spoke up: "We clean our own floors and benches . . . why the whole thing?" And Rosemary: "We got hired to set up and charge. If we were hired for cleaning, we weren't told about it." Fred, the foreman, strode over. "It's company policy," he said. Carla shocked everyone when she said, "It is not. I called the NLRB and they said we weren't hired for this." At this, Fred quickly defused the situation when he said, "Let me talk to personnel. I'll get back to you," and promptly left the department.

---

the stuff of this narrative, and they prove to be typical of strategies of resistance in the industry as a whole. For a discussion of the anthropologist-as-organizer in an industrial setting, see Bookman (1977: 6–9).

9. People did not mind cleaning their own benches but resented having to clean the department. Cleaning per se was not "beneath their dignity." Several workers mentioned other jobs they had cleaning offices, schools, and hospitals. They simply were not hired to clean the factory.

Griping and bickering about cleaning kept up all day. Lunch tables reflected the new alliances that had been made over the struggle. Yet planning remained at the individual level. By the day's end, Fred had not gotten back to anyone. Though they expected to be fired, Rosemary and Geri approached Fred once again before leaving for the day. Although Geri had worked there for three months, she said, "Fred, I'm one of the girls that talked to you this morning about the cleaning." "I know," he said. "Fred, they're making it into a personal thing. We don't mind cleaning our own benches, but we weren't hired for the other stuff. Is there any word from personnel yet?" "I'm waiting," he replied.

Later events proved that Fred had indeed consulted with personnel and prepared them for the storm that was brewing. He correctly identified for personnel the main point of contention—the sweeping—and communicated that "some of his girls were too old to push brooms." But his failure to get back to anyone revealed that management would use a stalling strategy in the hope that angry workers would, over time, cool off.

On the following Friday, a janitor appeared in the department and swept the floor and dusted the machines. People nudged each other and looked delighted. It appeared to be a clear victory: people would presumably have only their own benches to clean. Word traveled quickly through the department and then through the whole factory. Much to her surprise, workers from other departments, whom Rosemary did not even know, came up to her and said, "Hey, we heard you got a victory." There was a power struggle here that other workers had a clear stake in.

But the victory was short lived. The following Tuesday Bea the floor lady strategically placed herself next to me as she proceeded to cut into lots the list of names of girls who had not yet cleaned. While I did not realize it at the time, she was about to use me as a sounding board as well as a conduit to convey her intentions to my co-workers. She also did not miss the chance to separate me from my co-workers by noting that I did not have to worry about cleaning since I had done it already (when I first started work, before the struggle began).

This time, Bea told me, it was a "special" cleaning job since the "big shots" (owners of the company) were scheduled to tour the plant that afternoon. When I said it would probably cause trouble, she took that as an opportunity to pour out *her* story:

> I can't help it. I'm following orders from higher up. It's company policy. . . . If people don't like it, they can go to personnel or higher. . . . I try to be even handed and not play favorites. There's just not enough piecework to go around. . . . And this cleaning—I don't understand it. It's only for thirty minutes every three months. And there's no sweeping with the broom required.

Significantly, the issues Bea raised with me—favoritism, piecework, and cleaning—did not all relate directly to the struggle at hand; yet they were the areas of most contention in the labor process, and they all had in common the issue of control. In cleaning, however, the control issue was most clear cut. However much management tried to portray cleaning as a money issue alone, in fact it turned on the issue of control—specifically, job description and dignity. Where worker fightback in the form of griping, threatening, a joint verbal protest, and individual acts of defiance had been most intense—over *sweeping*—management had yielded. Workers were no longer required to push a broom. While Bea was sure to remind me of this concession, management reasserted control by requiring workers to clean shelves, machines, and other people's workbenches. In a brief talk, Bea had skillfully touched all the key points.

When I dutifully communicated Bea's message to my friends in the bathroom, Rosemary made me realize just how precise Bea's strategy was: "Bea told you this so the other girls will know they might have to clean this afternoon." Bea had avoided a confrontation, while *I* did her work for her.

This lead time gave people a chance to prepare, but the strategizing again took the form of individuals planning their own course of action, just as their co-workers did alongside them: "My heart is pounding. I don't know what I'll do." "It's up to the individual—if she's called on she'll quit rather than do it." "I hate to get fired. But if I have to, I have to. It's only right to refuse to clean." "I'm so bored, I'll do it. But if they take me off piecework to do it—I'll be mad." Most everyone at the lunch table individually braced herself for the possibility of standing up if her name were drawn by lot. But no strategy was planned to stand up *together*.

There had been suggestions of collective action, like Gloria's, who thought we would need one-half of the girls cleaning their benches with us to avoid getting fired, or Geri's, that we quit in sympathy for whomever's name was picked and had to refuse. "If we don't refuse, we won't finish what we started." But neither strategy was fully articulated, much less systematized. For the most part, alternatives were posed negatively—get fired or quit—and "what we started," in other words, preserving the integrity of our jobs, was never discussed positively.

But people tried. A group formed to support Gloria in her verbal protest to Bea. Others attempted individually to protest the indignities to which co-workers were subjected, as did Carla when Maria, a sixty-year-old Italian worker approached Carla's bench to clean it. In an act of passive resistance that would probably have been effective and dramatic had it been systematized, Carla stood up and refused to let Maria approach it. As Carla cleaned her own bench, she turned and stared at Fred to make sure he got the point. He turned away in embarrassment.

It became clear that the struggle over cleaning would be waged as individuals engaging in solitary acts of defiance, one after another. In frustration, Gloria had already stopped coming to work regularly and eventually quit altogether. It was now just a question of time until another of the "militants'" names would be drawn in the lot each Friday. A few weeks later, Rosemary's name was drawn. She got up and told Carla, "I'll see you." Carla told her to "wait until they tell you to go." But Rosemary got her things and went to personnel. Fred, saying he'd meet her there, grinned as he left the department. We later found out that the personnel manager told Rosemary it was not "unreasonable" for her to clean up once, "after all the time she'd been there" (six months), but Rosemary should "do what you have to do." Rosemary did not return. Carla and Geri did not wait long to follow. Geri quit that same day, not "wanting to give them the satisfaction of firing me." When Carla told a supervisor she was also quitting, the supervisor replied, "Everybody cleans. It's company policy." Carla said, "It is not. I polled this place—three people from *each* department—and no one does it." "You did *what*?? . . . . Carla, why don't you just go? Why do you have to go around stirring up trouble?"

And so, in a final and serious act of resistance, Gloria, Geri, Carla, and Rosemary, the "militant" leaders of the cleaning struggle, quit. It was a personal act of defiance, of dignity and an assertion, if for one last moment, of control. The other attempts had not worked. As one jewelry worker ironically remarked, "The only power we have is the power to quit." Most workers did not see the significance of quitting in these terms. As a result, the ones that remained could not get the ideological mileage out of their co-workers' defiance that might have countered management's portrayal of the latter as "troublemakers." In fact, management took back control of the quitters' actions by saying, for instance, that Gloria "had been terminated."

Thus far I have described quitting as a self-preserving resistance strategy whereby workers affirmed themselves by refusing to perform jobs for which they were not hired. But clearly, such a strategy in the end proved self-defeating. By not staying and collectively fighting for a better work situation, for themselves and others, those who quit robbed the shop of its militant leadership. Had these leaders stayed and organized the others to resist the assignment that everyone hated, few, if any, would probably have been fired. As it was, the struggle died through the attrition of its leaders. It was not a bloody death marked by the sort of militant walkout that makes news. Rather, it faded away, as leader after leader quit as individuals. In the weeks that followed, people continued to clean with a grim resignation that characterized jewelry workers in general.

The poignant failure of this strategy of resistance was brought home when Geri, perhaps the most militant worker, remarked to some of us: "We should all quit together and go work in another place and make sure its union this time so they can't pull this shit." The irony of this view, of course, is that it helps to keep jewelry shops "the pits" where no one stays to organize and improve working conditions. This reproduces the migrant-labor character of the jewelry work force, where workers go from one to another of the thousand jewelry shops in Rhode Island in search of better working conditions and dignity. It had happened in the setup and charge department of H&B Creations as it happens all the time in jewelry. Events transpired just as Rosemary, the voice of twenty years' experience in jewelry shops, had counseled: "Don't take this job seriously—just go from one to another." The sad irony remains, however, that she and others took the cleaning issue *seriously* enough to quit.

References

Bookman, Ann. 1977. "The Process of Political Socialization among Women and Immigrant Workers: A Case Study of Unionization in the Electronics Industry." Ph.D. diss., Harvard University.

Noble, David F. 1979. "Social Choice in Machine Design." In Andrew Zimbalist, ed., *Case Studies on the Labor Process*. New York: Monthly Review Press.

Shapiro-Perl, Nina. 1979. "The Piecerate: Class Struggle on the Shop Floor. Evidence from the Costume Jewelry Industry in Providence, Rhode Island." In Andrew Zimbalist, ed., *Case Studies on the Labor Process*. New York: Monthly Review Press.

Thompson, C. Bertrand. 1917. *The Taylor System of Scientific Management*. Chicago: A. W. Shaw.

12

NAOMI KATZ
SAN FRANCISCO STATE UNIVERSITY
and
DAVID S. KEMNITZER

Women and Work in Silicon Valley: Options and Futures

Some thirty miles south of San Francisco lies the Santa Clara Valley, until the 1960s a place of fruit orchards and canning, with the sleepy, sleazy city of San Jose its center, and now—thanks to the entrepreneurship of Stanford University and William Shockley, its most famous engineer—one of the two main centers in the United States for the burgeoning electronics industry. Its pear orchards having been replaced by large and small factories, and its hills covered with condominia for their employees, San Jose is now the third largest city in California and the fastest growing.

The popular image of this growth, fostered by the companies themselves, is of an immense bonanza, fueled by the futuristic marvels of the computer age, peopled by engineers and eccentric programmers cum promoters who graduate with B.S. and BMW to a $25,000-a-year job complete with stock options and lifestyle. Figures for average wages in the industry of thirty-five thousand to forty thousand dollars are frequently bandied about, and stories of entrepreneurs going from garage to multinational (like the Apple Computer Company) get great play in the papers. Moreover, all of this is seen as so *clean*. All of the cities in Silicon Valley have regulations requiring that factories look like anything but factories (suburban high schools and Store-It-Urself facilities seem to be the favorite models), and open space with ground-cover landscaping is everywhere despite record level real estate prices. There are no smokestacks. The area, which provides more industrial employment than any other part of Northern California, does not *look* industrial; although it is the major source of toxic wastes in California, Silicon Valley has the appearance of a carefully tended suburban landscape.

The irony of the electronics industry is not limited, however, to the contrast between industrial wealth and squalor played out against a backdrop of stucco and redwood rather than one of brick and steel.

Of the 155,000 people employed in electronics in Silicon Valley in 1980, 60 percent, or 93,000, were production workers. Of these, 75–80 percent, or 70,000–75,000, were women; in 1978 there were, for the first time, more women employed in the United States in electronics than in the garment industry. Of these women production workers, about half are Third World, and many of these latter are newly arrived Asian immigrants. These are the legal immigrants; undocumented workers are employed cash-payment fashion in the cottage industries that surround the major firms like satellites. Of the male production workers, many are also Third World and immigrant; white men, by all accounts, rise rapidly to technical or supervisory positions. Wages in general have not kept up with U.S. manufacturing wages as a whole (Snow, 1980: 6); in 1982, they averaged less than five dollars an hour. Union organizing has been slow and only minimally successful.

This essay derives from a field study, conducted in the Santa Clara Valley from 1979 to 1982, which focuses on women blue-collar production workers. We here consider, in part, the contrasting worker and management views of the work situation and of the industry and also some of the means whereby these are expressed. We discuss as well some of the implications of the changing production relations the industry is implementing, including its underground aspects, and their relation to women production workers.

When any assembly worker is asked, "Why are you working at this job?" she invariably answers, "I need the money." Although her answers immediately become more complex, the well-known facts of the inadequacy of a single income in a family, the large numbers of single mothers and other self-supporting women, and the recent layoffs in neighboring industries such as auto or canning have led, in Silicon Valley as elsewhere, to a large number of potentially employable women, many of whom in the last decade, and some even now, are seeking work for the first time. In addition, the very presence of this industry has drastically raised the cost of living in the Santa Clara Valley, adding to everyone's need for work. The industry, in its efforts to recruit these women to its lower paid jobs, uses gender stereotyping in a number of interesting ways.

In recruiting and training materials, the unskilled and therefore "easy" nature of the work is explained as a virtue. Bypassing the definitional problem that all assembly jobs are called "unskilled"—even rather complex soldering under microscopes that does require special training—trainers tell new recruits, and managers told us, that the work is "really easy," "just like following a recipe." The only skill one needed, we were told, was manual dexterity, which women had anyway, particularly Asian women, who had as well a high tolerance for tedious work. The tedious, "easy" work was, again, a virtue because women would not be so tired when they got home and had all those household chores—"naturally"—to do. In fact, the "nontiring" work, requiring little training, along with the "pleasant" surroundings, choice of shifts, and "the mothers' shifts" all combined, in the language of managers, to make these jobs ideal "supplementary" jobs for women.

As part of being supplementary, women's need for jobs is also portrayed as temporary: "until the orthodontist's bill is paid," "until the RV is purchased," "until she gets married" or marries again. Because their working is only temporary, women are said to desire and prefer an undemanding go-nowhere job. Thus women seldom get real and acknowledged on-the-job training, and some of the deepest resentments we heard expressed concerned just the issue of being an experienced assembly worker: ". . . and then a white man comes in," is soon up for advancement, and "you end up training your boss."

The woman's perception of the work situation as a whole is in many ways more complex than the expressed paternalistic managerial view. Interviews with women chronicle a subtle awareness of the benefits and disadvantages of their options. Ease of getting or changing a job is acknowledged, and choice of shifts is in fact a big plus, making possible shared child care for mothers, overtime, and moonlighting for everyone. But the low pay, necessitating regular overtime, moonlighting, or both and making the reality for almost everyone a six- or seven-day week, makes the management construct of "women's work as supplementary activity" both laughable and bitterly resented. For the interviewees, their job, far from being supplementary or temporary, represents, or is part of, a *lifelong* strategy for coping with or overcoming low class, or race, or sex positions.

If job benefits and disadvantages are somewhat coolly viewed by the women interviewed, much more highly charged are those issues having to do with status and class, specifically issues of condescension to them and devaluation of them as production workers, both on the job and in the outside world. Statements like "When you get on the production floor, you feel like less" and "It's easy to dump on someone who makes $3.85 an hour" were never far from the surface of people's conversations about work. Several times we were to hear comments about clerical personnel like "The secretaries think they're something with their skirts and high heels and going out to lunch with the managers, but with overtime, we make more." In one plant, an issue was raised over production workers' pictures displayed on a bulletin board *below* those of managers.

This seeming disjuncture between managerial statements communicating ethnic and gender stereotypes and the women's repeated emphasis on status and class was underlined for us when one of us applied for a production job in the Valley. In the course of seeking work, she had to admit that she had had some college education and that she had been married to a teacher. On three separate, independent occasions, she was told by personnel people—all women, as it happens, who were clearly trying to be helpful—"You won't like the work," and then, in a single breath, "They're a lower class of people—they don't even all speak English." Needless to say, it was the helpfulness of the co-workers that allowed her to survive her brief stint as a temporary, working graveyard; and it was they who were careful to remind her not to work even fifteen seconds into her break and to go to the bathroom, as permitted on "their" time, not during the lunch half hour. More to the point, however, is the fact that the off-the-cuff comments of the personnel managers, not for public consumption but to an apparently misguided "class" mate, revealed the core class condescension that underlies the more strategic management stereotyping—condescension that appears to be lost on no worker. Moreover, that very stereotyping—"it's easy, just like following a recipe"—defines the work not only as women's work but as trivial, insignificant, not even, properly speaking, work at all—and surely not a trade or skill. The gender stereotyping in this instance does not mask the status or class devaluation, as it so often does elsewhere, but rather, reinforces and communicates it.

The workers combat their devaluation as workers where possible by increasing their income with job hopping, overtime, moonlighting, or home work—thus, incidentally, revealing once again the symbolic as well as the practical attributes of money. Assertion of positive status and pride in themselves as persons are clearly tied to making more than survival pay. The most overwhelming example of this sort is provided by a Tongan woman who works three jobs and lives simultaneously, if tiredly, in three cultures. When we commented on how little sleep she must get, she answered that she gets top pay working graveyard at Lenkirk ("I'm trained and experienced, and it's a union plant"), top pay for cleaning houses (". . . and I only clean clean houses"), and that, moreover, in addition to sending money home to Tonga and participating generously in local Tongan celebrations, "I'm putting money away for my son's college." Similar sentiments were expressed by three women, all married with employed husbands, who regularly worked fifty-eight hours a week—also for top pay at Lenkirk: "Despite what we look like when we get off, with that big check you feel like somebody." "It's for the house payments. But we're buying a good house in a good neighborhood—for the children." "I dropped out of high school . . . my son goes to private school, won't have to do like me." The commitment to the strategies and symbols of mobility, for themselves, perhaps, and at least for their children, is once again a way out of, or at least a way to cope with, the practical difficulties of their lives. Simultaneously, it is a counterassertion of self and status in the context of the devaluation and condescension from above.

Although the workers clearly approach their work and work situations *as workers* in Silicon Valley, there is an entrepreneurial aspect to the relations many have to their jobs. In recent years, this approach has both encouraged and been reinforced by the resurgence, as the underside of this otherwise highly advanced industry, of the older manufacturing practice of home work, or cottage industry. We turn for a moment to how this cottage industry works and then to the practice of home work in conjunction with job hopping, moonlighting, and excessive overtime.

At first glance, the mushrooming of home work is a management strategy analogous to offshore (overseas) production, providing flexibility, a means of getting work done more cheaply—with no benefits, no sick leave, no paid breaks—with piecework rates and no unions. It is all this, and more. Many women view home work from another perspective, as a preferable option, revealing again many of the felt inadequacies of jobs on the production floor.

Home work appeals to many as a way of tailoring their work more closely to their life situations: to mothers who do not want to leave small children; to women who want, for whatever reason, greater flexibility than any shift allows; and to those who prefer continued isolation at home to spending all day in a closed-in, supervised plant. It also appeals to those women who *do* wish to define their paid work as supplementary: "I only do it after my husband has left for work in the morning, and after I've picked up the house." There are also many (the precise number being unavailable for obvious reasons) who can *only* work at home: the undocumented workers.

From a contrasting, more feminist perspective, the subcontracting side of home work is seen by some experienced workers as a way out of their low positions in the plant as women. Two young mothers emphasized that, for them, subcontracting was a means to independence and status, as well as to a less alienated relation to their work. They discussed becoming "independent" after having trained a series of bosses while they worked in the plants, stressing repeatedly that subcontracting was the only way that they, as intelligent women, could achieve outside the factory the levels of initiative, income, excitement, job satisfaction and "something to show for it" that capable men could achieve, via promotion, inside the plants. Of course, from a management viewpoint, two experienced, restless, dynamic women who might be just the ones to challenge authority effectively—as union organizers, for example—are diverted elsewhere.

Nonetheless, the conditions and costs of home work reflect an erosion of the protections and benefits we have come to associate with production work and thus merit some further attention. Plants may send work home with full-time workers on a cash-payment basis, as for example, rush orders. More usually, they will contract work out via subcontractors. Pay is by piecework or job lot, with no legally mandated protections such as unemployment insurance, workers' compensation, guaranteed overtime rates, or paid breaks, with no sick leave or paid holidays, and certainly no such benefits as health insurance. Workers can be, and are, fired on the spot. Independent employees frequently have to provide their own tools and equipment; they often have to pick up and return work at their own transportation cost and time; they are held responsible for the safety of the parts; and they always provide their own overhead, such as heat, electricity, and cleaning. Plants can thus be proportionately smaller, and save on both construction and maintenance, in effect transferring these costs to the workers. Finally, because the whole practice is at best semilegal, and thus not under the surveillance otherwise provided by government agencies, health and safety protection is nonexistent; instances have been documented of women heating toxic chemicals on their kitchen stoves. The advantages for management are clear: in the words of a state labor practices investigator, "They do it because they're getting away with something" (Personal interview, 1981).

The conventional wisdom in Silicon Valley—from managers, muckraking liberals, and Marxists alike—is that these entrepreneurial excesses and underground features of the Valley economy can be explained by the relative youth and competitiveness of this particular industry. It is thus interesting to note that, in a recent article, Mattera (1980) notes similar developments in Italy, in a variety of industries including textiles, apparel, footwear, and also metalworking, electronics, and automobile-parts construction. Mattera links, as do we, overtime, moonlighting, and home work. He points to the recent proliferation of practices almost identical to those just described. While not acquainted with our data, he discusses as well other features we found, which thus become exceedingly interesting for analysis in a comparative context: the increasing use of immigrant labor, both legal and illegal; the importance of the underground economy in the more highly industrialized and technologically advanced areas and industries; and the fact that, despite surface appearances, the independent or decentralized firms are not independent at all, but on a more basic level, "are external departments of the big plants or, to use the Italian term, a diffused factory" (72–73). He also strongly emphasizes, as we do, the critical importance of the lengthening of the working day and the erosion of workers' historically won benefits.

The similarity of the developments in the two areas seems to confirm both Mattera's and our suggestion that we are witnessing, not a recapitulation of earlier forms of capitalist development in a new industry, but the further development of contemporary capitalism as part of Capital's efforts to deal with current economic conditions. Moreover, industry's strategies are also political and related to the successful struggles of workers in the past; they affect both above-ground and "underground" workers by their individualizing and antiunion impact and are, properly speaking, part of the class struggle as traditionally understood.

The similarity between the situation Mattera describes and that in Silicon Valley suggests that at this juncture the initiative is in the hands of employers and that the options open to workers are not of their own making. While in one way this formulation is true, and available options allow workers to find a livable strategy only within narrow limits, this does not give "the system" total dominance, leaving no role for the perceptions, actions, and choices of real human beings. Indeed, quite the reverse is true; as we observed, individual workers quite knowingly take advantage of the contradictions and interstices of the situations they confront. Thus they make choices for themselves that permit not only survival but assertion of self and flexibility in the arrangement of their work so it is compatible with their life situation and with their definition and understanding of it. In this sense, they may, and frequently do, shape the form of their labor and expand the range of options open to them.

At the same time, the individualized choices workers *can* make have only the most limited potential for transforming the system. On a more fundamental level, however, the gains of the metropolitan working classes over the last century—economic, social, and political—have effected real structural changes in capitalism. It is to these changes, in significant part, that the current undermining and erosion of institutionalized workers' benefits is a response. Moreover, one element of this response is the displacement of class conflict, away from confrontation at the workplace and toward issues of social status which the workers confront as individuals, or as members of a cultural "type" (women, Vietnamese, etc.) in a broader, more diffuse arena. The increasing speedup and the transforming of labor relations, bolstered by the diffusion of class into social issues with other markers, such as gender or ethnicity, underscore the fact that the "institutionalized indirect wages" (Wolpe, 1975: 247) won by metropolitan workers over the last century are not so secure as had been previously assumed.

Part of the recent counterattack against labor has been a weakening of health, safety, and environmental standards and of the national and state agencies enforcing these standards. As noted, the electronics industry attempts to project an image of itself as "clean" in terms of both its impact on the environment and the risks to workers' health, an image considerably at variance with reality. In particular, many production processes in electronics involve the use of highly toxic chemicals and heavy metals that pose real risks to workers in the plant and grave problems of waste removal and contamination of soil, air, and water outside it. The response of the industry to criticism about these matters is twofold. On the one hand, industry threatens relocation to avoid environmental legislation; relative independence from supplies of raw materials and the portability of plant equipment make such mobility feasible. In fact, expansion of plants in California has lately been for the most part outside of Silicon Valley, for a number of reasons including "getting away from that damned Sierra Club atmosphere." On the other hand, the electronics industry is also a pioneer of the accommodative compromise with regulatory agencies, compromises that usually give considerable leeway to the company, bought with the promise to be good in the future; a large-sounding fiscal contribution to clean-up work; and a grandiloquent "study" of the problem.

In the absence of effective unions to represent them in the adversarial process of government "fact-finding" and regulation, it is not surprising that workers' responses to health issues on the job are for the most part individual and widely varied. Health hazards were frequently alluded to and always acknowledged by the women production workers we interviewed, although many preferred not to dwell on such risks at length, summing up the matter with fatalistic remarks such as "but every job has its hazards," or "when your number is called. . . ." At the same time, many workers have strong opinions on health and safety issues and risk supervisory disapproval by selecting very carefully on that basis the departments or plants in which they will work, by reporting infractions to supervisors and community or government agencies, and in some cases by seeking outside support and even suing. A particularly interesting case is that of a long-time production worker currently engaged in a suit who became militant about health issues upon learning that both her parents' deaths were due to asbestos poisoning in World War II shipyards.

It is important to note that workers' responses to health risks are dependent on their knowledge of dangers and that they are frequently underinformed, owing in part to the fact that information about some of the chemicals in use in electronics, especially in combinations, is frequently lacking.

The workers' relative atomization on the job appears to contrast with their activism as *citizens* and as "neighbors" of polluting or hazard-producing facilities. Production workers in concert with the Central Labor Council and environmental groups have been active both in filing suits and in protests to authorities. One recent, well-publicized case involves the pollution of groundwater in South San Jose by Fairchild, which resulted in a number of birth defects and late-term miscarriages and in a ban on drinking well water. A production worker who participated in this suit emphasized strongly in a TV interview that while she as an adult worker could evaluate the risks posed by chemicals in the plant and still choose to work there, her children had no such choice regarding the pollution of their neighborhood.

This duality of response to health and environmental issues—individual, fragmented, and variable on the job; more activist, confrontational, and collectivist off the job—recalls the earlier issue we raised about the entrepreneurial relation many production workers have to their jobs. This sort of response differs markedly from the assumptions and strategies of workers in other, older industries, where status mobility is tied to collective efforts and practices such as collective bargaining, seniority, job security, promotion, and pride in skill. Both aspects of electronics production workers' relationship to their jobs acknowledge the devaluation of work and the workplace as the basis for mobility, safety and security, or even self-esteem. At the same time, the struggle for these things continues; it has simply been displaced.

To some extent, this displacement acknowledges the power of employers to define the industry. Thus, production work is defined as nonindustrial and as women's work, and significant struggle with its conditions has *thus far* taken place largely outside the arena of class—as individual survival, or as "citizenship."

UPDATE: 1983

How has the current depression affected production workers in the year since the data for this essay were collected?

While electronics has suffered less than most older manufacturing industries, the last year has witnessed cutbacks of every kind. All the major companies have been cutting back in a variety of ways, ranging from a six-month wage freeze at Fairchild, to a one-year freeze at Signetics, to actual pay cuts at troubled Intel. Layoffs have hit most assemblers with less than one year's seniority, and a large number with less than two, resulting paradoxically in a slightly higher average wage for assemblers (now from $5.00 to $6.00 an hour, as most assemblers have three to seven years experience; starting rates are still posted at an average of $4.10 per hour). Layoffs, however, are not strictly by seniority; in many cases they are at the discretion of department heads, leading to many instances of punitive or racially discriminatory layoffs. One consequence is an environment in which workers increasingly fear antagonizing their supervisors, but there have been some cases in which such firings have been successfully challenged (significantly enough, mostly through appeal to outside agencies rather than through collective worker action). In the departments where workers have been reinstated, there has been a resurgence of worker militancy and even union activity.

Unemployment is generally high in Santa Clara County because other industries—especially canning and auto—have been hit even harder than electronics, leading to serious competition for the few jobs that do become available. One ongoing employment opportunity for experienced assemblers, however, is offered by small, start-up electronics firms. Both new businesses and business failures were exceptionally high in Santa Clara County in 1982; these start-up companies, while putatively independent, frequently arise to meet the specific needs of major firms (for specialty parts or services) and end up bearing the brunt of business fluctuations and price wars. Jobs with these firms tend to be short lived, and benefits, if not pay, correspondingly lower.

In addition to transferring risks to start-up companies and using the strategy of runaway shops (in Albuquerque, New Mexico—an area to which many companies are moving and which also has a large supply of female, Third World, and immigrant labor—the going wage for assemblers is the legal minimum wage, $3.35 an hour), industry is also increasing its profits by reordering its workday shifts. Shifts are changing without notice, a particular hardship for working mothers, and in the direction of a workweek of three 12-hour days or four 10-hour days. A successful struggle was waged in the Valley for time-and-a-half after eight hours' work on any given day, but the new shifts, in combination with the layoffs, have led to speedups and considerably less available overtime. All of this, in combination with the wage cuts, has led to notably smaller paychecks for production workers.

The outcome of all this is considerable reduction of the options available to workers, with less pay; less opportunity to hustle (and more people needing to do it); and less control over time, place, and conditions of work. At the same time that many workers in the Valley have become demoralized or plain exhausted by these worsening conditions and the extra burdens they imply, there are significant pockets of resistance emerging, coming out of defensive struggles, both inside and outside of the plants, against, for example, unfair firings, threats to overtime pay, and toxic waste pollution or job-safety issues. It is clear that not merely worsening conditions, but the decline of options other than confrontation, has contributed to this new and encouraging collective spirit.

References

Mattera, P. 1980. "Small Is not Beautiful: Decentralized Production and the Underground Economy in Italy." *Radical America* 14, no. 5.

Personal interview. 1981. With California Bureau of Labor Standards employee, January.

Snow, R. 1980. "The New International Division of Labor and the U.S. Workforce: The Case of the Electronics Industry." East-West Center, Honolulu. Mimeograph.

Wolpe, H. 1975. "The Theory of Internal Colonialism: The South African Case." In I. Oxaal, T. Barnett, and D. Booth, eds., *Beyond the Sociology of Development*. London: Routledge and Kegan Paul.

13

SUZANNE C. CAROTHERS and PEGGY CRULL
NEW YORK UNIVERSITY WORKING WOMEN'S INSTITUTE

Contrasting Sexual Harassment in Female- and Male-dominated Occupations

Sexual harassment is a social issue touching all working women. It has been around for as long as women have worked outside their homes. Only in recent years, owing to the efforts of grassroots organizations, has sexual harassment been publicly acknowledged and officially defined in the legislatures and courts. At Working Women's Institute,[1] a national organization instrumental in raising public consciousness about this phenomenon, we have come to define it in the following way:

> Sexual harassment in employment is any attention of a sexual nature in the context of the work situation which has the effect of making a woman uncomfortable on the job, impeding her ability to do her work or interfering with her employment opportunities. It can be manifested by looks, touches, jokes, innuendoes, gestures, epithets or direct propositions. At one extreme, it is the direct demand for sexual compliance coupled with the threat of firing if a woman refuses. At the other, it is being forced to work in an environment

1. The institute, located at 593 Park Avenue, New York, NY 10021, maintains the National Information and Referral Network on sexual harassment. The network serves as a central clearinghouse for information about sexual harassment for individuals, organizations, companies, unions, and attorneys across the country and makes referrals for those women needing assistance to people and organizations in their locality. For community groups, unions, educational institutions, and corporations, it offers a program of speakers and workshops on the nature and impact of sexual harassment in employment and how it can be prevented. The institute operates a crisis-counseling service for women in the New York metropolitan area who have been sexually harassed.

> in which, through various means such as sexual slurs and/or the public display of derogatory images of women, or the requirement that she dress in sexually revealing clothing, a woman is subjected to stress or made to feel humiliated because of her sex. Sexual harassment is behavior which becomes coercive because it occurs in the employment context, thus threatening both a woman's job satisfaction and security. (Working Women's Institute, n.d.)

Experience and research have shown that sexual harassment occurs in every kind of work setting. It has direct economic ramifications, influences women's images of themselves as workers, and can be a potential occupational hazard wherever it is found. The slowly growing body of theory has only recently began to address the question of how the work setting itself affects the forms and outcomes of sexual harassment. Recent anecdotal evidence and surveys indicate that there is a significant contrast in the forms, sources, and functions of sexual harassment in fields that are traditional for women as compared to those where women are beginning to do jobs formerly held by men. To explore this idea, the co-authors conducted a series of interviews of women who had been counseled at Working Women's Institute. This essay synthesizes some of the preliminary findings of those interviews and stories and comments from a conference on sexual harassment sponsored by United Tradeswomen in New York City in November 1981. We describe the differences we found, analyze the conditions that seem to give rise to them, contrast women's responses to both forms of harassment, and discuss how women have organized to protect themselves.

Research on Sexual Harassment

Briefly, previous research indicates the high incidence and significant economic impact of sexual harassment on women in the work force. One of the earliest surveys, conducted by *Redbook* in 1976, found that 88 percent of nine thousand female readers reported some form of unwanted sexual attentions in their work lives (Safran, 1976). A 1980 survey of government workers in Illinois showed that 59 percent of the women had been harassed on their jobs; in a massive study of federal government employees, 42 percent of the women told of sexual harassment within the last two years of their federal service (Hayler, 1980; U.S. Merit Systems, 1981). Two considerably smaller surveys have looked at blue-collar jobs. A telephone-interview study of 139 unskilled female auto workers revealed that 36 percent of the interviewees had experienced sexual harassment (Gruber and Bjorn, 1982). In a small survey of coal miners, 53 percent of the women had been propositioned by a boss, 76 percent by co-workers; 17 percent had been physically attacked (White, Angle, and Moore, 1981). Figures from survey data on loss of jobs and promotions from sexual harassment vary widely.

Nearly half of the nine thousand *Redbook* respondents said they or someone they knew had left or been fired from a job because of sexual harassment. In the federal government study, about 16 percent of the women reported that they had lost a promotion or job or had quit a government position because of sexual harassment. In the Illinois study, about 9 percent had been fired or denied a promotion because of sexual harassment, and 7 percent had quit. The issue of job loss was not addressed in the auto-work and coal-mining studies, but respondents in both indicated that sexual harassment had resulted in unfair handling of their promotions.

Finally, recent studies have explained the hidden effects of sexual harassment on productivity and health. At Working Women's Institute we have analyzed the counseling records of hundreds of women and found that they report a distinct pattern of psychological, physical, and work problems that they feel are caused by sexual harassment (Crull, 1982a). Similar inquiries were included in the federal government and auto-work studies with similar results.

Because the focus of these surveys has been to assess the incidence and economic impact of sexual harassment, they have not analyzed the forms harassment takes and how these may be related to kinds of workplaces. Nor have they probed women's perceptions of their experiences. We have begun such an analysis as a first step in developing specific programs to combat different forms of sexual harassment.

Sexual Harassment in Traditional and Nontraditional Settings

To gather information that would provide a deeper understanding of sexual harassment, we conducted exploratory interviews with twenty-eight women who had come to the institute for assistance. We were careful to include women both in occupations where women have traditionally been employed and in jobs where they do "man's work" because our counseling experience and reading of the survey research suggested their stories would be different. In our sample, the women doing what we considered traditional female work included secretaries, lower level managers, editorial assistants, clerks, nurses, and waitresses. The women in previously male-dominated occupations included those working on loading docks, on construction sites, in repair shops, and on assembly lines.[2] When we looked at the

2. We chose the terms *traditional* and *nontraditional* as the best available descriptions of the kinds of situations we list here, but there are problems with these terms. Some jobs that are nontraditional for women are not included in our present sample or in any that we have read about. For example, women surgeons are in a previously male-dominated field, but we have no record of their experiences with sexual harassment and are thus unsure whether their experiences would fit our hypotheses. Furthermore, all of the nontraditional jobs we list are blue-collar jobs. We do not, however, mean to imply that all blue-collar jobs where

interviews, it was obvious that each type of occupation had its own pattern of harassment.

Both the institute's definition and the guidelines passed by the Equal Employment Opportunity Commission (EEOC) in 1980 include the two extremes of sexual harassment: the threat of losing one's job for refusing to comply with demands for sexual favors, and being faced with a sexually demeaning work environment manifested by slurs and public displays of derogatory images of women. Our interviews indicate that traditional women's work is more likely to be characterized by one extreme, the threat of losing a job for failing to comply with sexual demands, whereas the other extreme, a sexually demeaning work environment, is the more typical mode of harassment for women working in formerly all-male settings. Women who are clerical workers, lab assistants, or lower level managers described subtle compliments and hints for dates that turned into work sabotage and sometimes job loss when turned down. For example:

> He always complimented me on what I wore. I thought he was just being nice. It got to the place that every time he buzzed for me to come into his office for dictation, my stomach turned. He had a way of looking at me as if he were undressing me. This time as his eyes searched up and down my body and landed on my breast, he said, "Why should your boyfriend have all the fun. You could have fun with me *and* it could pay off for you. *Good* jobs are really scarce these days."

Women on construction sites or loading docks, on the other hand, were more likely to describe hostile and sometimes threatening sexual remarks that were accompanied by other acts designed to let them know women were outsiders on their work site:

> I walked into the shanty. It was covered with pictures of naked women. All of a sudden, he grabbed me, picked me up, and said, "This is what happens to little girls who try to do men's work." I screamed and my foreman came running and asked me, "Connie, what are *you* doing?" I shouted, "It's not me, it's him." The foreman replied, "We didn't have these problems 'til you got here."

We began to ask ourselves What are the possible reasons for these differences in the modes of sexual harassment? One answer seemed to lie in the relationship of these occupations to traditional sex roles. The idea that man is the breadwinner and woman the bread baker is an inappropriate and incorrect model for many families in U.S. society. For example, black women in U.S. society have had a long tradition of combining seemingly incompatible roles of worker, mother, and wife (Dill, 1979; Epstein, 1973). Since World War II, nonblack women have

---

women work are nontraditional. Many jobs in light industry, like textiles, for instance, have been typically held by women. We would consider these traditional women's work and subject to the same types of harassment as jobs like clerical work.

increasingly joined this tradition owing to the rising divorce rate and the necessity for even middle-class families to bring in two salaries to survive. Nevertheless, an implied role difference in families still dictates how men and women are expected to relate to each other. It pervades the very structure of the work force and the content of work, and it seems to play a part in determining the mode of sexual harassment in particular settings.

The jobs commonly held by women, such as teaching, nursing, and clerical work, often include duties that tend to be continuations of their domestic role: they take care of children or sick people; they organize housekeeping details. It is in part because of this blurring of home and work roles that women are expected to perform work outside their job descriptions. As one secretary reported, "In addition to typing and screening his calls, I always made his morning coffee. Sometimes I went for his lunch." Furthermore, according to traditional sex roles, men are sexually aggressive, a masculine right, whereas women are supposed to be passive and there primarily for men's pleasure. Thus, when the boss propositions his secretary, he is only playing out the behaviors already suggested by the role divisions in the workplace. If he is playing a male role to her female role at work, it is easy to see how sexual aggression can become one of his ways of dealing with her.

But sex roles can only partially explain harassment in the traditional setting. Women in those jobs lack the power to determine almost any of the conditions of their work. They do not hold status, position, or earnings equal to men in their workplace. The men in these workplaces, however few they may be, are the bosses, and women have little choice but to serve them as a wife serves a husband and depend on them as children depend on a parent. The male boss can use his power over the women within the organizational structure to impose sexual attentions on a woman, just as he can coerce her into getting his coffee. They both know that if she does not go along, she is the one who will lose in terms of job benefits. In an earlier paper, Crull (1982b) has atttributed this type of harassment to "an overflow of power and roles," and Ellis (1981) has aptly described it as "exploitative harassment," suggesting that it is an abuse of power.

If sexual harassment arises from unequal power and sex roles, one might assume that it ceases when men and women have equal status and roles. In earlier studies and our own interviews, however, women who do the same work as men report a high incidence of sexual and work harassment. During World War II, women workers actively participated in heavy industry and skilled trades. When the war ended, women returned to unemployment, or to more typically female jobs. Many blue-collar jobs have historically been considered "men's work" because they involve stereotypical masculine tasks. When women enter these jobs, they step out of female roles. More significant, they demystify male work and the male role itself. A female surveyor for a construction company said, "The men out on the crew always talked about how hard their job was. After I was out there for two weeks, I could have taught a high school junior with one good year of algebra their 'difficult' work. Frankly, I wasn't impressed."

As in the traditional setting, sex roles are not the only contributor to sexual harassment in male-dominated workplaces. Status and power within the workplace and in the job market as a whole play a part in creating the behavior. Women's entrance into heavy industry, construction, police work, crafts, and other blue-collar areas poses a threat to men's monopoly over these relatively well-paying jobs. One way to discourage a woman from trying to compete in this domain is to remind her, through sexual remarks and behavior, of her female fragility.

Sexual harassment in these jobs, then, appears to be a form of retaliation against the women for invading a male sphere and threatening male economic and social status. Women in these positions become objects of harassment ranging from vulgar remarks to outright physical attacks. The sexual behavior they face is more intimidating and abusive than the acts of harassment to which secretaries are exposed. The men seem to use the teasing, comments, and grabs to express their resentment at the presence of women in their domain. Ellis (1981) labels this behavior "generalized harassment," drawing the analogy with racial epithets and slurs used to drive minorities out of jobs.

The contrast between harassment in traditional and nontraditional jobs is clear. Harassment of women workers in traditional jobs appears more often as hints and requests for dates which, when rejected, are followed by work retaliation. Harassment of women in male-dominated settings is typically more overtly hostile at the outset. The motive for harassment in the traditional setting appears to be exploitation of role and power differences, whereas in the nontraditional setting the motive seems to be a defense against what male workers take to be an implicit challenge to their gender power and work roles.

Women's Responses to Both Forms of Harassment

The two forms of harassment we have delineated elicit their own specific sets of responses from the targeted women, responses that are integral to the work setting. In traditional work settings women may be confused by behavior that appears complimentary but, in the long run, proves to be derogatory: "How nice you look Miss Jones. . . . What a lovely dress you're wearing. . . ." grades into "Helen, that sweater really shows what you've got. It's got to be more than a mouthful." On the other hand, women in nontraditional settings are often the butt of sexual jokes, slurs, and abusive, insulting remarks from the very beginning of their employment. But even this form of harassment is frequently taken as benign at the outset. Many women assume they are simply being hazed like any newcomer to a construction crew. When it continues long after they stop being newcomers, they realize that their initiation is different from that of their male counterparts. Because harassment of women in traditional jobs often starts with sexual come-ons, the woman may feel guilty, assuming it was something *she* did that created the problem in the first place. This socialized self-blame may make it difficult for her to see the reality of the situation. Even if she is able to separate out her own guilt, she may fear that others will blame her. Because of the overt hostility in the sexual remarks and advances directed at women in nontraditional jobs, these women tend not to be confused by guilt. They often feel, however, that their pioneering positions mean that they cannot admit the embarrassment and fear aroused by their plights. The stance they take is to try to ignore the remarks and the feelings: "We're tough. We can handle it." To come to terms with these feelings, which impede clarity and flexibility of thought, women need to talk with other women, on and off their jobs, who may be experiencing similar difficulties.

Women in traditional jobs may be more hesitant to attempt to organize than women in male-dominated settings, who tend to be conscious of the overt hostility and alienation they face at work. This encourages them to come together and organize. The traditional work setting fosters a false sense of safety, comfort, and complacency among women, even when sexual harassment has disrupted it temporarily. It is easier for a woman in a job where women are "naturally" tracked to tell herself, "I'm only doing this until I get something better" and to deny her commitment. A tradeswoman who has had to go against the tide to get her job approaches it with the attitude of "this is what I have chosen to be," so she cannot deny her investment in the job or the implicit consequences of such an investment.

The power relationships in the two different settings play a part in determining how women attempt to resolve their situations. In a mainly female work setting, the harasser is likely to be a superior, someone in management, because that is where the men are. Therefore, traditional workers may have less internal conflict about bringing the harasser up on charges and less difficulty garnering support from other women for instituting sanctions against potential harassers. Blue-collar and tradeswomen workers may have more internal conflict about what to do, since their harassers are more likely to be co-workers and fellow union members. Bringing charges feels more divisive in such a situation; and it is usually not possible for one union member to grieve against another. In these cases women may need to create within their union new mechanisms for gaining protection from harassment.

Protections against Sexual Harassment

Because of the efforts of many women both as individuals and in groups, protections against sexual harassment already exist at many levels for women throughout the work force. Whether she is a construction worker or a secretary, a woman is covered by Title VII of the 1964 Civil Rights Act, which prohibits sexual discrimination, and by the EEOC guidelines that define sexual harassment as a form of discrimination. Court decisions on sexual harassment have been generally favorable. Black women have been at the forefront of litigating sexual harassment cases. They have been instrumental in establishing that sexual harassment is discriminatory because it happens to women based on their sex. The EEOC's guidelines are progressive because they include protections against an "intimidating, hostile, and offensive" work atmosphere (Working Women's Institute, 1980). This is especially important for nontraditional workers, who are often forced to quit under such conditions.

While women have gained legal leverage, litigating sexual harassment cases often requires considerable time, money, and perseverance. An emerging risk involved in these cases is the possibility of being countersued for defamation of character or slander. In addition, not every lawyer is willing, interested, or informed enough to handle such cases. Not every judge is sympathetic or sensitive to the issue, nor is every sexual harassment complaint a strong enough case to fight in court. Because of this, other measures to support and protect women before legal action becomes necessary have been and must continue to be developed. Toward this end, education, service, and advocacy groups have sprung up all over the country, including Working Women's Institute in New York, the Alliance Against Sexual Coercion in Cambridge, the Coalition Against Sexual Harassment in Minneapolis, and the Women's Alliance for Job Equity in Philadelphia. In addition, many YWCAs, community groups, and women's crisis centers have extended their service to include sexual harassment. Many established women's and workers' rights groups, professional associations, and unions have also undertaken programs to serve women trying to deal with sexual harassment and to educate their members. Such diverse groups as the Coal Employment Project, the American Federation of State, County, and Municipal Employees (AFSCME), and the Modern Language Association have published handbooks explaining the issue and possible protections. Organizations like United Tradeswomen in New York City, the Coalition of Labor Union Women, Office Workers of New Haven, and the American Federation of Government Employees (AFGE) have made sexual harassment the topic of their workshops, task forces, and training sessions.

Important organizing efforts have taken place both within established unions and outside of them. At the urging of their female members, unions have sought to provide permanent protections in several ways. United Auto Workers, AFSCME, and AFGE have issued policy statements condemning sexual harassment of employees by supervisors and, in some cases, by co-workers. United Auto Workers was one of the first unions to include a sexual harassment clause in a contract and presently has such clauses in its contracts with Chrysler and Ford. District 65, Distributive Workers of America, also has a sexual harassment clause in its contract at Boston University. These official actions have been supported and pushed forward by rank-and-file and grassroots initiatives. In a number of instances, union members have rallied to the support of women in their ranks who are being harassed. For example, members of Local 201 of the International Union of Electrical Workers walked off their jobs when a secretary at their plant was harassed by two managers (Hams, 1981). A similar situation in a lumber mill in Washington State served to raise discussions among members about whether or not sexual harassment of even a single woman is a breach of their contract. In California a sexual harassment incident in which a lawyer grabbed the breast of a receptionist spurred a group of legal service workers to organize the California Rural Legal Assistance Workers. To date the policies and contract clauses have treated sexual harassment as an issue of sex discrimination and urged that grievances be carried out under that approach, but because of the recent recognition that sexual harassment creates stress and impairs health, unions are beginning to look at the possibility of including it in contract provisions for worker health and safety.

References

Crull, Peggy. 1982a. "Sexual Harassment and Male Control of Women's Work." *Women: A Journal of Liberation* 8, no. 2: 3–7.

———. 1982b. "The Stress Effects of Sexual Harassment on the Job: Implications for Counseling." *American Journal of Orthopsychiatry* 52, no. 3: 539–544.

Dill, Bonnie. 1979. "The Dialectics of Black Womanhood." *Signs* 4, no. 3: 543–555.

Ellis, Judy. 1981. "Sexual Harassment and Race: A Legal Analysis of Discrimination." *Journal of Legislation* 8, no. 1: 30–45.

Epstein, Cynthia. 1973. "Positive Effects of the Multiple Negative: Explaining the Success of Black Professional Women." In Joan Huber, ed., *Changing Women in a Changing Society*, 150–173. Chicago: University of Chicago Press.

Gruber, James, and Lars Bjorn. 1982. "Blue Collar Blues: The Sexual Harassment of Women Autoworkers." *Work and Occupations* 9, no. 3: 271–298.

Hams, Marcia. 1981. "Electrical Workers Wildcat over Sexual Assault on Union Member." *Labor Notes* (June 25): 7.

Hayler, Barbara. 1980. "Testimony before the House Judiciary II Committee, State of Illinois." (March 4): 1–5. Memo.

Safran, Claire. 1976. "What Men Do to Women on the Job." *Redbook*, November.

U.S. Merit Systems Protection Board, Office of Merit Systems Review and Studies. 1981. *Sexual Harassment in the Federal Workplace: Is It a Problem?* Washington, D.C.: GPO.

White, Connie, Barbara Angle, and Marat Moore. 1981. "Sexual Harassment in the Coal Industry: A Survey of Women Miners." Coal Employment Project, Oak Ridge, Tennessee. Mimeo.

Working Women's Institute. 1980. "Comments" (on E.E.O.C.'s Proposed Amendments to Its Guidelines on Discrimination because of Sex) (37 FR 6836, April 5, 1972 as amended). To Add Sec. 1604.11, Sexual Harassment. Written for the Institute by Joan Vermeulen.

———. n.d. "Sexual Harassment: Questions and Answers." Mimeo.

14

MARÍA PATRICIA FERNÁNDEZ KELLY
UNIVERSITY OF CALIFORNIA, SAN DIEGO

Maquiladoras: The View from the Inside

Since the end of World War II, and particularly during the last two decades, there has been an increasing trend for the large monopolies of the highly industrialized nations to transfer more parts of their manufacturing operations to underdeveloped areas of the world (Palloix, 1975: 57–63). The industrial countries have thus become administrative and financial headquarters for the international management of refined manufacturing activities (Fröbel, Heinrichs, and Kreye, 1976). Large numbers of working people throughout the underdeveloped world are experiencing directly the impact of multinational investment.

There is a somewhat mechanical tendency to interpret social events in underdeveloped areas as an automatic effect of the requirements of capital accumulation at a global level, without regard for local diversity or independent activity, particularly among working classes and class fractions (O'Brien, 1975). Participant observation contributes to understanding the effects of, and workers' responses to, the international political and economic system at the level of the factory and the household. It shows workers as more than the cheap labor they appear to be when viewed from a global demands-of-capital viewpoint. Yet insights derived from political economic theory can inform ethnographic data collection and illuminate the details often missed in broader analytical efforts.

Along the Mexican side of the United States–Mexico border, there has been a huge expansion of manufacturing activities by multinational corporations. This has incorporated large numbers of women into direct production in the last fifteen years. As a result of implementation of the Border Industrialization Program since 1965, more than one hundred assembly plants, or *maquiladoras*, have sprung up in Ciudad Juarez, across the border from El Paso, Texas. This set of programs has made it possible for multinational firms to collaborate with Mexican state and private enterprise to foster the emergence of a booming export industry along the border. More than half of the plants are electric or electronic firms. Most of the rest are apparel assembly plants (see Newton and Balli, 1979).

The importance of the program in recent years may be appreciated by noting that *maquiladoras* account for about half of U.S. imports from underdeveloped countries under assembly industry tariff provisions, as compared with only 10 percent in 1970. In 1978 they provided the Mexican economy with more than ninety-five thousand jobs and $713 million in value added in this class of production in all of Latin America (Newton and Balli, 1979: 8). They rank third, behind tourism and petroleum sales, as a contributor to Mexican foreign exchange. The objective circumstances that have determined the growth of the *maquiladora* industry are the availability of what appears to be an inexhaustible supply of unskilled and semiskilled labor, and extremely high levels of productivity.

The plants themselves are small, and most subcontract from corporations with their headquarters in the United States. Although nationally recognized brands are represented in Ciudad Juarez, the vast majority of these industries are associated with corporations that have regional rather than national visibility. The low level of capital investment in the physical plant often results in inadequate equipment and unpleasant working conditions.

While all *maquiladoras* employ an overwhelming majority (85 percent) of women, the apparel industry hires women whose position in the city makes them especially vulnerable to exploitative labor practices. They tend to be in their midtwenties, poorly educated, and recent migrants to Ciudad Juarez. About one-third of the women head households and are the sole supports of their children.

Looking for a Job: A Personal Account

What is it like to be female, single, and eager to find work at a *maquiladora*? Shortly after arriving in Ciudad Juarez, and after finding stable lodging, I began looking through the pages of newspapers, hoping to find a want ad. My intent was to merge with the clearly visible mass of women who roam the streets and industrial parks of the city searching for jobs. They are, beyond doubt, a distinctive feature of the city, an effervescent expression of the conditions that prevail in the local labor market.

My objectives were straightforward. I wanted to spend four to six weeks applying for jobs and obtaining direct experience about the employment policies, recruitment strategies, and screening mechanisms used by companies to hire assembly workers. I was especially interested in how much time and money an individual worker spent trying to get a job. I also wanted to spend an equal amount of time working at a plant, preferably one that manufactured apparel. This way, I expected to learn more about working conditions, production quotas, and wages at a particular factory. I felt this would help me develop questions from a workers' perspective.

In retrospect, it seems odd that it never entered my head that I might not find a job. Finding a job at a *maquiladora* is easier said than done, especially for a woman over twenty-five. This is due primarily to the large number of women competing for jobs. At every step of their constant peregrination, women are confronted by a familiar sign at the plants—"no applications available"—or by the negative responses of a guard or a secretary at the entrance to the factories. But such is the arrogance of the uninformed researcher. I went about the business of looking for a job as if the social milieu had to conform to my research needs.

By using newspapers as a source of information for jobs, I was departing from the common strategy of potential workers in that environment. Most women are part of informal networks which include relatives, friends, and an occasional acquaintance in the personnel management sector. They hear of jobs by word of mouth.

Most job seekers believe that a personal recommendation from someone already employed at a *maquiladora* can ease the difficult path. This belief is well founded. At many plants, managers prefer to hire applicants by direct recommendation of employees who have proven to be dependable and hard working. For example, the Mexican subsidiary of a major U.S. corporation, one of the most stable *maquiladoras* in Juarez, has an established policy not to hire "outsiders." Only those who are introduced personally to the manager are considered for openings. By resorting to the personal link, managers decrease the dangers of having their factories infiltrated by unreliable workers, independent organizers, and "troublemakers."

While appearing to take a personal interest in the individual worker at the moment of hiring, management can establish a paternalistic claim on the worker. Workers complain that superintendents and managers are prone to demand "special services," like overtime, in exchange for granting personal "favors" such as a loan or time off from work to care for children. Yet workers acknowledge a personal debt to the person who hired them. A woman's commitment to the firm is fused with commitment to the particular personnel manager or superintendent who granted her the "personal favor" of hiring her. Anita expressed the typical sentiment, "If the group leader demands more production [without additional pay], I will generally resist because I owe her nothing. But if the *ingeniero* asks me to increase my quota on occasion, I comply. He gave me the job in the first place! Besides, it makes me feel good to know that I can return the favor, at least in part."

Only those who are not part of the tightly woven informal networks rely on impersonal ways to find a job. Recently arrived migrants and older women with children looking for paid employment for the first time find it especially difficult. As a "migrant" to Ciudad Juarez, I too lacked the contacts needed for relatively stable and well-paid jobs in the electronics industry. Instead, I too entered the apparel industry.

This was not a random occurrence. Ciudad Juarez electronics *maquiladoras* tend to employ very young, single women, a preferred category of potential workers from management's point of view. Workers also prefer electronics because it has large, stable plants, regular wages, and certain additional benefits. In contrast, the apparel-manufacturing sector is characterized by smaller, less stable shops where working conditions are particularly strenuous. Many hire workers on a more or less temporary basis, lack any commitment to their employees, and in the face of a fluctuating international market, observe crude and often ruthless personnel recruitment policies.

One such firm advertised for direct production workers in the two main Juarez newspapers throughout the year, an indication of its high rate of turnover. Despite a grand-sounding name, this small plant is located in the central area of the city rather than in one of the modern industrial parks, hires only about one-hundred workers, and is surrounded by unpaved streets and difficult to reach by public transportation. The shoddy, one-story plant, with its old-fashioned sewing machines and crowded work stations, reflects the low level of capital investment made in it.

I went into its tiny office in the middle of summer to apply for a job. As I entered, I wondered whether my appearance or accent would make the personnel manager suspicious. He looked me over sternly and told me to fill out a form now and to return the following morning at seven o'clock to take a dexterity test. Most of the items were straightforward: name, age, marital status, place of birth, length of residence in Ciudad Juarez, property assets, previous jobs and income, number of pregnancies, and general state of health. One, however, was unexpected: what is your major aspiration in life? All my doubts surfaced—would years of penmanship practice at a private school in Mexico City and flawless spelling give me away?

I assumed the on-the-job test would consist of a short evaluation of my skills as a seamstress. I was wrong. The next morning I knocked at the door of the personnel office where I filled out the application, but no one was there. In some confusion, I peeked into the entrance of the factory. The supervisor, Margarita, a dark-haired woman wearing false eyelashes, ordered me in and led me to my place at an industrial sewing machine. That it was old was plain to see; how it worked was difficult to judge. I listened intently to Margarita's instructions. I was expected to sew patch pockets on what were to become blue jeans from the assortment of diversely cut denim parts on my left. Obediently I started to sew.

The particulars of "unskilled" labor unfolded before my eyes. The procedure demanded perfect coordination of hands, eyes, and legs. I was to use my left hand to select the larger part of material from the batch next to me and my right to grab the pocket. There were no markers to show me where to place the pocket. Experienced workers did it on a purely visual basis. Once the patch pocket was in place, I was to guide the two parts under a double needle while applying pressure on the machine's pedal with my right foot.

Because the pockets were sewed on with thread of a contrasting color, the edge of the pocket had to be perfectly aligned with the needles to produce a regular seam and an attractive design. Because the pocket was diamond shaped, I also had to rotate the materials slightly three times while adjusting pressure on the pedal. Too much pressure inevitably broke the thread or produced seams longer than the edge of the pocket. The slightest deviation produced lopsided designs, which then had to be unsewed and gone over as many times as it took to do an acceptable pocket. The supervisor told me that, once trained, I would be expected to sew a pocket every nine to ten seconds. That meant 360 to 396 pockets every hour, or 2,880 to 3,168 every day!

As at the vast majority of apparel-manufacturing *maquiladoras*, I would be paid through a combination of the minimum wage and piecework. In 1978 this was 125 pesos a day, or U.S. $5.00. I would, however, get a slight bonus if I sustained a calculated production quota through the week. Workers are not allowed to produce less than 80 percent of their assigned quota without being admonished, and a worker seriously endangers her job when unable to improve her level of output. Margarita showed me a small blackboard showing the weekly bonus received by those able to produce certain percentages of the quota. They fluctuated between 50 pesos (U.S. $2.20) for those who completed 80 percent of the quota, to 100 pesos for those who completed 100 percent. Managers call this combination of steep production quotas, minimum wages, and modest bonuses an "incentive program."

I started my test at 7:30 A.M. with a sense of embarrassment about my limited skills and disbelief at the speed with which the women in the factory worked. As I continued sewing, the bundle of material on my left was renewed and slowly grew in size. I had to repeat the operation many times before the product was considered acceptable. I soon realized I was being treated as a new worker while presumably being tested. I had not been issued a contract and therefore was not yet incorporated into the Instituto Mexicano del Seguro Social (the national social security system). Nor had I been told about working hours, benefits, or system of payment.

I explained to the supervisor that I had recently arrived in the city, alone, and with very little money. Would I be hired? When would I be given a contract? Margarita listened patiently while helping me unsew one of many defective pockets and then said, "You are too curious. Don't worry about it. Do your job and things will be all right." I continued to sew, aware of the fact that every pocket attached during the "test" was becoming part of the plant's total production.

At 12:30, during the thirty-minute lunch break, I had a better chance to see the factory. Its improvised quality was underscored by the metal folding chairs at the sewing machines. I had been sitting on one of them during the whole morning, but until then I had not noticed that most of them had the Coca Cola label painted on their backs. I had seen this kind of chair many times in casual parties both in Mexico and in the United States. Had they been bought, or were they being rented? In any event, they were not designed to meet the strenuous requirements of sewing all day. Women brought their own colorful pillows to ease the stress on their buttocks and spines. Later on, I was to discover that chronic lumbago is a frequent condition among factory seamstresses (Fernández, 1978).

My questions were still unanswered at 5 P.M., when a bell rang to signal the end of the shift. I went to the personnel office intending to get more information. Despite my overly shy approach to the personnel manager, his reaction was hostile. Even before he was able to turn the disapproving expression on his face into words, Margarita intervened. She was angry. To the manager she said, "This woman has too many questions: Will she be hired? Is she going to be insured?" And then to me, "I told you already, we do piecework here; if you do your job, you get a wage; otherwise you don't. That's clear isn't it? What else do you want? You should be grateful! This plant is giving you a chance to work! What else do you want? Come back tomorrow and be punctual."

This was my initiation into applying for a job. Most women do not job-hunt alone. Rather, they go with friends or relatives and are commonly seen in groups of two or three around most factories. Walking about the industrial parks while following other job seekers was especially informative. Very young women, between sixteen and seventeen, often go with their mothers. One mother told me she sold burritos at the stadium every weekend and that her husband worked as a janitor but that their combined income was inadequate for the six children. Her daughter Elsa was sixteen. "I can't let her go alone into the parks," the mother explained. "She's only a girl and it wouldn't be right. Sometimes girls working in the plants are molested. It's a pity they have to work, but I want to be sure she'll be working in a good place."

At shift changes, thousands of women arrive at and leave the industrial parks in buses, taxis, and *ruteras* (jitney cabs). During working hours only those seeking jobs wander about. Many, though not the majority of these, are "older women." They face special difficulties because of their age and because they often support their children alone. Most of them enter the labor force after many years dedicated to domestic chores and child care. Frequently, desertion by their male companions forces their entry into the paid labor force. A thirty-one year old mother of six children explained, "I have been looking for work since my husband left me two months ago. But I haven't had any luck. It must be my age and the fact that I have so many children. Maybe I should lie and say I've only one. But then the rest wouldn't be entitled to medical care once I got the job." Women need jobs to support their children, but they are often turned down because they are mothers.

I finally got a job at a new *maquiladora* that was adding an evening shift. I saw its advertisement in the daily newspapers and went early the following morning to apply at the factory, which is located in the modern Parque Industrial Bermudez. Thirty-seven women preceded me. Some had arrived as early as 6 A.M. At 10, the door that separated the front lawn from the entrance to the factory had not yet been opened, although a guard appeared once in a while to peek at the growing contingent of applicants. At 10:30 he finally opened the door to tell us that only those having personal recommendation letters would be permitted inside. This was the first in a series of formal and informal screening procedures used to reduce the number of potential workers. Thirteen women left immediately. Others tried to convince the guard that, although they had no personal recommendation, they knew someone already employed at the factory.

Xochitl had neither a written nor a verbal recommendation, but she insisted that her diploma from a sewing academy gave her claim to a particular skill. "It is better to have proof that you are qualified to do the job than to have a letter of recommendation, right?" I wondered whether the personnel manager would agree. The numerous academies in Ciudad Juarez offer technical and vocational courses for a relatively small sum of money. The training does not guarantee a job because many *maquiladora* managers prefer to hire women with direct experience on the job, or as one manager put it to me, "We prefer to hire women who are unspoiled, that is, those who come to us without preconceptions about what industrial work is. Women such as these are easier to shape to our own requirements."

Xochitl's diploma was a glossy document dominated by an imposing eagle clutching a terrestrial globe. An undulating ribbon with the words "labor, omnia, vincit" complemented the design. Beneath it was certification of Xochitl's skills. A preoccupied expression clouded Xochitl's face while she looked at her certificate again. The picture on its left margin, of a young girl with shiny eyes, barely resembled the prematurely aged woman in line with me. At thirty-two, Xochitl was the mother of four children. She took up sewing at home to supplement the money her husband made peddling homemade refreshments. When there was work available (which was not always), she sewed from 6 A.M. until 3 P.M. She could complete three beach dresses, for which she received 22 pesos (U.S. $0.80) a day. The dresses were then sold in the market for approximately 150 pesos. She resented her contractor's high profit but felt she had no other choice. Most of her income was spent on food, clothing, and in attempts to furnish her two-room adobe house. She had already been standing outside the factory for over 3½ hours. All this time she could have been sewing at home and minding the children. Her husband might not approve of her looking for work in the factory, either. He felt it was one thing to sew at home, another to work in a factory.

The young, uniformed guard seemed unperturbed by the fluctuating number of women standing by the door. To many of us, he was the main obstacle lying between unemployment and getting a job from someone inside. To the women, he appeared arrogant and insensitive. "Why must these miserable guards always act this way?" nineteen-year-old Teresa asked. "It would seem that they've never had to look for a job. Maybe this one thinks he's more important than the owner of the factory. What a bastard!"

Teresa turned to me to ask if I had any sewing experience. "Not much," I told her, "but I used to sew for a lady in my hometown."

"Well then, you're very lucky," she said, "because they aren't hiring anyone without experience." She told me that she and her sister worked with about seventy other women for three years in a small shop in downtown Juarez. They sewed pants for the minimum wage but had no insurance. When the boss could not get precut fabric from the United States for them to sew, he laid them off without pay. For the last three months they had been living on the little their father earned from construction work, painting houses, selling toys at the stadium, or doing other odd jobs. "We are two of nine brothers and sisters (there were twelve of us in total but three died when they were young)."

"I am single, thanks be to God, and I do not want to get married," she informed me. "There are enough problems in my life as it is!" But her sister Beatriz, who was standing in line with us, had married an engineer when she was only fifteen. Now she is divorced and has three children to support. "They live with us too. Beatriz and I are the oldest in the family, you see; that's why we really have to find a job."

"I also used to work as a maid in El Paso. I don't have a passport, so I had to cross illegally as a wetback, a little wetback who cleaned houses. The money wasn't bad. I used to earn up to thirty-five dollars a week, but I hated being locked up all day. So I came back and here I am."

I asked Beatriz if her husband helped support her children.

"No," she said emphatically, "and I don't want him to give me anything, not a cent, because I don't want him to have any claim or rights over my babies. As long as I can support them, he won't have to interfere."

I asked if there were better jobs outside of *maquiladoras*. "I understand you can make more money working at a *cantina*; is that true?"

Both of them looked at me suspiciously. *Cantinas* are an ever-present reminder of overt or concealed prostitution. Teresa acknowledged that she could earn more there but asked:

> What would our parents think? You can't stop people from gossiping, and many of those "*cantinas*" are whorehouses. Of course, when you have great need you can't be choosey, right? For some time I worked there as a waitress, but that didn't last. The supervisor was always chasing me. First he wanted to see me after work. I told him I had a boyfriend, but he insisted. He said I was too young to have a steady boyfriend. Then, when he learned I had some typing skills, he wanted me to be his secretary. I'm not stupid! I knew what he really wanted; he was always staring at my legs. So I had to leave that job too. I told him I had been rehired at the shop, although it wasn't true. He wasn't bad looking, but he was married and had children. . . . Why must men fool around?

The guard's summons to experienced workers to fill out applications interrupted our conversation. Twenty women went into the narrow lobby of Camisas de Juarez, while the rest left in small, quiet groups. For those of us who stayed, a second waiting period began. One by one we were shown into the office of the personnel manager, where we were to take a manual dexterity test, fitting fifty variously colored pegs into fifty similarly colored perforations on a wooden board in the shortest possible time. Clock in hand, the personnel manager told each woman when to begin and when to stop. Some were asked to adjust the pegs by hand; others were given small pliers to do so. Most were unable to complete the test in the allotted time. One by one they came out of the office looking weary and expressing their conviction that they would not be hired.

Later on, we were given the familiar application form. Again, I had to ponder what my greatest aspiration in life was. But this time I was curious to know what Xochitl had answered.

"Well," she said, "I don't know if my answer is right. Maybe it is wrong. But I tried to be truthful. My greatest aspiration in life is to improve myself and to progress."

Demonstrating sewing skills on an industrial machine followed. Many women expressed their doubts and concern when they rejoined the waiting women in the lobby. Over the hours, the sense had increased that all of us were united by the common experience of job seeking and by the gnawing anxiety that potential failure entails. Women compared notes and exchanged opinions about the nature and difficulty of their respective tests. They did not offer each other overt reassurance or support, but they made sympathetic comments and hoped that there would be work for all.

At 3:30 P.M., seven hours after we arrived at the plant, we were dismissed with no indication that any of us would be hired. They told us a telegram would be sent to each address as soon as a decision was made. Most women left disappointed and certain that they would not be hired. Two weeks later, when I had almost given up all hope, the telegram arrived. I was to come to the plant as soon as possible to receive further instructions.

Upon my arrival I was given the address of a small clinic in downtown Ciudad Juarez. I was to bring two pictures to the clinic and take a medical examination. Its explicit purpose was to evaluate the physical fitness of potential workers. In reality, it was a pregnancy test. *Maquiladoras* do not hire pregnant women in spite of their greater need for employment. During the first years of its existence, many pregnant women sought employment in the *maquiladora* program knowing they would be entitled to an eighty-two day pregnancy leave with full pay. Some women circumvented the restrictions on employing pregnant women by bringing urine specimens of friends or relatives to the clinic. Plant managers now insist on more careful examinations, but undetected pregnant women sometimes get hired. The larger and more stable plants generally comply with the law and give maternity leave, but in small subcontracted firms, women are often fired as soon as the manager discovers they are pregnant.

After my exam at the clinic, I returned to the factory with a sealed envelope containing certification of my physical capacity to work. I was then told to return the following Monday at 3:30 P.M. to start work. After what seemed like an unduly long and complicated procedure, I was finally hired as an assembly worker. For the next six weeks I shared the experience of approximately eighty women who had also been recruited to work the evening shift. Xochitl, Beatriz, and Teresa had been hired too.

WORKING AT THE *Maquiladora*

The weekday evening shift began at 3:45 and ended at 11:30 P.M. A bell rang at 7:30 to signal the beginning of a half-hour dinner break. Some women brought sandwiches from home, but most bought a dish of *flautas* or *tostadas* and a carbonated drink at the factory. On Saturdays the shift started at 11:30 A.M. and ended at 9:30 P.M., with a half hour break. We worked, in total, forty-eight hours every week for the minimum wage, an hourly rate of about U.S. $0.60.

Although wages are low in comparison to those of the United States for similar jobs, migrants flock to zone 09, which includes Ciudad Juarez, because it has nearly the highest minimum wage in the country (only zone 01, where Baja California is located, has a higher rate). Legally, *maquiladoras* are also required to enroll their workers in the social security system and in the national housing program (Instituto Nacional a la Vivienda). As a result, investment per work hour reached U.S. $1.22 in 1978. For women who have children, the medical insurance is often as important as the wage.

Newcomers receive the minimum wage but are expected to fulfill production quotas. My new job was to sew a narrow bias around the cuff openings of men's shirts. My quota of 162 pairs of sleeves every hour meant one every 2.7 seconds. After six weeks as a direct production operator, I still fell short of this goal by almost 50 percent.

Sandra, who sat next to me during this period, assured me that it could be done. She had worked at various *maquiladoras* for the last seven years. Every time she got too tired, she left the job, rested for a while, then sought another. She was a speedy seamstress who acted with the self-assurance of one who is well-acquainted with factory work. It was difficult not to admire her skill and aloofness, especially when I was being continuously vexed by my own incompetence.

One evening Sandra told me she thought my complaints and manner of speech were funny and, at the end of what turned out to be a lively conversation, admitted to liking me. I was flattered. Then she stared at my old jeans and ripped blouse with an appraising look and said, "Listen Patricia, as soon as we get our wage, I want to take you to buy some decent clothes. You look awful! And you need a haircut." So much for the arrogance of the researcher who wondered whether her class background would be detected. Sandra became my most important link with the experience of *maquiladora* work.

Sandra lived with her parents in "las lomas" in the outskirts of the city. The area was rugged and distant, but the house itself indicated modest prosperity. There were four ample rooms, one of which was carpeted. The living room walls were covered with family photographs. There were an American television and comfortable chairs in the room. There were two sinks in the kitchen as well as a refrigerator, blender, beater, and new American-made washing machine (waiting until the area got its hoped-for running water). Sandra's father was a butcher who had held his job at a popular market for many years. Although in the past, when his three daughters were small, it had been difficult to stay out of debt, better times were at hand. He had only two regrets: his failing health and Sandra's divorce. He felt both matters were beyond his control. He considered Sandra a good daughter because she never failed to contribute to household expenses and because she was also saving so she could support her two children, who were currently living with her former husband. Sandra had left him after he beat her for taking a job outside the home.

Even with Sandra's help, I found the demands of the factory overwhelming. Young supervisors walked about the aisles calling for higher productivity and greater speed. Periodically, their voices could be heard throughout the workplace: "Faster! Faster! Come on girls, let's hear the sound of those machines!"

My supervisor, Esther, quit her job as a nurse for the higher wages as a factory worker because she had to support an ill and aging father after her mother's death three years earlier. Although her home was nice and fully owned, she was solely responsible for the remaining family debts. She earned almost one thousand pesos a week in the factory, roughly twice her income as a nurse.

The supervisor's role is a difficult one. Esther, like the other supervisors, often stayed at the plant after the workers left, sometimes until one in the morning. She would verify quotas and inspect all garments for defects, some of which she restitched. She would also prepare shipments and select materials for the following day's production. Management held supervisors directly responsible for productivity levels as well as for workers' punctuality and attendance, putting the supervisors between the devil and the deep blue sea. Workers frequently believed that supervisors were the ones responsible for their plight at the workplace and regarded abuse, unfair treatment, and excessive demands from them as whims. But while workers saw supervisors as close allies of the firm, management directed its dissatisfaction with workers at the supervisors. Many line supervisors agreed that the complications they faced on their jobs were hardly worth the extra pay.

One young woman at another factory told me, "Since I was promoted to a supervisory capacity I feel that my workmates hate me. We used to get along fine. I would even go so far as to say that we shared in a genuine sense of camaraderie. Now, they resent having to take orders from me, a former assembly worker like themselves. They talk behind my back and ask each other why it was I and not one of them who was promoted" (Fernández, 1978).

For some months this woman labored under considerable stress. Her problems were compounded when she had to decide who among her subordinates would have to be laid off as a result of plant adjustments. Caught between the exigencies of management and the resentful attempts of workers to manipulate her, she came close to a nervous breakdown. A short time afterward she asked to be transferred to her old job. From her point of view it was not worth being "a sandwich person."

Although my supervisor, Esther, was considerate and encouraging, she still asked me to repair my defective work. I began to skip dinner breaks to continue sewing in a feeble attempt to improve my productivity level. I was not alone. Some workers, fearful of permanent dismissal, also stayed at their sewing machines during the break while the rest went outside to eat and relax.

I could understand their behavior; their jobs were at stake. But presumably my situation was different. I had nothing to lose by inefficiency, and yet I felt compelled to do my best. I started pondering upon the subtle mechanisms that dominate will at the workplace, and about the shame that overwhelms those who fall short of the goals assigned to them. As the days passed, it became increasingly difficult for me to think of factory work as a stage in a research project. My identity became that of a worker; my immediate objectives, those determined by the organization of labor at the plant. I became one link in a rigidly structured chain. My failure to produce speedily had consequences for others operating in the same line. For example, Lucha, my nineteen-year-old companion, cut remnant thread and separated the sleeves that five other seamstresses and I sewed. Since she could only meet her quota if we met ours, Lucha was extremely interested in seeing improvements in my level of productivity and in the quality of my work. Sometimes her attitude and exhortations verged on the hostile. As far as I was concerned, the accusatory expression on her face was the best work incentive yet devised by the factory. I was not surprised to find out during the weeks I spent there that the germ of enmity had bloomed between some seamstresses and their respective thread cutters over matters of work.

Although the relationship between seamstresses and thread cutters was especially delicate, all workers were affected by each other's level of efficiency. Cuffless sleeves could not be attached to shirts, nor could sleeves be sewed to shirts without collars or pockets. Holes and buttons had to be fixed at the end. Unfinished garments could not be cleaned of lint or labeled. In sum, each minute step required a series of preceding operations effectively completed. Delay of one stage inevitably slowed up the whole process.

From the perspective of the workers, the work appeared as interconnected individual activities rather than as an imposed structure. Managers were nearly invisible, but the flaws of fellow workers were always present. Bonuses became personal rewards made inaccessible by a neighbor's laziness or incompetence. One consequence of these perceptions was that workers frequently directed complaints against other workers and supervisors. In short, the organization of labor at any particular plant does not automatically lead to feelings of solidarity.

On the other hand, the tensions did not inhibit talk, and the women's shared experiences, especially about longings for relief from the tediousness of industrial work, gave rise to an ongoing humorous dialogue. Sandra often reflected in a witty and self-deprecatory manner on the possibility of marriage to a rich man. She thought that if she could only find a nice man who would be willing to support her, everything in her life would be all right. She did not mind if he was not young or good looking, as long as he had plenty of money. Were there men like that left in the world? Of course, with the children it was difficult, not to say impossible, to find such a godsend. Then again, no one kept you from trying. But not at the *maquiladora*. Everyone was female. One could die of boredom there.

Sandra knew many women who had been seduced and then deserted by engineers and technicians. Other women felt they had to comply with the sexual demands of fellow workers because they believed otherwise they would lose their jobs. Some were just plain stupid. Things were especially difficult for very young women at large electronics plants. They needed guidance and information to stay out of trouble, but there was no one to advise them. During the first years of the *maquiladora* program, sexual harassment was especially blatant. There were *ingenieros* who insisted on having only the prettiest workers under their command. They developed a sort of factory "harem." Sandra knew of a man—"Would you believe this?"—who wanted as much female diversity as possible. All of the women on his crew, at his request, had eyes and hair of a different color. Another man boasted that every woman on his line had borne him a child. She told me about the scandals, widely covered by the city tabloids, about the spread of venereal disease in certain *maquiladoras*. Although Sandra felt she knew how to take care of herself, she still thought it better to have only female fellow workers. The factory was not a good place to meet men.

Fortunately, there were the bars and the discotheques. Did I like to go out dancing? She did not think I looked like the type who would. But it was great fun. Eventually Sandra and I went to a popular disco, the Cosmos, which even attracted people from "the other side" (the United States), who came to Juarez just to visit this disco. It had an outer-space decor, full of color and movement, and played the best American disco music. If you were lucky, you could meet a U.S. citizen. Maybe he would even want to get married, and you could go and live in El Paso. Things like that happen at discotheques. Once a Jordanian soldier in service at Fort Bliss had asked Sandra to marry him the first time they met at Cosmos. But he wanted to return to his country, and she had said no. Cosmos was definitely the best discotheque in Juarez, and Sandra could be found dancing there amidst the deafening sound of music every Saturday evening.

The inexhaustible level of energy of women working at the *maquiladoras* never ceased to impress me. How could anyone be in the mood for all-night dancing on Saturdays after forty-eight weekly hours of industrial work? I had seen many of these women stretching their muscles late at night trying to soothe the pain they felt at the waist. After the incessant noise of the sewing machines, how could anyone long for even higher levels of sound? But as Sandra explained to me, life is too short. If you don't go out and have fun, you will come to the end of your days having done nothing but sleep, eat, and work. And she didn't call that living. Besides, where else would you be able to meet a man?

Ah men! They were often unreliable, mean, or just plain lazy ("wasn't that obvious from the enormous number of women who had to do factory work in Ciudad Juarez?"), but no one wanted to live alone. There must be someone out there worth living for—at least someone who did not try to put you down or slap you. Sandra could not understand why life had become so difficult. Her mother and father had stayed married for thirty years and they still liked each other. There had been some difficult times in the past, but they had always had each other. She knew a lot of older folks who were in the same situation. But it was different for modern couples.

At 11:15, Sandra's talks about men stopped, and we prepared to go home. We cleaned up our work area and made sure we took the two spools and a pair of scissors we were responsible for home with us to prevent their being stolen by workers the following morning. As soon as the bell rang at 11:30, we began a disorderly race to be the first to check out our time cards. Then we had to stand in line with our purses wide open so the guard could check our belongings. Women vehemently resented management's suspicion that workers would steal material or the finished products. The nightly search was an unnecessary humiliation of being treated as thieves until proven innocent by the guard.

Once outside the factory, we walked in a group across the park to catch our bus. There was a lot of laughing and screaming, as well as teasing and exchanging of vulgarities. Most of the time we could board an almost-empty bus as soon as we reached the main avenue. Sometimes, when we had to wait, we became impatient. In jest, a woman would push another worker toward the street, suggesting provocative poses for her to use to attract a passerby to offer a ride. When a car did stop, however, they quickly moved away. To joke was one thing, but to accept a ride from a man, especially late at night, was to look for trouble.

Individually, the factory women appeared vulnerable, even shy, but as a group, they could be a formidable sight. One night a man boarded the bus when we were already in it. His presence gave focus to the high spirits. Women immediately subjected him to verbal attacks similar to those they often received from men. Feeling protected by anonymity and by their numerical strength, they chided and teased him; they offered kisses and asked for a smile. They exchanged laughing comments about his physical attributes and suggested a raffle to see who would keep him. The man remained silent through it all. He adopted the outraged and embarrassed expression that women often wear when they feel victimized by men. The stares of whistling women followed him as he left the bus.

Although I only saw one such incident, I was told that it was not uncommon. "It is pitiful," a male acquaintance told me; "those girls have no idea of what proper feminine behavior is." He told me he had seen women even paw or pinch men while traveling in buses and *ruteras*. According to him, factory work was to blame: "Since women started working at the *maquiladoras* they have lost all sense of decorum." The women see it as a harmless game fostered by the temporary sense of membership in a group. As Sandra liked to remind me, "Factory work is harder than most people know. As long as you don't harm anybody, what's wrong with having a little fun?"

Conclusions

In telling of my experience, I have tried to acquaint the reader with a new form of industrial employment from a personal viewpoint. Textile and garment manufacturing are, of course, as old as factories themselves, but *maquiladoras* epitomize the most distinctive traits of the modern system of production. They are part of a centralized global arrangement in which central economies such as the United States have become the locus of technological expertise and major financial outflows, while Third World countries increase their participation in the international market via the manufacture of exportable goods.

This global system of production has had unprecedented political and economic consequences. For example, the fragmentation of labor processes has reduced the level of skill required to perform the majority of assembly operations required to manufacture even the most complex and sophisticated electronics products. In turn, the geographical dispersion of production has curtailed the bargaining ability of workers of many nationalities vis-à-vis large corporations. At times, workers in Asia, Latin America, and the Caribbean seem to be thrust into competition against one another for access to low-paying, monotonous jobs. Labor unions and strikes have limited potential in a world where factories can be transferred at ease to still another country where incentives are more favorable and wages cheaper.

More than two million workers are presently employed in export-processing zones located in less developed countries. Perhaps most significant is the fact that between 85 percent and 90 percent of them are women. Under the Border Industrialization and *Maquiladora* Programs, Mexico is participating in this global arrangement by offering attractive stimuli and customs leeway to multinational corporations mainly involved in electronics and garment manufacturing. More than 156,000 women are employed in *maquiladoras*. In spite, or perhaps because, of Mexico's increasing economic difficulties, the number of such plants will increase in the next years. Several devaluations of the Mexican currency have placed the country in a competitive position with respect to Taiwan and Hong Kong as a source of cheap labor.

From the point of view of business, *maquiladoras* are a great success. But as the preceding narration suggests, the experiences of working women employed at the plants give reason for concern. Low wages, strenuous work paces, the absence of promotions, the temporary nature of employment, and unsatisfactory working conditions combine to make *maquiladoras* a precarious alternative. Such factories thrive only in labor markets characterized by very few occupational choices.

It is evident from the testimony of workers that women seek *maquiladora* jobs compelled by their need to support families whether they be formed by parents and siblings or by their own children. Male unemployment and underemployment play an important part in this. Multinationals tend to relocate assembly operations to areas of the world where jobless people automatically provide an abundant supply of cheap labor. Sandra's longing for male economic support and regrets over the irresponsibility of men represent a personal counterpoint to a structural reality where men are unable to find remunerative jobs while women are forced, out of need, to join the ranks of the industrial labor force.

The same testimony demonstrates that *maquila* women would prefer to withdraw from the exhausting jobs available to them and give full attention to home and children. Husbands and fathers frequently press women to leave their jobs to adjust to a conventional understanding of what gender roles should be. Nevertheless, when women retire from wage labor to become housewives and mothers, they often face dire alternatives. Later, they may have to seek new forms of employment because of the inability of their men to provide adequately for their families. Older and with children to provide for, they then face special constraints in a labor market that favors very young, single, childless women. The life profile of *maquiladora* women is, then, a saga of downward mobility, a fate contrary to the optimistic expectations of industrial promoters.

The segregation of the labor market on the basis of sex tends to weaken the bargaining position of both men and women as wage earners. But perhaps more important is the observation that the same segregation produces a clash between ideological notions about the role of women and their actual transformation into primary wage earners. This has given rise to tensions perceived both at the household and community levels. *Maquiladora* workers have become notorious in that they challenge conventional mores and values regarding femininity. Concerns about young women's morality, virtue, and sexual purity are, in part, reflections of widespread anxiety and fear that, as a result of wage earning, women may end up subverting the established order. *Maquiladora* workers may see their riotous behavior toward a man in a bus as an innocuous diversion. Others, however, see it as a clear sign that women are losing respect for patriarchy.

Maquiladoras are hardly a mechanism for upward mobility, hardly the bold entrance to middle-class respectability, hardly the key to individual economic autonomy. All these are issues that should be of concern to government officials and social planners. Yet, while *maquiladoras* have taken advantage of women's vulnerability in the job market, they have also provided a forum where new forms of consciousness and new challenges are present. For younger *maquila* workers who are living with parents and siblings and have few or no children of their own, wage labor offers the cherished possibility of retaining at least part of their income for discretionary purposes.

References

Fernández, M. P. 1978. "Notes from the Field." Ciudad Juarez, Mexico. Mimeo.

Fröbel, J. R., J. H. Heinrichs, and O. Kreye. 1976. "Tendency Towards A New International Division of Labor Force for World Markets Oriented Manufacturing." *Economic and Political Weekly* 11: 71–83.

Newton, J. R., and F. Balli. 1979. "Mexican In-Bond Industry." Paper presented to the seminar on North-South Complementary Intra-Industry Trade. UNCTAD United Nations Conference, Mexico, D.F.

O'Brien, Philip. 1975. "A Critique of Latin American Theories of Dependency."

In I. Oxaal, T. Barnett, and D. Booth, eds., *Beyond the Sociology of Development*. London: Routledge and Kegan Paul.

Palloix, C. 1975. "The Internationalization of Capital and the Circuit of Social Capital." In H. Radice, ed., *The International Firms and Modern Imperialism*. New York: Penguin.

15

LOUISE LAMPHERE
BROWN UNIVERSITY

On the Shop Floor: Multi-Ethnic Unity against the Conglomerate

I came to understand the complexities of today's industrial jobs for women when I took a job in 1977 in a large sewing plant that manufactured children's clothes in a New England city. During a period of five months (interrupted by a work stint in the plant's warehouse and two months' layoff), I was trained to "set sleeves" on little girls' dresses and toddler's t-shirts. The plant where I worked, like virtually all garment plants in the country, is paid on the piece-rate system.

As a new worker, I came to learn, not only the technical skills necessary for my job, but more important, how women workers deal with the piece-rate system and management's attempts to control their work and increase productivity.

One of the first lessons I learned was an appreciation of the skills necessary to sew sleeves fast enough to be able to attain higher and higher levels of "efficiency" in the context of the firm's training program and the piece-rate system of pay. Even by August, after four months as a sewer, I was only making about "60 percent efficiency" and still had trouble learning to sew new styles of sleeves.

My field notes were filled with descriptions of mistakes I had made, of troubles with the sewing machine, and of spending my lunch hours

---

Some of the ideas presented here were adapted from my article entitled, "Fighting the Piece-Rate System," in *Case Studies on the Labor Process*, ed. Andrew Zimbalist (New York: Monthly Review Press, 1981).

Throughout the essay, the real names of the people have been changed.

repairing rejected sleeves. Most of my mistakes were a result of inexperience and trying to work faster under the pressure of having to increase my production and eventually "make the piece rate," or achieve 100 percent efficiency with a wage of $3.31 an hour.

A second set of lessons I learned were that women were not passive accepters of their situations but active strategists. On the shop floor there is a subtle conflict between management's attempt to control work and workers' attempts to preserve their own autonomy and maximize their own interests. I discovered workers' strategies for dealing with management policy by watching other women and by taking tips from them. I began to realize that women workers socialized new workers to see their shared interests, to develop a sense of trust, and to outguess management efforts to make them work harder. New workers were always being brought into the plant to be trained as sewers. In addition, at each change in style season, production often increased or decreased, and new garments were put into production. These changes meant considerable shifting of workers from job to job, or even layoffs. Both management and workers were always in the position of socializing workers to their respective views of work and production. I identified four strategies for dealing with shifting management policy: first, socializing new workers in the context of the training program; second, creating ties among workers in the face of ethnic conflict by humanizing and "familizing" the work context; third, socializing new workers to informal work rules within the department; and fourth, outguessing new management policy with regard to the organization of production and worker layoffs.

In a capitalist labor market, women are hired individually and placed in a job in accordance with management's assessment of their skills and production needs, without regard to their age, marital status, ethnicity, friends, or kin among the work force. During the course of working in the same department within a plant, workers develop both social ties and cultural understandings that bridge the gaps between individuals who were strangers and who are potentially divided by ethnic background, age, and marital status. Historians of women's work have called these social ties and cultural understandings a "women's work culture." The women's strategies I discuss here help both to create a work culture and to distance workers from management's views of production, creating an alternative. These are strategies of resistance, but they also create cohesive bonds between workers.

In a unionized shop, women's strategies of resistance, which focus on the day-to-day details of work and social relations, may parallel the formal union structure and strengthen it. Or the union may be a very weak institution, basically a set of officers and shop stewards who handle grievances but who have relatively little to do with the cohesiveness of the work force. In 1977 in the plant where I worked, the union seemed somewhere between these two extremes.

The union seemed barely visible in the day-to-day struggle with the piece rate (although I did hear of several official grievances) and had not drawn Portuguese workers into active participation. Management notices were both in Portuguese and in English, while notices about union meetings and recent contract benefits were only in English. Union leadership was drawn primarily from the ranks of the older, non-Portuguese workers; and the union organized some social activities (a 20-Club lottery and a Christmas dinner-dance), but Portuguese workers seemed less involved in them. The wildcat strike which erupted in 1979 was probably a product of worker resistance against management, on the one hand, and the union's inactivity, on the other. Both Portuguese and non-Portuguese participated in the strike, eventually forcing the union to be more receptive to worker demands and eventually voting in new union leadership.

Daily resistance strategies and informal ties among workers are often fragile and elusive. There are many forces that tend to push women workers apart, since some workers become socialized to management's view rather than the alternative. And there are always occasions where ethnic conflict comes to the fore, breaking apart ties of solidarity between members of different ethnic groups. Whether informal resistance strategies can be transformed into more formal means of resistance (such as a successful union drive or a strong contract) depends on a host of factors including management's antiunion campaign, the nature of an industry, and the state of the local and national economy. Yet, the daily struggle between management's efforts to socialize workers to their own organization of work, and worker's strategies of resistance and attempts to socialize new co-workers, illustrates the potentials of women's work culture for initiating change.

The Shop Floor

The plant where I worked had been established in the 1930s when a manufacturer of children's wear moved his production facilities from New York to New England to take advantage of the work force made available by widespread mill closings in the textile industry. The plant was unionized in the 1950s and taken over by a large conglomerate in the 1970s. As the older women workers retired, rather than moving production facilities South, the management hired recent Portuguese and Latin American immigrants.

Much of the sewing took place on the second floor of an old silk mill which contained seven of the twelve departments. Work came down from the cutting room in lots of 80 to 120 dozen garments. At the row of machines close to the back of each department, women performed the first operations in the process: sewing the shoulder seams, neck bindings, and collars. As the bundles progressed to the front, other women attached labels, and then others joined the tops and bottoms of girls' dresses. Different workers set the sleeves and seamed the sides. Finally, across the center aisle, the garments were hemmed, pressed, folded, and pinned. They were then taken off the floor to be boxed and sent to the distribution center, where shirts and pants were assembled into outfits and orders from across the country were filled.

The lots were divided into bundles of 2½ or 5 dozen garments, with smaller packets of sleeves, collars, sides, and other unsewn parts. On each bundle, a "ticket" specified the operations that had to be done to make a complete dress or t-shirt. Each operation had a number, and each style of garment had a pay rate for each operation. For Operation 37, "set sleeves," for example, the piece rates varied depending on the size of the garments in the bundle and on whether the garment was a dress or t-shirt.

Piece rates were based on the decimal system, so that they were easy to computerize. But they were also calculated to baffle the workers, since garments were batched in dozens and most sewers kept their eyes on a clock that ticks away in sixty-minute hours. In the official system, the hour is divided into 100 parts, so that 10 minutes is really .167 of an hour. Thus, a piece rate of .073 meant that an operation had to be performed on a dozen garments in 4.38 minutes if the sewer was to earn $3.31 an hour in 1977 or $4.05 an hour in 1979: both *base rates* on which the piece rates were figured. Following the example of our training instructors, I always used a pocket calculator (at home) to figure out how well or how badly I was doing, and I marveled at other workers who seemed to be able to translate all the decimal figures into real dollars and cents. I figured that to earn the minimum wage in 1977 ($92.00 a week before deductions) by working all day on the same t-shirts with a rate of .073, I would have to sew a dozen garments (setting two sleeves each) every 6.3 minutes, completing 76 *dozen* garments in a day.

Women workers realized that the piece-rate system could be used against them. It induced individuals to speed up, which caused individualism rather than collectivism among workers, shortened the season by encouraging workers to get the work out faster and earlier, and lowered the wage by allowing rates to be based on the times of the faster workers. On the one hand, the piece-rate system forced the sewer to work as rapidly as possible without making a mistake. On the other hand, because of the way in which management enforced the system, women were under constant threat of being further underpaid (if the rates dropped) or having their jobs eliminated (if styles were simplified or operations cut out).

The women developed several strategies for dealing with the piece-rate system. First, they kept track of how many dozen pieces they had sewn each day, and they kept a sharp eye out for rates that were too low for the difficulty of the style. Each worker kept a little notebook in her machine drawer listing the number of bundles finished so that she could accurately fill out her punch card at the end of the day and recheck the amount on her paycheck when she received it on Thursday afternoon.

Second, women watched to see that cutting-room mistakes were not blamed on individuals and that individuals were treated fairly by the floor lady or the training instructor. In some instances, women covered over the mistakes of others by "just letting the work go through" so that a woman did not lose wages by having to do the work over.

These daily strategies for coping with the piece-rate system were, of course, taught to new workers. They were the most obvious strategies of resistance that emerged on the shop floor. New workers first encountered management views and organization of work as part of the training program, however, and only later did they begin to discover alternatives as they got to know older employees and were transferred from the training program to the shop floor.

Socializing the Worker through the Training Process

The firm's training program was a worker's first introduction to sewing. Management used the program both to give the skills needed to become a sewer and to instill the correct attitudes toward work and toward the company. Training also provided a method of weeding out workers who "did not fit," because they either had difficulty gaining the skills or exhibited the wrong attitudes.

The conglomerate initiated the training program in January 1976 to standardize training in plants throughout the company. Each of the sewing operations was categorized as an A, a B, or a C job. A sewer was trained for an A job (neck binding, collars, sleeve bindings) in six weeks, for a B job (e.g., labeling) in twelve weeks, and for a C job (setting sleeves, seam sides, hemming) in eighteen weeks.

The training supervisor and her three bilingual assistants gave new employees a battery of tests and assigned them to a particular job. One of the training assistants taught the "new girl" a job (e.g., setting sleeves) according to a prescribed method (worked out by the supervisor). After about a week they placed the trainee in her future department, where they continued to monitor her work by an efficiency chart tied to her machine.

Use of bilingual instructors made the training program an extremely effective way of integrating Portuguese women into the production system. Since the trainer could act as a mediator if the "new girl" made mistakes that affected the work and wages of others, the program reduced conflict with older workers. It also helped control the high turnover rate by spotting and encouraging "good workers" while replacing those who left with a minimum of disruption.

Throughout the training program, the supervisor and her assistants worked toward reinforcing the company line about work. Lucia, a second-generation Portuguese woman and supervisor of the program, felt she was training girls to work as efficiently as possible, which was in both the company's and the workers' interest. "Let's face it. It's for the company, but it helps the girls make more money too." She explained that the company wanted to improve production and to save wasted motion. "You see some girls who *look* like they are working hard," she told me while imitating a girl shaking out a garment before sewing it, looking as if she were rapidly working, "but they are really wasting a lot of time. Others hardly look like they are working: it's almost automatic. *And* they are the ones that are making money."

"Making money" was the code word in the culture of both management and workers for making over the minimum wage—in 1977 a vast terrain above $2.30 an hour that was only limited by a worker's lack of experience from the management point of view. Lucia was always pointing out women who were doing well. After my fifth day at work, she told me I was improving (up to 37 percent efficiency) and that she was "proud of all her girls." "That little Spanish girl reached 100 percent and graduated (from the training program) just a couple of days ago." Christina, one of the instructors, told me about a woman who had just started the week before and was already up to 88 percent efficiency and already making $22.00 a day. Accounts of women who were able to "make money" were held out as the ideal, and making money was the prize to be won by any worker who applied herself to the task at hand.

The training program during the peak of the season handled a large number of women, most of whom did not stay. For example, two of us started work on February 2, another six started the next Monday, and on Valentine's Day, fourteen showed up to be trained. Some women lasted only a few days. One, I remember, said that she had done badly on the tests they gave the first day—on purpose. She wanted an easy job, and she received one: gathering sleeves. She found it boring and did not show up the next day. Another trainee had worked for the company before, in the section where machines automatically embroidered designs on the clothes. She had not had previous experience sewing, and her reaction to the first day's tests were that they were "bullshit tests, just like in grammar school." These women clearly looked with scepticism on the training program, the management ideology of hard work, and the constraints of sewing; they quickly left the job.

Management used workers' personal qualities along with their inability to keep up with the pace of the training program to discourage trainees. Alice, a heavyset woman, was having a difficult time learning to set sleeves. Her efficiency had been up to 19 percent (about right for the second week of training) but had dropped to 11 percent when she received a difficult batch of sleeves to set. During the next week, she was called down to the nurse's office and told to take two baths a day and to use a particular deodorant since her body odors had been so offensive. Alice explained that because of her weight she perspired a lot and most deodorants did not work. She could not take a bath every day; with the weather as cold as it was, she did not want to catch a cold. "The awful thing is, they don't tell you directly; they told the nurse. It really hurt." And after she got home, she cried. She left the job soon after, perhaps convinced that her boyfriend, who encouraged her to quit, would help support her, with the help of her food stamps.

Another example was Cindy, a young woman who had started the training program before I did and who was still in the training area long after I had been assigned to a department. On February 11 she said she was still in the same place and did not know why. "I really don't care how fast I go and sometimes I'm just fed up with the whole thing," she said. Two weeks later she had done several bundles of shirts all wrong and had to do them all over again. The next day she was "hauled down to the office" and told that she "must not want her job." If she did not improve, they would let her go. She was furious at the trainee supervisor (Lucia), who had stood quietly behind the production manager while he talked to her about her behavior.

Cindy said if she was doing something wrong, "I'd like to hear it from the bitch, herself. That bitch, I could punch her in the mouth. I've never met anyone like her. But then I'd lose my job for sure." She *had* done the shirts wrong but felt that the instructor had not checked her work. "They" also complained that she took too much time off from work and was always in the ladies room. "Well," Cindy said, "they told me that whenever I wanted, I could get up and go to the bathroom and have a cigarette." She insisted that she did not do this too often, but her supervisor countered, "She's in there all the time." The production manager gave her two days to shape up. He said he would see on Friday if she still wanted to keep her job. On Wednesday, she was working hard and had done twenty-nine dozen sets of sleeves by the end of the morning. Cindy continued to work until the layoffs a week later but declined to work at the warehouse and did not reappear in June when we were called back to the sewing operation.

The training program effectively weeded out workers like Alice and Cindy who were having difficulty working fast enough and with enough skill, but whose demeanor and attitudes also did not fit with the work environment. Cindy often did not care how hard she worked, and she was defiant, not willing to assume responsibility for her mistakes (which are very common in the first weeks of sewing). Lucia, the trainee supervisor, always had a cheery attitude and encouraged hard work, "sticking to it." In contrast, older workers were more cynical about the management view that hard work made it possible to "make money." They cautioned trainees not to accept management ideas, especially after a trainee was assigned to her permanent job on the sewing floor. Mrs. Januz, an older Polish woman, asked how a Polish trainee was doing. The instructor, Christina, said, "She's a smart girl and doing really well." Mrs. Januz retorted, "Pretty soon she'll be working really fast, but *she still won't be making any money.*"

The older workers in my department counseled me about the job itself, how to do it, and when not to get discouraged. Rose, who had been setting sleeves for twenty-two years, said, "It's a good little job . . . just take your time and the speed will come to you." Several times when I was having trouble putting sleeves on inside out or not catching the first two inches of the sleeve, she encouraged me, saying that she had had the same difficulties at first. "Just keep going . . . it will come to you." At the same time she made no bones about her feeling that it was difficult to make money. "If you are satisfied with $2.30 an hour, you'll do all right. You really have to push yourself to make more. . . . The one thing about this place is that the work is steady. . . . If you keep improving, it will be okay. As long as you do a dozen or so more each day."

While the trainee supervisor implied that an average worker was timed in setting the rates, older workers scoffed at this idea. Angela pointed out the management efficiency expert by saying, "That's the one we hate." When I asked whom he timed, she said, "They usually pick out the fastest girl. They're not dumb, you know."

The piece-rate system itself pits workers against each other in a competitive race for wages. Women are fairly secretive about how much they are making. I sensed, however, that some of the rates were easier to make than others. In setting sleeves, I was told Rose made about $3.00 an hour, whereas Angela and Anita seemed to be making more nearly the minimum wage. The women sewing tops and bottoms together were reputed to be making $33.00 a day, or $4.12 an hour. The rate on sides was also supposed to be good: "We fought hard to get them a high rate."

Worker attempts to put "new girls" straight about the realities of the way management enforces the piecework system was illustrated by the following incident. My instructor came by to tell me that my card indicated that I had done only 17 dozen sleeves the previous day. She thought there must have been some mistake, since I had been doing more like 36 dozen a day. My handwriting had been misread so that, for one style, only 2 dozen sleeves, rather than 24 dozen, had been counted. She wrote this down on her pad and left, presumably to correct the mistake in the office. Angela, thinking that the instructor had been criticizing the level of my work, gave me the following advice: "Don't let her tell you that 17 dozen isn't enough. She hinted at it, you know. She ought to try it sometime. The girl who used to be at your machine, she used to tell them."

Angela and Rose reminded me that my predecessor had quit because she could not make more than the minimum wage. She had reached a plateau in two or three months and just could not make any more. I explained that I had been told I would be able to make $3.31 an hour (the base rate) by the end of my training period. Angela scoffed at this. "I've been here ten years and I don't make that." Rose said, "You tell them that if an *old girl* who's been here twenty-two years can't make that, then you can't do it." Angela concluded, "You just let what they tell you go in one ear and out the other. Just keep going along as best as you can."

Thus from the management perspective, the training program helped give women workers the appropriate skills and weeded out those who could not acquire those skills fast enough, as well as those who did not have the appropriate attitudes toward their work. Older workers often blamed trainees for making mistakes and for making their own jobs more difficult or for interrupting their work by asking for help. They were also careful, however, to socialize trainees to a different view of the work and the piece-rate system. During the first few days at work, the trainee supervisor and her assistants were in frequent contact with the trainees and offered their view of working hard and making money. When the worker was placed in the department, she heard a different view: that it would be difficult to make over the minimum wage and that the piece-rate system often worked against you. Workers were cautioned to be wary of management promises.

Humanizing the Workplace

As a new trainee assumed her position in a particular department, she both felt the rapid pace of the work and met more and more of her fellow workers. I soon noticed relatively stable groups that met at the breaks and during the lunch period. These groups were formed among workers of the same age and ethnic group who worked near each other. The major division, between Portuguese and non-Portuguese workers, was created partly by the fact that most of the recent Portuguese immigrants did not speak English well, if at all. Those Portuguese speakers who mingled with non-Portuguese were either second-generation women or those whose command of English was fluent.

In some ways these small groups illustrated the ethnic divisions in the workplace—largely between Portuguese and non-Portuguese. But in addition there were often clusters of Continental Portuguese, as opposed to those from the Azores, and there were several groups of Polish workers, many of whom were first-generation immigrants. Women of second- and third-generation French, Italian, Irish, or English background were often part of mixed groups. For example, in our row of sleeve setters, Rose (a French Canadian) and Angela (an Italian) were the center of a little cluster that included another Italian woman (a pinner) and the quality-control woman (whose ethnic background I could not determine). In the department behind me, one lunch group included two Polish women and a French Canadian. Age was the most important divider among the non-Portuguese ethnics. The young, unmarried high school graduates formed a group of their own that included two girls of French Canadian descent, a second-generation Portuguese, and a girl who said she was of several different ethnic backgrounds, "Heinz 57 varieties," as she put it.

Women in these groups often expressed a fair amount of anti-Portuguese sentiment. A week after I started work, and on one of my first days in the department, Rose and Angela were upset that the two Portuguese sisters sewing tops and bottoms of dresses (the operation just before ours) had not told them they were working on two different lots of the same style dresses. Rose and Angela had inadvertently mixed up the bundles from the two lots and later had to stop work to sort them out into different chutes. After explaining all this to me, Rose said, "I'm glad they are hiring some of our own kind [obviously referring to me]. There are too many Portuguese being hired now."

There were interethnic tensions around the piece-rate system as well. Employers hired Portuguese women because of their reputation as hard workers, and the Portuguese women fulfilled their expectations. Some workers thus saw Portuguese women as working too hard, sometimes cutting corners to keep their wages up or engaging in "rate busting." One worker commented that the Azorean woman sewing the elastic band that joined the top and bottom of dresses "ruined that job for everyone." In other words, she worked so fast that the piece rate was lowered, and the workers had to increase their output to make the same pay. "She doesn't miss a dime," and "She makes more money than anyone else on the floor," another worker commented. For their part, Portuguese workers often felt discriminated against and said that U.S. workers do not work hard enough.

The divisions apparent in the structure of break and lunch groups and in attitudes expressed within them were cross-cut by a number of ways in which women joined together around their family roles and life-cycle events. Workers celebrated marriages and the birth of children with showers, usually organized by a group of friends, who collected a small amount from members of the women's department or other acquaintances. The organizers then presented wrapped gifts as a surprise during the lunch break. Retirement celebrations were more extensive. Friends brought pastry and baked goods for morning break and a cake for lunch. Orders were taken for a fast-food lunch of hamburgers, cole slaw, potato chips, and pop. Retirements and sometimes showers were organized along department lines, often through the help, and certainly with the knowledge, of the management (i.e., the floor lady). In both the department-organized and friendship-based functions, the monetary contributions and the signatures on the card cut across ethnic lines.

Leslie's baby shower provides a good example of how such non-work-time events integrate workers of diverse ages and ethnic backgrounds. It was organized by her two friends, who collected the money from a wide range of women as well as from her department, and who went out to buy the gifts: a car seat, a high chair, and a baby carriage. During lunch break, they brought the huge, wrapped boxes down the center aisle and placed them by her machine and waited until she returned from the ladies room. Halfway down the aisle, she realized what was happening. Perhaps a little embarrassed by all the attention, she let one of her friends begin helping her open all the gifts. One of the Portuguese women picked up the yellow ribbon that came off the first package and pinned it on Leslie. She exclaimed, "Oh, Jesus," on opening the gifts and finally pulled the card out to look at it. She thanked everyone, and newcomers to the crowd peered over others to see what the gifts were. "Let's see what we got you," the woman who served morning coffee said, while Leslie's floor lady looked on. More admirers came by as Leslie's two friends began to stuff the gifts back in their boxes. The buzzer rang, ending the lunch break and sending everyone scurrying back to their machines. Though organized by the clique of young high school graduates, Portuguese women in Leslie's department clearly had contributed to the gifts and stood by admiring them.

Rose's retirement party was an all-day event, and our work was almost more interspersed between the breaks than the other way around. We had prepared for the party by each contributing $1.00 for Rose's gift and $1.50 for a fast-food hamburger for lunch, all at times when Rose was not around to find out about the surprise celebration. The celebration began when our floor lady came around before the morning break and told us that they had the pastry all set out. We were to come to the table at the front of the department before the break. Just before the break, Edna, the floor lady, brought over a corsage for Rose—with blue bachelor buttons, red carnations, two little pink roses, some bridal wreath, and a multicolored bow. Rose seemed appropriately surprised. One of the young Portuguese women came over and gave Rose a congratulatory kiss, while one of the Portuguese girls gestured excitedly.

Edna motioned us over to eat the pastry, so we all lined up to get doughnut holes, doughnuts, and homemade coffee cakes. Edna presented Rose with two cards, which she opened. One contained about sixty dollars and was signed "From all the girls in Department #11," and the other contained about the same amount, "From all your Colleagues." The department card said, "Use this to kick up your heels and enjoy." Everyone spent the rest of their break enjoying the pastry in their usual groups, while Rose was surrounded by her usual clique of friends, discussing the last retirement party, which Rose herself had organized for her friend Angela.

The half-hour lunch break brought another round of partying, with the floor lady's assistant bringing each of us a paper bag with our hamburger. Angela, Rose's friend, arrived to join the party just as the buzzer rang, and everyone lined up near the floor lady's desk to get potato salad, cole slaw, potato chips, and soda pop. Again, everyone sat in their usual groups, but several women, both Portuguese and non-Portuguese, came by to talk with Angela or Rose. Angela had lots of tips to give out about retirement and said that she "missed the people more than the place," but, "you get used to it." After lunch, she made the rounds of the department, stopping by each machine and talking to each of her ex-co-workers, whether English or Portuguese speaking. One of the Portuguese workers brought over a picture of her grandson to show Angela. She traded stories about grandchildren with the head mechanic, a Portuguese man in his fifties. Her general comment on leaving was that she "missed all my girls." The mood of the whole day was one of departmental festivity. In contrast to the underlying tensions between Rose and Angela, and some of their Portuguese co-workers, which had surfaced several times over the spring and summer months, the retirement party was an occasion for crossing ethnic lines and expressing, even across a language barrier, feelings of solidarity.

On other occasions women brought their family lives into the work situation, by showing family pictures to those who worked at nearby machines, by sharing news about an illness in the family, by discussing vacation plans, and by recounting an important event, like a wedding or confirmation. Showing pictures, usually during morning or afternoon breaks, enabled women to communicate across ethnic lines. Several weeks after I had started work in my department, Anita, an older Portuguese woman who set sleeves at the machine behind me, brought in her family pictures to show me. I had talked with her several times in my halting Portuguese about her children and grandchildren. She carefully showed me each picture and explained who each person was. She was particularly proud of the first-communion picture of her two granddaughters—a studio picture taken of them in their white dresses with curled hair topped with little white veils—"two little angels," she said.

Other times, women showed family pictures to a wide variety of workers, their closest acquaintances as well as those around them with whom they may have only a nodding acquaintance. Several weeks after the summer vacation, Vivian brought to work her wedding pictures, taken during her trip to Portugal, where she married the man she had been engaged to for several years. During morning break, she showed them to our floor lady and her clique (including two of the pinners). Then she returned to her own Portuguese-speaking group and turned the pages for them, explaining who the godparents and various relatives were. Several Portuguese women came over from adjacent tables when they saw Vivian open the album, so she started her explanation over. Sharing the wedding pictures thus crossed ethnic lines and seemed appropriate as a follow-up to the wedding present the department had given her two weeks before.

When Lucille's sister died, we all heard immediately, guessing that something was wrong when she failed to show up for work one Tuesday morning. A sheet was circulated for each to sign and put down a contribution (usually twenty-five or fifty cents) for flowers. The following Monday, as Lucille came around to each person delivering their repairs, she thanked each one, greeting many with a kiss, even those who did not speak English well. Such department-wide expressions of support brought workers of different ethnic backgrounds together.

Celebrating special events and sharing family pictures "humanized" the workplace, bringing family life into the industrial setting. Almost all the collections were for life-cycle events (weddings, baby showers, retirements, and deaths), some of them specifically celebrating women-centered events (such as a marriage or a birth of a baby). In bringing family life into the workplace, women workers made connections with others, making strangers into acquaintances, and within the circles of one's break group, making acquaintances into friends. In a work setting where the piece-rate system drove workers apart and where ethnic divisions were clear, with interethnic tensions just beneath the surface during everyday work, these events might be termed part of a strategy of worker consolidation.

Socializing the Worker through Informal Work Rules

Another set of strategies that united women involved the informal work rules devised to insure that the work was divided evenly. These rules arose from the clear understanding that the piece-rate system divided workers and could be used by individuals to "make money" unfairly, that is, at the expense of others. A worker's various tricks for getting more garments completed during the day were seen as "cheating." Forms of cheating included sewing only the small sizes in a lot and leaving the larger sizes for other workers, or reporting a fake number of dozens on the work card handed in at the end of the day.

One of the clearest examples of how these informal rules worked revolved around the informal agreement, among those of us who were setting sleeves, that everyone would "work by sizes." Two days after I was out on the shop floor, Rose, who had worked for the company for twenty years, told me how to work with different sizes to share the work more evenly. She said, "Well, you do a bundle of size 4 (the smallest size) and then an 8 (the largest size on t-shirts) and then a 5 and a 6, and kind of let the 7s go in between. Otherwise a girl might get a whole chute of 6- and 7-sized bundles and it will take her longer. This way, then each does her fair share." During my first months at work, the older workers often split up a lot for the whole line, filling a chute near our machines with the appropriate mix of bundles.

By the end of the summer, however, two of these workers had retired and a third had been moved to another job. Three or four new workers had appeared in the line, leaving only one of the Portuguese women and myself with a knowledge of the rule system. A running struggle developed over a two-week period in August shortly after a new Portuguese woman entered our department. Frieda and Vivian, both older women who were new to sewing, had been fighting about the size problem before the new trainee entered the scene. Vivian complained that she always did the larger sizes, which explained her low production (sometimes only twenty-five dozen a day). Frieda accused Vivian of doing all the size 4s in one lot. Other workers suggested that Frieda complain to the floor lady or ask the floor lady to give out the work. An older Polish woman tried to mediate, counseling Vivian to take some of each size and to have the floor lady give her the work.

I explained the size rules to Eva, the trainee, as soon as she sat down at her machine, as did one of the older workers who spoke both Portuguese and English. Even the trainee instructor came in to make sure that Eva understood the rules. Things went fine for several days, until one afternoon, Vivian started sewing sleeves on a lot of pink dresses Eva had begun sewing earlier in the day. After rifling through the chutes of remaining dresses, Vivian accused Eva of taking all the bundles of size 4s. Then Carlotta, the label girl, checked with the floor lady to make sure there were only four bundles of size 4 in the lot and maintained that she had seen Eva doing all four bundles of size 4s. By afternoon break, it was clear that she had indeed done all the size-4 bundles, but in the end she only admitted to doing two of them. Finally, I sorted out the remaining bundles so that Eva would have more 6s and Vivian more 5s, trying to make up for the earlier inequality. After this and a number of other instances where Eva's mistakes were brought to the attention of her Portuguese-speaking instructor, the floor lady, and other workers, she began to be more careful about the size bundles she took, stacking her garments after completing the sleeves, and not mixing garments from several bundles into the same stack.

This shows how women worked to socialize new workers to an informal set of rules that would distribute the work fairly and thus alleviate some of the divisive competition that can develop under the piece-rate system. Both Portuguese speakers and non-Portuguese speakers enforced these rules, the Portuguese speakers explaining to those who spoke little or no English. Some women acted as mediators between disputing workers. At other times, management (the floor lady or the instructor or the trainee supervisor) was called in to repeat the rules or to work out an equitable solution. The rules were important in socializing Portuguese workers, many of whom came from rural small-holder backgrounds and who were used to working long, hard hours. In the factory context, the piece-rate system induced them to act on their rural values and push themselves as hard as possible to "make money." The socializing pressures of other workers, those who were more aware that the system could be used against them, allowing management to lower the rates, for example, began to alter the new worker's behavior, bringing her into line with others.

A final set of strategies, which I have labeled "outguessing the conglomerate," pertained to the workers' attempt to understand and react in a more unified way to changes in management policy.

Outguessing the Conglomerate

During breaks and lunch, women often talked about recent management policy and what was happening in the workplace. Since the apparel industry is extremely seasonal, layoffs are frequent when work for one season is ending and before the orders for the next season come in. Thus the periods between style seasons prompt intense discussion about how or what management might do. Our plant had been bought by a conglomerate in 1974, which by 1977 had changed a number of the top and middle management. We were concerned about the policies these new men would adopt.

In early March, as the end of the spring style season approached, rumors flew through the plant. Already several women had been laid off. Others had been sent to the warehouse to help with pinning, boxing, and filling the last spring orders. A woman who had worked for the company for seventeen years said, "There have never been layoffs like this before. It's this new company."

Some workers felt that there was some chance that the plant would close. Angela maintained that they had been working several months without a contract, and with a temporary extension. She suspected something funny was going on. "You know, they could just close up this place and move South." Even Christina, the instructor, felt there was some chance they would close the plant down and just use it for offices and part of the headquarters. "They are sending all the good work down South and leaving all the junk for up here." Other older workers also speculated about a shutdown. Angela said that wages down South were very cheap, about $1.60 or $1.70 an hour. Nancy, who did quality control for several departments, felt there was trouble coming. She was not in favor of a strike but said, "We'll have to fight for things." "We need them more than they need us" was her comment on a possible plant closing.

Both workers and lower level management felt that the new management was handling production badly. My floor lady blamed the sudden lack of work in early March on the engineers. "They aren't coordinated and don't seem to know what they are doing." I overheard her and the floor lady of the next department characterize a recent meeting with the "higher-ups" as "another bunch of bullshit." One older worker felt the management had planned badly. "They took so many girls on. They know how many lots they need to make each season. They could plan better, instead of taking lots of people on and then laying them off."

Such gossip and rumor trading was not just a matter of bad-mouthing the management. It served as part of a strategy for trying to outguess the management and to figure out what was going on in the absence of information management preferred to withhold. Outguessing the management included: socializing new workers to a sense that things were different and to be critical of management policies; speculating about what was likely to happen so that individuals could be prepared for layoffs or being shifted to new jobs because of lack of work and thus better manage the connection between their work and family lives; and spreading the word from one part of the shop to another so that workers who experienced management policy in isolated ways would understand that their situation might be part of a larger pattern.

Such outguessing had the effect of raising workers' consciousness and helping formulate work-related issues for the union. If the union did not respond, then such consciousness helped workers push the union to be responsive. Several women from the warehouse raised a number of issues pertaining to the company's hiring and transfer policies in the warehouse at the union meeting in September 1977. The company had been hiring temporary workers through agencies (paying the agency $4.50 an hour), which reduced the possibility of sewers or those working part time on the second shift transferring to the $4.25-an-hour "order-picking jobs" at the warehouse. At the same time, hiring temporaries kept a segment of the labor force out of the union. The business agent maintained such a practice was against the contract, especially if there were permanent company employees who wanted work, and promised to look into the issue.

I do not know if this issue was resolved, but two years later, when the contract was being renegotiated, at least ninety local issues remained unresolved, including a number of grievances concerning piece rates. Just three days before the vote on the contract, a wildcat strike erupted. Workers from the knitting mill and warehouse apparently spearheaded the strike, but a number of sewers who called in sick the first day participated in a picket line for the next two days and even defied a back-to-work court injunction on the last day of the wildcat. Workers voted down the national contract by an overwhelming 834 to 118 votes, although it was accepted on a national level. The vote indicated both the severity with which management had stepped up its tactics to squeeze workers' wages and the workers' feeling that the union had not been dealing effectively with these new policies. As one worker said, "The union won't fight for us. The union's the company" (*Providence Journal*, Wednesday, September 5, 1979).

Conclusions

I have emphasized that women are active strategists at work. Their attitudes are conditioned in the workplace itself, through a day-to-day struggle against a pay system that divides workers from each other (by pushing them to make money individualistically) and against management manipulation of that system which, over the long run, operates to keep the wage bill down. I have emphasized worker strategies that are aimed at socializing other workers, making them sceptical of management ideology concerning the benefits of the piece-rate system, and making them aware that management may work to cut pay, eliminate jobs, keep workers out of the union, or lay off sewers.

Women industrial workers come from a wide variety of age, marital, and ethnic backgrounds, and the piece-rate system exacerbates and sharpens these divisions, often playing on prejudices, especially against recent immigrants who do not speak English. Celebrations of life-cycle events and the "familizing" of the workplace, on the one hand, and the socialization of workers to an informal set of work rules, on the other, both operate, though in different ways, to bridge those ethnic divisions.

The effectiveness of the wildcat strike in all departments of the plant also illustrates the themes I have developed in this essay. Neither the piece-rate system nor ethnic divisions stifled worker protest. Production-related strategies such as the informal work rules softened the competitive effects of working on piece rates, while the nonproduction strategies, nourished by women's collective celebration of life-cycle events, blunted ethnic hostility.

These strategies indicate that women, including recent immigrant women, are not passive accepters of management tactics but engage in day-to-day struggle to maintain and even improve their economic situation against very impressive odds.